The Apostle Paul
and the Pauline Tradition

Stephen Finlan

A Michael Glazier Book

LITURGICAL PRESS
Collegeville, Minnesota

www.litpress.org

A Michael Glazier Book published by Liturgical Press

Cover design by David Manahan, OSB. Mosaic illustration of Saint Paul from the dome of the Capella Arcivescovile, Ravenna, Italy.

1	2	3	4	5	6	7	8

Library of Congress Cataloging-in-Publication Data

Finlan, Stephen.
   The apostle Paul and the pauline tradition / Stephen Finlan.
     p. cm.
   "A Michael Glazier book."
   Includes bibliographical references and indexes.
   ISBN 978-0-8146-5271-8 (pbk.)
1. Bible. N.T. Epistles of Paul—Criticism, interpretation, etc.   I. Title.
   BS2650.52.F56   2008
   227'.06—dc22
                                                  2008005852

Contents

Abbreviations

1 En.	*First Enoch*, a non-canonical Jewish work
AB	Anchor Bible
Abr.	Philo of Alexandria's "On Abraham"
AcBib	Academia Biblica (a dissertation series of Society of Biblical Literature and Brill)
ACCS	Ancient Christian Commentary on Scripture
Ari. *Eth.*	Aristotle, *Nicomachean Ethics*
BCE	Before the Common Era
BAGD	Bauer, Arndt, Gingrich, and Danker, *A Greek-English Lexicon of the New Testament and Other Early Christian Literature*, 1979
BECNT	Baker Exegetical Commentary on the New Testament
CE	Common Era (= AD)
CBQ	*Catholic Biblical Quarterly*
Det.	Philo of Alexandria, "The Worse Attacks the Better"
DSS	Dead Sea Scrolls
Ep. Mor.	Seneca, *Epistulae Morales*
EQ	*Evangelical Quarterly*
ESEC	Emory Studies in Early Christianity
HTR	*Harvard Theological Review*
Ign. Eph.	Ignatius of Antioch, letter to the Ephesians

Ign. Magn.	Ignatius of Antioch, letter to the Magnesians
Ign. Phld.	Ignatius of Antioch, letter to the Philadelphians
Ign. Poly.	Ignatius of Antioch, letter to Polycarp
Ign. Rom.	Ignatius of Antioch, letter to the Romans
Ign. Smyrn.	Ignatius of Antioch, letter to the Smyrneans
Ign. Trall.	Ignatius of Antioch, letter to the Trallians
JBL	*Journal of Biblical Literature*
JETS	*Journal of the Evangelical Theological Society*
Jos.	Philo of Alexandria, "On Joseph"
Jos. *Ant.*	Josephus, *Antiquities of the Jews*
JSJ	*Journal for the Study of Judaism*
JSNT	*Journal for the Study of the New Testament*
JSNTSup	*Journal for the Study of the New Testament*, Supplement Series
Jub.	*Jubilees*, a non-canonical Jewish work
KJV	King James Version (= Authorized Version)
LCL	Loeb Classical Library
LSJ	H. G. Liddell and Robert Scott, rev. H. S. Jones, *A Greek-English Lexicon*, 1940
LXX	Septuagint, the Greek translation of the Jewish Scriptures (Old Testament)
Met.	Ovid, *Metamorphosis*
Mig.	Philo of Alexandria, "On the Migration of Abraham"
Mos.	Philo of Alexandria, "Life of Moses"
NAB	New American Bible
NASB	New American Standard Bible
NICNT	New International Commentary on the New Testament
NIGTC	New International Greek Testament Commentary
NIV	New International Version
NJB	New Jerusalem Bible
NovTSup	*Novum Testamentum* Supplements

NRSV	New Revised Standard Version
NT	New Testament
NTS	*New Testament Studies*
Opif.	Philo of Alexandria, "On the Creation"
OT	Old Testament
Plant.	Philo of Alexandria, "On Noah's Work as a Planter"
PTMS	Princeton Theological Monograph Series
RSV	Revised Standard Version
SBLDS	Society of Biblical Literature Dissertation Series
SBLSBS	Society of Biblical Literature Sources for Biblical Study
SBLSP	Society of Biblical Literature Seminar Papers
Sib. Or.	*Sibylline Oracles*
SNTSMS	Society for New Testament Studies Monograph Series
Som.	Philo of Alexandria, "On Dreams"
SP	Sacra Pagina (series)
Spec. Leg.	Philo of Alexandria, "The Special Laws"
T. Levi	*Testament of Levi*, one of the *Testaments of the Twelve Patriarchs*
T. Naph.	*Testament of Naphtali*, one of the *Testaments of the Twelve Patriarchs*
T. Reub.	*Testament of Reuben*, one of the *Testaments of the Twelve Patriarchs*
TDNT	Gerhard Kittel and Gerhard Friedrich, eds., *Theological Dictionary of the New Testament*
TNIV	Today's New International Version
TNTC	Tyndale New Testament Commentaries
WBC	Word Bible Commentary
WUNT	Wissenschaftliche Untersuchungen zum Neuen Testament

The Pauline Letters

Paul the apostle is the church's most influential theologian, yet most Christians have only a hazy concept of his actual teachings. He was controversial in his day, was opposed by some Christian leaders, and was even treated with disrespect by some within the congregations he founded, yet his teaching proved persuasive, shaping the church's stance on many issues. His letters, designed to instruct particular churches, eventually became teaching instruments for the whole church, and his theology is the starting point for all later systematic theologies.

The importance of the Pauline letter tradition in Christian theology is exceeded only by that of the gospels, yet many people read and interpret the gospels through the lens of the Pauline tradition. Certain concepts derived from the letters ("Jesus died for my sins") have become dominant in popular theology, even among people who know very little about Paul's teaching as a whole. The church's image of Paul is largely derived from the Acts of the Apostles, where the wonder-working Paul is a main character. There are many doubts, however, about the historical accuracy of Acts. The letters must be central to any study of Paul.

The Tradition behind the Tradition

What is "the Pauline tradition"? It can refer to the thirteen epistles (letters) in the New Testament that are said to have been written or cowritten by Paul.[1] But "Pauline tradition" could also mean the Pauline

---

1. The prescripts of the letters identify the purported authors, as in "Paul, a servant of Jesus Christ" (Rom 1:1), and "Paul, an apostle . . . and Timothy our brother" (2 Cor 1:1). I use NRSV as the default translation.

letter collection that existed long before there was a New Testament. Yet the Pauline collection itself underwent changes. Thus, "tradition" includes both the original core that was preserved from generation to generation and the changes and additions made over time by the tradents (people who hand on a tradition). "Tradition" can also refer to the social setting and means by which the teachings and texts were transmitted. Finally, "tradition" can signify the meanings and values the community understands itself to be deriving from these literary works. This would be the community's summary of Paul, and it might differ from Paul's own recorded view.

Thus "Pauline tradition" can mean four different things: the teachings and writings of the apostle Paul himself; the assimilation and, often, simplification of these ideas by the people who handed on the tradition; some new letters added to the collection by those tradents; and the final form of the thirteen or fourteen letters that churches have labeled as Paul's. There is what *started* the tradition, what *came into* the tradition, and the final (expanded) literary collection. Scholars have often spoken of the seven "undisputed letters" of Paul,[2] but each of the other letters has its defenders as regards Pauline authorship.

Each meaning of "tradition" flows into the next, and there is some uncertainty as to the exact facts about each level, and even the final form, since there is no universal agreement among churches about whether or not to consider the letter to the Hebrews to be Paul's. Hebrews itself makes no claim to being written by Paul, and its style is more complicated and literary than Paul's own style. But some early church fathers in Alexandria (Egypt) attributed Hebrews to Paul, and although some important Latin fathers doubted it,[3] Pauline authorship came to be accepted by many churches. It was a post-biblical conversation that led these churches to consider Hebrews to be Pauline.

"Tradition" turns out to be a fluid thing, constantly being reinterpreted, explained, and expanded. Paul's congregations discussed and restated Paul's teachings, inevitably reshaping the original message as they attempted to comprehend it. Certain ideas and slogans emerged as summaries, and new letters were written (and attributed to Paul), at-

2. 1 Thessalonians, 1 Corinthians, 2 Corinthians, Galatians, Romans, Philippians, and Philemon.

3. Erik M. Heen and Philip D. Krey, *Hebrews*. ACCS NT 10 (Downers Grove, IL: InterVarsity Press, 2005), xvii. Origen considered it to be based on notes taken by a follower of Paul (p. xviii).

tempting to clarify his meaning (and to shut off other po
interpretations).

Does this mean it is impossible to recover the teachings of the real
Paul? No, it is not impossible, but it sometimes is difficult. We need to
become educated in possible ways of discerning the different layers
within a literary tradition, and we must always be prepared to rethink
and revise our prior conclusions if necessary. The church has usually not
bothered to make these distinctions, accepting the thirteen or fourteen
letters as authentically Pauline. But since the mid-twentieth century the
Roman Catholic Church has openly accepted biblical scholarship as a
valid part of the church's study and teaching.[4] An educated questioning
and investigating becomes a valid part of the life of faith—not *replacing*
faith, but joined to it.

Biblical scholarship sets out to understand what biblical texts, and
particular expressions within them, meant in their original setting, how
the symbols and metaphors are to be understood, who wrote the texts,
who read them, how they were handed on, and what may have been
added to the original text in this process of "traditioning."

Covering the Letters

This book is designed for students, and each chapter should be read
in conjunction with the letter it concerns. This does not mean that each
letter is of equal importance or complexity. Rather, I use the chapters on
the shorter letters to discuss particular themes that apply to all the letters.
For instance, the chapter on 1 Thessalonians discusses Paul's use of
recognizable patterns of argument found in popular Hellenistic philosophies (Cynicism, Stoicism). Given the introductory nature of this book,
these discussions are necessarily brief. In fact, many more footnotes and
much longer discussions could have been provided throughout, but they
have not been, in order to avoid making this a lengthy book.

The footnotes provide just a glimpse into the possibilities for further
research. Almost every verse in the Pauline corpus is surrounded by
debate, but we touch on these debates only for selected passages.

---

4. Pius XII's encyclical *Divino afflante spiritu* (1943) allowed new translations of the Bible
from the original languages (see Eugene H. Maly, "The Purpose of the Bible," in *The New
American Bible* [Nashville: Thomas Nelson, 1987], xii) and extended freedom of investigation to biblical scholars.

By and large, the order of chapters follows the likely sequence of the letters' composition. Philemon works well in final position, although it may have been written before Philippians. Galatians may or may not have been written after the Corinthian letters. Placing it after them enables Galatians to be examined before Romans, which has similar subject matter (though a very different emotional tone). The so-called deutero-Pauline letters are placed after the undisputed letters.

Chapter 1

The Social
and Literary Settings
of the Letters

Jewish Messianic Hope

Many passages in the NT indicate that there was a lively messianic hope among the Jewish people—actually *several* hopes, since there were different and competing messianic concepts. First we need to know that "Messiah" means "anointed one" in both Hebrew and Aramaic.[1] In seeking to discover what a Messiah might be, we need to notice which leaders in Jewish society were anointed at the beginning of their public roles. We are not surprised to find that the three types of anointed leaders correspond to the three main kinds of messianic hope: for a new king, a new priest, or a new prophet.

These represent three very different value systems and expectations. Those who hoped for a kingly Messiah were desiring political rescue and vindication for Judea and military revenge against Rome and even against weaker neighbors such as the Samaritans and Idumeans. The

---

1. Aramaic had been the international diplomatic language under the Assyrian, Chaldean, and Persian empires and became the daily language of some peoples, such as Galilean Jews. Outside of Palestine, however, many Jews spoke Greek as their first language. Greek was the international language in the first century CE. The Greek word for Messiah was "*christos.*"

Jews took a great deal of pride in the stories of the long-lived Davidic dynasty of Judah,[2] and many of them hoped for a Davidic Messiah who would lead a political and military revival. Even though, by Jesus' and Paul's time, there had not been a Davidic king for over six hundred years, many people hoped for a return of this dynasty. Although not led by any pretender to the throne, the Jews had, in fact, successfully revolted against the oppressive Seleucids only two centuries earlier,[3] and some hoped to do the same—and more—against Rome. A Davidic or royal messianic hope was very much alive in the first century CE, even among Jesus' first followers. In the gospel accounts, the disciples reveal their political cast of mind by arguing about which positions they would occupy in the coming kingdom (Mark 9:33-34; 10:37; Matt 18:1). Simon the Zealot (Luke 6:15) shows, in his name, his affinity to the nationalistic party, while Peter's readiness to take up the sword against Jesus' enemies (John 18:10) is Zealot-like behavior. Jesus repudiates using the sword (Matt 26:52; John 18:36) and turns away from a king-making crowd (John 6:15); he may not have wanted to be considered the Messiah (answering a messianic question ambiguously in Matt 26:63-64; 27:11, and Luke 22:67-68, unlike the definite affirmative in Mark 14:61-62).

Jesus cleverly uses the fact that Middle Eastern fathers never call their sons "lord" to attack the idea that the Messiah should be called "son of David" *at all.* Since David calls the Messiah "lord," the Messiah cannot be David's son (Mark 12:35-37; Matt 22:42-45; Luke 20:41-44). Christians nevertheless promoted a son-of-David Messiah, after having denationalized and (partially) de-militarized the idea, understanding themselves to be witnessing the fulfillment of the promises that "many nations shall join themselves to the LORD on that day" (Zech 2:11) and "I am coming to gather all nations and tongues" (Isa 66:18). The spiritualized "Son of David" concept, then, affirmed a Jewish background and a universal destiny.

Those Jews who yearned for a priestly Messiah, on the other hand, were hoping for the triumph of religious institutions and practices and for strict observance of purity rules, which included separation from the Gentiles. Thus the priestly Messiah (sometimes called the Messiah of Aaron) implies hostility to Gentiles, for somewhat different reasons than

---

2. Early tenth to early sixth century BCE.

3. The Maccabean revolt, recounted in 1 Maccabees. The Jews regained control of their land and ritually cleansed the Temple, a story now memorialized in the celebration of Hanukkah.

the hostility in the royal-messianic idea. The important documents known as the Dead Sea Scrolls express hope for two distinct Messiahs: "until there shall come the prophet and the messiahs of Aaron and Israel."[4] The second-century BCE *Testaments of the Twelve Patriarchs* also envision a "dual messiahship," royal and priestly, but foresee a future prophet as well.[5]

Thus we see a hint of the third messianic (or related-to-messianic) concept: the idea of a new prophet, rooted in the prophetic books. This concept shows much more openness to the Gentiles than the other two ideas. "Many peoples shall come" to Jerusalem to learn about the Lord (Isa 2:3); a "shoot . . . of Jesse" will be endowed with the spirit of counsel and wisdom, will rule with justice, and "the earth will be full of the knowledge of the LORD" (Isa 11:1-5, 9); God will bless Egypt and Assyria as well as Israel (Isa 19:24-25); the whole Jewish nation will be "a light to the nations" (Isa 49:6); "nations that do not know you shall run to you" (Isa 55:5; cf. 60:3). Obviously this is a powerful (and accelerating) theme within Isaiah, the greatest prophetic book. Usually it is *God* who will make these things happen, but the shoot of Jesse or the Servant of the Lord plays a key role in some of these texts and (over time) many readers understood these to be messianic figures, although much of our evidence for that is from Christian sources. We see both a relatedness and a distinction between Messiah and new prophet in the questions asked of John the Baptist, whether he was the Messiah, Elijah, or "the prophet" (John 1:20, 21, 25).

The *Testaments of the Twelve Patriarchs* speak of "the unique prophet," an agent of the Most High (*T. Benj.* 9:2). Evidently some Jews hoped for an eschatological ("end-times") prophet and for fulfillment of the prophetic ideals. Even though they did not usually use the term "Messiah," I will refer to this as a "prophetic Messiah" concept because it is usually seen to merge with messianic ideas. Jesus was identified by followers as "the prophet" (John 7:40; Matt 21:11) at the same time as being called "Messiah" or "Son of David" (John 7:41; Matt 21:9, 15). The hope for a new prophet or teacher who proclaims the new age is seen in a number

---

4. *1QS* 9:11 (the Community Rule); cf. *CD* 12:23; 14:19 (the Damascus Document). See John J. Collins, *Apocalypticism in the Dead Sea Scrolls* (London: Routledge, 1997), 75, 77.

5. Howard Clark Kee, "Testaments of the Twelve Patriarchs," in James H. Charlesworth, ed., *The Old Testament Pseudepigrapha.* 2 vols. (Garden City, NY: Doubleday, 1983–1985) 1:777–78; see the varying concepts in *T. Dan* 5:10; *T. Levi* 18:2-3; *T. Reub.* 6:7; *T. Jud.* 24:1-6; *T. Naph.* 4:5.

of sources, including the Qumran (Dead Sea) scrolls. The Melchizedek Scroll speaks of an instructor in truth, "the anointed of the spirit" who "brings good news . . . to comfort all who mourn" (*11QM* 2:18-20), citing Isaiah 61:1-2. The "anointed one" (*messiah*) of Isaiah 61 is a liberator, healer, and teacher. No wonder that, according to Luke, Jesus chose Isaiah 61 to announce the beginning of his own public ministry, ending with "Today this scripture has been fulfilled in your hearing" (Luke 4:18-21). Isaiah 61 itself may envision a prophetic Messiah: "The spirit of the Lord GOD is upon me, because the LORD has anointed me; he has sent me to bring good news to the oppressed, to bind up the brokenhearted, to proclaim liberty to the captives, and release to the prisoners . . . to comfort all who mourn . . ." (61:1-2).

The description of a peace-king in Zechariah 9:9 ("triumphant and victorious is he, humble and riding on a donkey") may also have prophetic messianic implications, and according to the gospel accounts Jesus deliberately fulfilled this scripture when he rode into Jerusalem on a donkey (a poor person's steed, instead of a horse, appropriate for a warrior-king). Interestingly, only Matthew 21:5 and John 12:15 indicate that Zechariah 9:9 lies behind this action; Mark 11 and Luke 19 simply tell the story without mentioning that scripture. It may be that it took awhile for people to pick up on some of Jesus' uses of scripture.

Some Jews understood Deuteronomy 18:18, the promise of a Moses-like prophet, messianically. There God tells Moses: "I will raise up for them a prophet like you from among their own people; I will put my words in the mouth of the prophet, who shall speak to them everything that I command." This is probably "him about whom Moses . . . wrote" referred to in John 1:45. Deuteronomy 18:18 was probably meant to describe what *any* true prophet would look like, but such anticipations grow with time and it is a small step from expecting a prophet to expecting "the" prophet.

The prophetic idea clearly stood for a different set of hopes than did the royal and priestly ideas. A prophet would teach and heal, would bring in the Gentiles and inaugurate peace, while a royal Messiah would punish the Gentiles and a priestly Messiah would exclude them from sacred territory.

Prophetic ideals are crucial even before the beginning of Jesus' ministry. John the Baptizer, the predecessor of Jesus, articulates prophetic ideas and, even more, *embodies* them, dressing like a prophet and speaking of "one . . . coming after me" (Matt 3:11; Mark 1:7; John 1:27). The Messiah idea was powerful but highly fluid, and even when early Christianity started to solidify it through identification with Jesus we can discern different emphases in different authors.

Hellenistic Universalizing

In the fourth century BCE Alexander the Great conquered numerous cultures stretching from northern Greece, through Asia Minor and the Middle East, southward to Egypt, and eastward to Iran and western India. After he died, his empire broke up into several large empires and a few smaller realms, but a Greek cultural umbrella remained over the whole region. From Egypt to India people were reading Greek literature and philosophy, imitating Greek artistic styles, adopting and universalizing Greek ideas. We call these post-Alexandrian cultures and cultural products "Hellenistic"—a *cultural,* not an ethnic term. If we want to refer to the classical culture of Athens before the Alexandrian conquests we use the word "Hellenic" (which simply means "Greek").

Hellenistic culture was universalistic in a way that Hellenic culture was not. Hellenistic culture was multi-racial: anyone who could read or even speak Greek could make a contribution to Hellenistic culture. "Hellenistic" is a cultural category—actually a *super*-cultural category, since it is used to describe cultures from southwest Asia to the Middle East to southeastern Europe. After Alexander, Greek became the international language in a way that no other language had ever functioned. Aramaic had previously been the international language for business and diplomacy and had become the daily language of many people, but it did not have the philosophical and cultural influence that Greek took on. In the Hellenistic period, for the first time, people on different continents who had never even encountered each other could read the same works of literature and philosophy, or even read each other's newly created works.

When Rome exerted control over the Mediterranean region in the third and second centuries BCE it conquered Greece and most of the Hellenistic world. Rome became Hellenized through intimate contact with these Hellenistic cultures. Rome saw the Greek culture as its predecessor and was willing to absorb ideas and values from Hellenism, so we can call the territory conquered by the Roman republic and the early Roman Empire a *Hellenistic* empire.

The most important book to have a multi-cultural effect during this period was the Bible itself. The Hebrew Scriptures (what Christians refer to as "the Old Testament") were translated into Greek. Undertaken by scholars in Alexandria, this translation was called the Septuagint. Some other Jewish works circulating only in the Greek language were added to the collection. Now for the first time Gentiles could read the Jewish Scriptures in the universal language, Greek.

The Septuagint fostered the adaptation of Jewish thought to a Gentile framework. The important Jewish philosopher Philo of Alexandria re-stated and framed Jewish beliefs in Hellenistic philosophic categories, describing Moses as the embodiment of virtue; "his mind was unable to admit any falsehood . . . he exhibited the doctrines of philosophy in all his daily actions . . . Moses . . . displayed . . . the genius of the phi-losopher and of the king."[6] Philo tried to convince readers of Greek to study the first five books of the Bible as the greatest philosophy. Of course, in order to do this he had to interpret the many local customs and detailed stories as allegories, symbolic of deeper meanings. When Abraham left Ur, for instance, it meant he left behind the sensual, selfish life for the life of philosophy (*Mig.* 1-3; *Det.* 159). When Genesis says "all the families of the earth shall be blessed" (12:3; 28:14), it means all the parts ("families") of a person will be purified if the *mind* is purified (*Som.* 1.177).

In order to say more about Philo of Alexandria or any other thinker of this period we must look at the popular philosophies that were known throughout the Hellenistic world and were more widely followed than Platonism, which most people considered too brainy. The three most important Hellenistic philosophies were Cynicism, Stoicism, and Epicureanism. Although our words "cynical," "stoical," and "epicurean" descend from these schools of thought, the meanings of these words have undergone considerable change, and we should not prejudge these philosophies on the basis of our current usage of these terms.

Cynicism was very radical, teaching that society was a domineering and enslaving influence from which the true philosopher needed to free himself. (Nearly all the Cynic philosophers were men, but some of the later Stoics and Epicureans were women.) Cynicism taught that it was important to get in tune with nature, which meant shedding the artificial and confining trappings of society. Some Cynics rejected all concepts of commerce, government, and marriage. To dramatize the seriousness of their rejection of customs the early Cynics did shocking things, such as urinating in public, thus earning the nickname "dogs." *Kynos* is Greek for "dog," and gives us our word "Cynic." The ancient Cynics yearned

6. *Mos.* 1.24, 29; 2.2.

for honesty and fairness in one-to-one dealings between people. They were not "cynical" in our modern sense, but one can see how the term got its current meaning, when more cautious and conformist people lost patience with what seemed extreme and antisocial views.

The Stoic philosophy was by far the most important one of this period, and in fact it is still with us today. Stoics also advocated living in harmony with nature, but they did not conclude that one had to reject human institutions in order to do so. The Cynics sought outward freedom, but the Stoics taught that true freedom was inward; they taught courageous devotion to duty, and some of the martyr traditions that come down to us were written by Stoics. The Stoics in fact borrowed an essential idea from Plato, although they were not Platonists; they accepted the idea that there was a "spark of divinity" in every person, that the *logos* or reason within the individual was the same as the *Logos* or rationality in the universe.[7] "You have in yourself a part of [God]. . . . You bear God about with you, poor wretch, and know it not."[8] This spiritual insight led to the Stoic concept of human brotherhood. Since one's deepest instincts about right and wrong derive from the *logos,* and everyone's *logos* is plugged into the same source, all true and unconfused moral perception will agree. The Golden Rule is thus a "natural" principle. Many of these ideas became a part of Christian thought and go under the general heading of "natural law" or "natural theology."

Stoicism lives on within Christianity! But before Christians ever absorbed it, Stoicism was adapted by some Jews. All of Philo's writings and the Septuagint works *4 Maccabees* and the Wisdom of Solomon[9] show this blending of Judaism with Stoicism. The focus in *4 Maccabees* is on martyrdom. Even though the main story line has to do with the courage of a family of martyrs who refuse to reject the Jewish law even when they are viciously tortured by the Seleucid king, the founding principle of the work is this Stoic one: "reason is dominant over the emotions" (*4 Macc* 1:7), and the martyrs repeatedly lecture the king that they are not afraid of pain or death. *Reason*—understood as loyalty to the Law of

7. I am making a point by using the English distinction of capitalization, which is not present in Greek.

8. Epictetus, *Disc.* 2.8, in Whitney J. Oates, ed. and trans., *The Stoic and Epicurean Philosophers* (New York: Modern Library, 1940), 295.

9. *4 Maccabees* is not in the Bible, so it is italicized. Wisdom is not italicized because it is in the Roman Catholic and Eastern Orthodox Bible. Protestants follow Luther (and the Jewish tradition) in rejecting works that are preserved only in Greek.

Moses—has conquered their fear-emotions. But all of this is communicated in Hellenistic thought categories, and written in Greek.

The Wisdom of Solomon, often referred to simply as Wisdom, is a remarkable blend of Platonic, Stoic, and Jewish thought. We are told that "righteousness is immortal" (Wis 1:15), but "the ungodly will be punished as their reasoning deserves" (3:10). Wisdom touches on the issue of judgment in the afterlife,[10] which *4 Maccabees* makes a major pillar of its argument for remaining strong in the face of persecution: "we, through this severe suffering . . . shall have the prize of virtue and shall be with God . . . but you . . . will deservedly undergo from the divine justice eternal torment by fire" (*4 Macc* 9:8-9). There is no Old Testament verse like this. This clear-cut heaven and hell theology was new for the Jews in the second century BCE, but it had existed in the Zoroastrian religion for centuries.[11] The only other OT verse that is at all similar is Daniel 12:2, and Daniel is one of the last books in the OT to be written.

The final Hellenistic philosophy we must mention is Epicureanism, much less important to us but considered a strong rival of Stoicism in Hellenistic times. Philosophers of these two schools often debated in public. The Epicureans believed in reason but rejected Stoicism's idealism, its belief in a connection between an inward *logos* and a transcendent *Logos*. Epicureans believed in honesty, friendship, and scientific investigation, but most of them did not believe in an afterlife.

All these philosophies had an instinct that there was such a thing as *truth,* and that what was true at all was true everywhere. For the Epicureans this truth had to do with decent character, loyalty to one's friends, and scientific principles. With the Stoics and Cynics there was a universal moral law, the law of "nature," that needed to be recognized. Jews could re-express their ancestral beliefs through Stoic categories, saying, as Philo did, "this world is a sort of large state, and has one constitution, and one

10. John J. Collins, *Jewish Wisdom in the Hellenistic Age* (Louisville: Westminster John Knox, 1997), 165, 183–88.

11. Scholars are fiercely divided over the possibility of Zoroastrian influence on Jewish afterlife beliefs. One thoughtful appraisal, accepting Persian religious influence on Qumran thought, is John R. Levison, "The Two Spirits in Qumran Theology," in James H. Charlesworth, ed., *The Bible and the Dead Sea Scrolls: The Princeton Symposium on the Dead Sea Scrolls,* vol. 2: *The Dead Sea Scrolls and the Qumran Community* (Waco, TX: Baylor University Press, 2006), 169–94.

law, and the word of nature enjoins what one ought to do."[12] All who love wisdom are "fellow citizens" of "the whole world."[13]

Once people have begun to think that way, they might accept what Paul would say: ". . . there is no distinction between Jew and Greek; the same Lord is Lord of all" (Rom 10:12). The universalizing streak in Judaism started to unite with Hellenistic universalizing and then was electrified with spiritual certainty at the hands of Jesus and Paul. There is a natural progression here: "the earth will be filled with the knowledge of the glory of the LORD, as the waters cover the sea" (Hab 2:14); "you are all brothers"; "there will be one flock, one shepherd" (Matt 23:8 NAB; John 10:16); "When all things are subjected to . . . the Son . . . God may be all in all" (1 Cor 15:28).

Rhetoric and Paul's Letters

Letters in the ancient world could serve the same purposes that letters serve today in personal, political, and business matters, but they sometimes had a teaching purpose as well. The Cynic philosophers made use of the letter genre to convey their ideas about rejecting artificial social rules and being loyal to nature. Some similarities between Paul's and the Cynics' letters will be mentioned in the chapter on 1 Thessalonians.

Rhetoric, the art of public debate, was taken very seriously in Hellenistic cultures. Ancient rhetorical handbooks divided rhetoric into three categories: *judicial* (for accusation and defense), *deliberative* (for persuasion, instruction, and advice), and *epideictic* (for praise or blame of particular persons), and these distinctions are sometimes discernible in letters as well. Paul is clearly familiar with the forms of rhetoric but is not tied to any conventional category. Although most of his effort is aimed at persuading and instructing ("deliberative"), he often defends himself against accusations ("judicial"), and also holds up himself and others as characters to be emulated ("epideictic"). Scholarly attempts to force some of Paul's letters into just one category have proved unconvincing; Paul is quite flexible and capable of moving back and forth

---

12. *Jos.* 29, Yonge translation. See also Richard A. Horsley, "The Law of Nature in Philo and Cicero," *HTR* 71 (1978): 37.

13. *Spec. Leg.* 2.45.

between different types of argument.[14] Nevertheless, he does seem to use certain recognizable syllogistic rhetorical forms.[15]

Some of Paul's letters are sent to discipline, correct, and instruct congregations he had founded: those at Corinth, Thessalonica, and Philippi, and in the region of Galatia. Paul's greatest writing, Romans, is more cautiously and thoroughly formulated, since he is writing to a congregation he did not found but still aims to correct and instruct. Sometimes his concern is to reiterate his message that believers are saved by faith, not by fulfillment of the rules of the Torah, and that the Jewish Torah must not be imposed on Gentiles, who constitute the majority of Christ believers. He also wants believers to conceive of themselves as being directed by the Spirit, not by the flesh, which requires that they repudiate their old fleshly life, including loose sexual behavior, idolatry, and pride of status. He offers a number of different metaphors to describe how "Christ died for us" (Rom 5:8), "died for our sins" (1 Cor 15:3), "becoming a curse for us" (Gal 3:13), using the imagery of martyrdom, sacrifice, and scapegoat. These will be discussed in the chapters on the individual letters.

Paul also wants his congregations (and the Roman congregation, which is not "his") to understand that the coming of Jesus the Messiah was foretold in the Jewish scriptures, and that God always intended to bless and save the Gentiles. He marshals OT texts to this task, arguing that they foretold this day when "in Christ Jesus the blessing of Abraham [would] come to the Gentiles" (Gal 3:14). Thus there is a convergence between Paul's soteriology (teaching about salvation), his interpretation of the OT (which prefigured these events), and his social message (full inclusion of Gentiles, no worldly status within the kingdom at all [Gal 3:28], and everyone showing sensitivity to others in the congregation). We will examine all these teachings, motivations, and social settings as we study the letters, rediscovering the often forgotten teachings of the apostle Paul.

But first a glance at the career of Paul is in order.

---

14. See Calvin Roetzel, *Paul: The Man and the Myth* (Edinburgh: T&T Clark, 1999), 78–81.

15. These include the *epicheireme,* which produces a sequence of premise, proof, minor premise, proof, and conclusion, according to Fredrick J. Long, "From Epicheiremes to Exhortation: A Pauline Method for Moral Persuasion in 1 Thessalonians," in Thomas H. Olbricht and Andres Eriksson, eds., *Rhetoric, Ethic, and Moral Perusasion in Biblical Discourse.* Emory Studies in Early Christianity (New York: T&T Clark International, 2005), 179–95.

Chapter 2

An Outline of the Life of Paul

This chapter will give the briefest of summaries of Paul's career. It is very difficult to glean much biography from Paul's letters. The Acts of the Apostles, which follows the four gospels in the NT, is the principal source of early stories about Paul, but scholars are generally wary of its historical reliability. Paul does mention some of the important events in his career in his letters, but he always has more to say about the *significance* of these events than about the details. For instance, Acts retells the story of Paul's call experience on the Damascus road three times, with much more detail than is found in Paul's own letters.

Distinguishing the Acts of the Apostles from the Letters of Paul

Acts begins in a way similar to the Gospel of Luke, with the author addressing his reader: "In the first book, Theophilus, I wrote about all that Jesus did and taught from the beginning until the day when he was taken up to heaven" (1:1-2). Luke is signaling that Acts is a sequel to the Gospel of Luke, which also begins with an address to Theophilus ("friend of God" in Greek).

Most scholars are willing to accept Lukan authorship for Acts but are cautious regarding its historical accuracy. It draws heavily on oral tradition and miracle stories that built up around the apostles. Some scholars say the miracle stories and wondrous escapes in Acts resemble those in entertaining Hellenistic romances.[1] Others consider this kind of view to be overly skeptical,[2] but many scholars would agree that Luke downplays the conflict between Paul and other apostles (quite visible in 1 Corinthians 1, 3–4; 2 Corinthians 11–12; Galatians 2;[3] and also in Acts 15, though there it is somewhat smoothed over).

For the most part, scholars prefer Paul's own statement that he did not visit the Jerusalem apostles right after his conversion (Gal 1:17) to the story in Acts 9:17-26 that has Paul go there right after his initial training. They rely on the hints and statements in the letters more than on the stories in Acts. Unfortunately there is nothing in the letters to either confirm or contradict much of the Acts narrative. Some will trust the general outline of events and persons in Acts, but not its details, which reflect Luke's theological agenda.

Acts gives almost no indication of the main social conflict Paul took on: the issue of the admission of Gentiles into the believing community on an equal basis.[4] Some Jewish believers insisted that the Gentiles undergo conversion to Judaism, symbolically enacted by males through undergoing the dangerous procedure of adult circumcision. Paul argued vigorously against this policy, especially in his letter to the Galatians. The coming of the Messiah changes everything, Paul said; what matters is recognition of the Messiah. "Christ is the end of the law" (Rom 10:4) probably means Christ is the *goal* and *completion* of the Jewish law, which makes Christ more important than the Law! To recognize the Christ and the values he embodies is to fulfill the Law.[5] On the other hand, Acts may accurately reflect Paul's early teachings, before the issues of law and circumcision became a primary concern.[6]

1. Richard I. Pervo wants to emphasize fictionality (Pervo, *Profit with Delight: The Literary Genre of the Acts of the Apostles* [Philadelphia: Fortress Press, 1987], 7, 11–22, 132–38). Howard Clark Kee highlights the messages communicated by miracle stories (*Miracle in the Early Christian World* [New Haven: Yale University Press, 1983], 193).

2. Such as I. Howard Marshall, *The Acts of the Apostles: An Introduction and Commentary*. TNTC (Leicester, England: InterVarsity Press, 1980), 34–37.

3. All these designate whole chapters, not verses.

4. I will generally avoid saying "Christian" since Paul never uses this term (it first appears in Acts 11:26), but will not be overly rigid about this, as though there were *no* connection between Paul and "Christian" developments not long after his time.

5. Gal 2:16; 5:13-16; 6:2.

6. This is the view of Karl P. Donfried (*The Theology of the Shorter Pauline Letters* [Cambridge: Cambridge University Press, 1993], 65–68).

Paul's policy, though contested in his lifetime, did triumph, and this made it possible for Gentiles to convert in large numbers, which would not have been possible if fastidious observance of the Law had been enforced.

The Damascus Road Experience

Paul's birth name was Saul, and the story begins with the activities of the zealous Pharisee, Saul of Tarsus, who "made havoc" among the Christians in Jerusalem and "violently persecuted" them (Acts 9:21; Gal 1:13). The Pharisees were a Jewish religious party that focused on scrupulous observance of all the laws of the Torah; they also read the prophets and the wisdom literature and believed in an afterlife. I think it likely that Pharisees were a visible and importance presence in Judah and Galilee.[7]

Saul was apparently authorized by some authorities in Jerusalem to travel to synagogues outside the city and convince the synagogue leaders to expel, and even to arrest, members of their congregations who believed in Jesus as Messiah. Paul would then "[bring] them bound before the chief priests" (Acts 9:21) in Jerusalem. In the course of his duties Saul was on hand when a "Hellenist"[8] deacon named Stephen (Acts 6:1-5) was being confronted by the chief priests, a scene witnessed by a large crowd. Stephen's speech recounted the biblical story, but when he said "the Most High does not dwell in houses made with human hands" (Acts 7:48), the priests and crowd took this as an insult to the Temple, and when he reminded them of prophets who had called them "stiff-necked" and "uncircumcised in heart and ears" (7:51; Deut 9:6; Jer 4:4; 6:10), the crowd turned ugly. Saul found himself holding their cloaks while the mob stoned Stephen to death. This was the first killing of a Christian "martyr," that is, "witness" (*martys* means witness).

Evidently the burden of the mob's cloaks on Saul's arm was as nothing compared to the burden of this event on his soul. Later, the converted Paul is merciless with himself: he is "unfit to be called an apostle, because

---

7. The standard scholarly position largely accepts Morton Smith's and Jacob Neusner's complete rejection the gospels' and Josephus's statements on early Pharisaic influence. A more balanced approach is found in James D. G. Dunn, "Pharisees, Sinners, and Jesus," in Jacob Neusner, et al., eds., *The Social World of Formative Christianity and Judaism* (Philadelphia: Fortress Press, 1988), 274–75, 283.

8. The "Hellenists" and "Hebrews" may have been the predominantly Greek-speaking and Aramaic-speaking Jews, respectively, within the Jerusalem church.

I persecuted the church of God" (1 Cor 15:9); "I was violently persecuting the church of God and was trying to destroy it" (Gal 1:13; cf. Phil 3:6). Saul had his comeuppance in his experience on the Damascus road when, according to Luke's telling, "suddenly a light from heaven flashed around him," Saul fell off his mount, and a voice said "Saul, Saul, why do you persecute me?" (Acts 9:3-4), and again, "I am Jesus, whom you are persecuting" (9:5). This reference to his persecuting activities may have touched Saul's heart. He offers no resistance to the instruction to go into the city where "you will be told what you are to do" (v. 6). Saul is struck blind by the experience (v. 8), but has his companions take him into the city. A disciple named Ananias receives instructions from the Lord (Christ), goes and speaks to Saul, telling him that he has been sent so "'that you may regain your sight and be filled with the Holy Spirit.' And immediately something like scales fell from his eyes, and his sight was restored. Then he got up and was baptized" (vv. 17-18), and shortly thereafter "he began to proclaim Jesus in the synagogues" (v. 20). So begins the career of the most influential apostle. In Acts 13:9 we hear that he is "also known as Paul,"[9] without further explanation, and he is not again called "Saul" except in flashbacks (such as 22:7).

Paul does not give any of this detail. In Galatians he says that he received the Gospel "through a revelation of Jesus Christ" (1:12), and after that experience he did not "go up to Jerusalem to those who were already apostles before me, but I went away at once into Arabia, and afterwards I returned to Damascus. Then after three years I did go up to Jerusalem to visit Cephas and stayed with him fifteen days" (1:17-18), and aside from that two-week visit he did not again return to Jerusalem for fourteen years (Gal 2:1), though the fourteen is probably meant to include the three. This will be discussed further in the chapter on Galatians. Paul does not mention Ananias, who is not an apostle; his concern in Galatians is to establish that he was not commissioned by Peter ("Cephas" in Aramaic) or any other apostle.

Thus the same incident can be described very differently in Acts and in the letters.[10] Further, there are many stories in Acts that cannot be

---

9. *Paulus* was a common Latin *cognomen,* the third part of a Roman's name (Jerome Murphy-O'Connor, *Paul: A Critical Life* [Oxford: Oxford University Press, 1997], 42). The name may have been meant to show Paul's Roman citizenship, or simply to present a familiar-sounding name.

10. Indeed, it is described rather differently on each of the three occasions when it is recounted in Acts (9:1-22; 22:4-16; 26:9-20).

verified from Paul's letters, such as Paul's preaching at Athens (Acts 17). Such stories will not be covered in this book. Other incidents will be discussed in the chapters on the individual letters. We will not attempt to construct a detailed itinerary of Paul's career, but we can summarize some of the scholarly reconstructions of the main events and missionary journeys.

Paul's Preaching Career

The chronology of the apostolic career of Paul is notoriously complicated. Scholars face the difficult task of coordinating Acts with the letters and trying to link both with events and dates from Roman records. Paul's longer trips are usually referred to as the three missionary journeys. Antioch (in Syria) was his long-term base of operations, but Ephesus, Corinth, and other cities were secondary bases for his extensive mission work in the regions around the Aegean Sea. In the midst of this activity there was an event commonly called the Apostolic Council or Jerusalem Council (Acts 15), in which some compromises were reached between the Jerusalem-based apostles and the apostles who were mainly teaching Gentiles (Paul and Barnabas).

In Acts (3:26; 13:46; 18:5-6; 26:20) Paul and his fellows preach first to the Jews in any given town, going to the Gentiles only after they have been rejected by the Jews. It takes on a somewhat artificial appearance, this repeated going to the Jews to be beaten and rejected, and then going to the Gentiles. On the other hand, it would be "implausible" to suggest that Paul did not preach to Jewish communities at all, especially in cities with sizable Jewish populations such as Corinth.[11]

No consensus on dating has ever been reached. Even the date of Paul's call experience is disputed, with estimates ranging from 30 (the same year as Jesus' death and resurrection) to 36 C.E. Martin Hengel and Anna Schwemer assign it to the year 33, followed by three years in Arabia and Damascus, a brief visit to Jerusalem in 36, and then preaching in Tarsus and surrounding areas from 36 to 40[12] (not counted as a "missionary journey").

---

11. David G. Horrell, *The Social Ethos of the Corinthian Correspondence: Interests and Ideology from 1 Corinthians to 1 Clement* (Edinburgh: T&T Clark, 1996), 75.

12. Martin Hengel and Anna Maria Schwemer, *Paul Between Damascus and Antioch: The Unknown Years* (Louisville: Westminster John Knox, 1997), xi.

Hengel and Schwemer date the first missionary tour of Paul and Barnabas to Syria, Cyprus, and southern Galatia from 41 to 46 or 47 C.E.[13] F. F.
Bruce places it from 47 to 48, and Robert Jewett advocates 43 to 45.[14] There
is no agreement on whether the Apostolic Council took place before, during, or after the second tour. Hengel and Schwemer put the Apostolic
Council at the end of 48 or beginning of 49, with the second tour beginning
in 49. Gerd Theissen agrees in placing the Apostolic Council before the
second tour, but puts it somewhere between 46 and 48.[15] Several scholars
place the Apostolic Council toward the *end* of the second tour, in 51.[16]

Paul is accompanied on the second tour by Silas instead of Barnabas,
with whom he had a dispute (Acts 15:37-40). The tour is eventful, with
hostile receptions and beatings in some cities, but with the founding of
many new churches. The apostles go through Asia Minor to Greece,
spending over two years in Thessalonica and Corinth, in 52–53 journey-
ing east to Asia Minor and then the Syrian coast, possibly going inland
to visit Jerusalem, then traveling north to Antioch, where Paul confronts
Peter for refusing to eat with Gentiles (Gal 2:11-15).[17] He may have written his Thessalonian correspondence during this tour.

On the third missionary journey Paul proceeds through Asia Minor
to such coastal cities as Ephesus (where Paul writes Galatians and the
Corinthian letters)[18] before moving into northern Greece and down to
Corinth, where Paul writes Romans in 55, 56,[19] or 57,[20] and then on to
Jerusalem to deliver the collection for the poor, where Paul is arrested.
He is held in prison in Caesarea for two years (Acts 23:33; 24:27). Still a
prisoner, Paul is taken to Rome, where he is held for two years according

13. Ibid., xii–xiii.

14. Summarized in Calvin Roetzel, *Paul: The Man and the Myth* (Edinburgh: T&T Clark,
1999), 179, 181.

15. Gerd Theissen, *The New Testament: History, Literature, Religion,* trans. John Bowden
(London: T&T Clark, 2003), 55.

16. Robert Jewett, summarized in Roetzel, *Paul: The Man and the Myth,* 181; Robin Griffith-
Jones, *The Gospel According to Paul: The Creative Genius Who Brought Jesus to the World* (New
York: HarperCollins, 2004), x; Murphy-O'Connor, *Paul: A Critical Life,* 28.

17. Hengel and Schwemer, *Paul Between Damascus and Antioch,* xiii.

18. First Galatians, *then* the Corinthian letters (Roetzel, *Paul: The Man and the Myth,*
182–83, 227 n. 5). The Corinthian letters, *then* Galatians (Hans-Josef Klauck, with the collaboration of Daniel P. Bailey, *Ancient Letters and the New Testament* [Waco, TX: Baylor
University Press, 2006], 313).

19. Griffith-Jones, *Gospel According to Paul,* xii–xiii; Theissen, *New Testament,* 56; Roetzel,
Paul: The Man and the Myth, 182–83.

20. Klauck, *Ancient Letters,* 301.

to Acts 28:30. He may have written Philemon and Philippians, and co-written Colossians,[21] during this imprisonment (some of which was really house arrest—"at his own expense," Acts 28:30). The Acts narrative breaks off without finishing the story of Paul. It is not known whether Luke understood Paul to have been released from supervised confinement. Some even think he may have made a journey to Spain before being re-arrested.[22] All our post-biblical Christian sources attest to the tradition that he was beheaded in Rome during Nero's reign.[23]

Paul's status as a Roman citizen (according to Acts) helped him through some of his encounters with the authorities.[24] This is never mentioned in the letters of Paul, but mentioning Roman citizenship might have been more of a negative than a positive for "a Hebrew born of Hebrews" (Phil 3:5) claiming to be part of "the Israel of God" (Gal 6:16).

The Apostolic Council

A major issue in the early church was the inclusion of Gentiles and exactly what provisions of Torah, if any, they would be required to observe. There were some on the conservative side who wanted to require circumcision and full Torah observance by all Gentile converts. Luke's main interest in his account of the Apostolic Council in Acts 15 is to show harmony between the Jerusalem apostles and Gentile-focused apostles such as Paul. Paul's interest is to show that his Gentile mission was "recognized" by other apostles (Gal 2:9), affirming that he "had been entrusted with the gospel for the uncircumcised, just as Peter . . . for the circumcised" (Gal 2:7).

According to Luke, James (the brother of Jesus) asked that the Gentiles follow a minimal Torah requirement—the rejection of idolatry, of unlawful marriage, of the meat of strangled animals, and of blood-eating. This policy was accepted and published (Acts 15:20-30), though some do not believe that Paul would have acquiesced to any list of Torah-requirements. The council's statement was an important compromise, for the

21. Regarding authorship issues, see the sub-chapter on Colossians.

22. Hengel and Schwemer, *Paul Between Damascus and Antioch,* xiv; Murphy-O'Connor, *Paul: A Critical Life,* 31.

23. In 62 or 64 (Hengel and Schwemer, *Paul Between Damascus and Antioch,* xiv); "probably" in 67 (Murphy-O'Connor, *Paul: A Critical Life,* 31).

24. Acts 16:37; 22:25; 23:37. Roetzel is skeptical about the claim of Roman citizenship (*Paul: The Man and the Myth,* 19–22).

conservative Jerusalem church was able to come to an agreement with the liberal-leaning mission of Paul and Barnabas. This willingness to compromise, in fact, shows that James and Peter were not the most extreme conservatives on the Gentile question, nor was Paul the most extreme liberal. There seems to have been a "Hellenist" wing that attacked such traditional symbols as the Temple, as Stephen does in Acts 7,[25] and an even more extreme Gnostic wing that completely repudiated traditional religion (Jewish or otherwise).

There was no well-organized "Gnosticism," but there was a Gnostic trend within Hellenistic religions that had penetrated both Judaism and Christianity, claiming to have a hidden wisdom and "knowledge" (*gnōsis*) unavailable to traditional religion, including orthodox Christianity. Gnostics were deeply suspicious of authority, clergy, religious law, and social institutions. Gnostic approaches were characterized by a sense of alienation from tradition, from the world, and from the body.[26] It is likely that this reflects the viewpoint of socially mobile urban professionals who were uncomfortable with religious traditionalism. They resonated with the idea that there was a special knowledge that ordinary people and traditional cultures did not have.

To summarize (and oversimplify), I would postulate the existence of the following six versions of Christianity in Paul's time, arranging them according to their attitude toward Jewish tradition: on the far right are "people . . . from James" or "the sect of the Pharisees" (Gal 2:12; Acts 15:5) who require Gentile men to undergo circumcision (which also implies a male-led community). These are the foes we see Paul fighting in Galatians and in Philippians 3. Not as far to the right is James himself, who is willing to impose only a partial Torah observance (without circumcision) on Gentiles. In the middle is a group, apparently led by Peter, that preaches to both Jews and Gentiles and believes that God "has made no distinction between them and us" (Acts 15:9). On the liberal side is Paul, with his refusal to impose any ritual rules from Torah (though he may want to retain some sexual rules, but even here he appeals to natural law [1 Cor 5:1] and to "the truth about God" [Rom 1:25] rather than to Torah). Paul has some limited respect for James and Peter, but only contempt for the most conservative group. Close to Paul but a little

---

25. William W. Meissner, *The Cultic Origins of Christianity: The Dynamics of Religious Development* (Collegeville, MN: Liturgical Press, 2000), 115.

26. Meissner, *Cultic Origins*, 165, 184. On narcissism and paranoia in the psychodynamics of cultic organizations, see ibid., 182–208, 218–22.

further to the left are the "Hellenists," who are more distant from Palestinian Judaism than is Paul, and perhaps speak only Greek. Furthest to the left are the Gnostics or proto-Gnostics.[27] Of course, this speculative reconstruction needs to be subject to revision in light of new evidence or new interpretations.

With this as a background picture we can begin examining the letters, the one thing that will enable us to get acquainted with Paul.

---

27. "Proto-Gnostic" is a term to signify first-century movements that seek secret wisdom and are suspicious of world and body, but lack the intensely anti-orthodox and systematic theology of second-century Gnosticism. The *Gospel of Thomas* would be proto-Gnostic (e.g., Sayings 56, 87, 108, and 110).

Chapter 3

First and Second Thessalonians

FIRST THESSALONIANS

All of Paul's letters were written to particular audiences to deal with particular problems, sometimes following a report heard by Paul about events going on in the congregation. Scholars use the term "occasional" to refer to the fact that each letter was stimulated by a particular occasion or situation. Thus the letters are not examples of systematic theology (with the partial exception of Romans), but of practical advice and of attempted rectification of particular problems. We are bound to be frustrated, therefore, if we try to find Paul's answers to all theological questions in the letters, even in Romans.

On the other hand, it can be difficult to reconstruct the occasion of a particular letter, as scholars disagree on the challenges faced by Paul. First Thessalonians may be easier than some other letters because Paul makes it clear he is trying to encourage his readers and, later in the letter, that he is responding to questions about the general resurrection (the resurrection of believers).

Reciprocity, Patronage, and Perseverance: 1:1–4:1

Paul opens the letter in a way that was standard in his day:[1] with a greeting, a "grace" blessing, and a thanksgiving for the friendship of the

---

1. See John L. White, *The Apostle of God: Paul and the Promise of Abraham* (Peabody, MA: Hendrickson, 1999), 63–65.

addressees. The greeting is from "Paul, Silvanus, and Timothy" (1 Thess 1:1), but numerous places in the letter (including "I, Paul" in 2:18) indicate that Paul does the writing. Silvanus and Timothy were fellow-workers of Paul's, personally known to the Thessalonian Christians. Timothy went to Thessalonica once when Paul was unable to do so (3:1-2).

Almost immediately in 1 Thessalonians we see evidence of the network of personal relationships between Paul and the Thessalonians. There were bonds of friendship and reciprocity, signaled by the frequent reference to them as brothers and sisters (1:4; 2:1, 9, 14, 17, etc.) who are "very dear" (2:8). But there is also an unequal relationship. Since Paul is responsible for their salvation (he preached in Thessalonica and founded the congregation there), he is their "father," and they are obligated to him. Paul was "entrusted with the message of the gospel" (2:4), and the Thessalonians "learned from us how you ought to live and to please God" (4:1).

This includes the ability to stand firm in the face of oppression: "For you, brothers and sisters, became imitators of the churches of God in Christ Jesus that are in Judea, for you suffered the same things from your own companions as they did from the Jews" (2:14). Evidently their Gentile neighbors are getting them into trouble with the authorities, just as Jewish neighbors were doing to the Jerusalem believers. It can be very dangerous to be a religious nonconformist, as many would find out centuries later in Christian lands! The odd remark that "God's wrath has overtaken" the Jews (2:16) "who killed both the Lord Jesus and the prophets" (2:15) has seemed out of place to many scholars, but it is the same view commonly found in prophetic and apocalyptic literature, that Israel is fundamentally rebellious and must be punished.[2] The past tense (aorist) verb *ephthasen* ("has overtaken") has led many scholars to assume that these verses were added by a later hand, after the Roman suppression of the Jewish revolt in 70 CE, but some lesser, local trouble could be in view. Jewish relations with the Roman overseers were quite troubled throughout the decade of the 50s.

Paul perceives a pattern: those who follow the way of Christ will be persecuted, but they will be empowered if they follow the right examples. Hearing "our message of the gospel," the Thessalonians "became imitators of us and of the Lord, for in spite of persecution you received

---

2. Sigurd Grindheim, "Apostate Turned Prophet: Paul's Prophetic Self-Understanding and Prophetic Hermeneutic with Special Reference to Galatians 3.10-12," *NTS* 53 (2007): 549.

the word with joy inspired by the Holy Spirit" (1:5-6). Paul has shown them how to endure. His own liveliness depends on their perseverance: "For we now live, if you continue to stand firm in the Lord" (3:8). Paul is reminding them that he is their patron and they are the clients. He helped them, and they are now obligated to him. "As you know, we dealt with each one of you like a father with his children" (2:11). Relations of patronage and clientage were so well known to ancient people that a mere reminder was usually enough. One in the position of a patron could afford to be subtle, even gentle, in reminding people of their inferior and obligated status in relation to oneself.

So Paul is able to emphasize that his leadership is considerate (2:12), gentle, even motherly (2:7), and not motivated by greed (2:5). Further, Paul makes it clear that he is under the leadership of God; he answers to God (2:4); the word he preaches is "the word of God" (2:13). But he wants the Thessalonians to remember their obligations to him, heightened by the fact that he has suffered for the Gospel (2:2; 3:4, 7), that he labored "night and day" for them (2:9), and prays "night and day" for them (3:10). He rejoices to learn that they are resisting temptation, persevering in "faith and love" (3:6). They have shown "love and steadfastness of hope" (1:3), and this reassures Paul (3:7, 9).

All these reminders and compliments strengthen Paul's hand when he comes to mention to them "what is lacking in your faith" (3:10), which may include sexual lust and exploitation (4:4-6), but certainly their confusion about the general resurrection (4:13-17), which Paul sets out to dispel in the last third of the letter.

Acquiring a Vessel: 4:2-8

Before that, though, there is the challenging passage in 4:2-8, where Paul tells them that it is God's will "that you abstain from fornication; that each one of you know how to control your own body [or: how to take a wife for himself] in holiness and honor, not with lustful passion" (4:3-5). "Take a wife" in 4:4 is a translator's guess; what it actually says is "acquire a vessel," and Beverly Roberts Gaventa advocates translating it that way, to preserve Paul's ambiguity.[3] Translators, even from early times, debated the meaning of the phrase. Does "acquiring a vessel"

---

3. Cited in Jennifer A. Glancy, *Slavery in Early Christianity* (Oxford: Oxford University Press, 2002), 61.

mean that a man should acquire self-control over his sexual organs,[4] or does it mean that a man should acquire (one) sexual vessel (a wife)? In either case, the implied reader is a male. In 1 Corinthians 7 Paul shows some respect for marriage. Referring to a wife as a "vessel [*skeuos*]" may not seem overly flattering, but it was common usage. Paul's point is that Christians should not be lustful like "the Gentiles" (4:5, *ta ethnē*, rendered "the nations" in NJB).

The ethical crux is in 4:6: one is not to "wrong or exploit a brother [or sister] in this matter." Women would have to be included within the label "brother" or else this does not follow from what precedes it. "The Lord is an avenger in all these things" (4:6), for example, these sexual matters.[5] Paul's lack of clarity is not due to a lack of seriousness. Modesty restrains him from being clearer. Presumably his original audience understood him better than we do. "God did not call us to impurity but in holiness" (4:7) certainly implies sexual purity. The spiritual basis of this exhortation is that "whoever rejects this rejects not human authority but God, who also gives his Holy Spirit to you" (4:8). Ethics are undergirded by spiritual principles. One must be clear about the principles and then practice them in one's relationships.

The Second Coming and Believer Resurrection: 4:13–5:10

The *parousia* (return) of Christ is mentioned several times in 1 Thessalonians, especially in the last section. Jesus' lordly status will be clear at his return: Paul speaks of the coming of "our Lord Jesus" or "our Lord Jesus Christ" at 2:19 and 5:23, and of "the coming of our Lord Jesus with all his saints" at 3:13 (the last idea echoing Zech 14:5).

No one knows when the Lord will come again. Echoing a line from Matthew, Paul says "the day of the Lord will come like a thief at night" (5:2; cf. Matt 24:43-44; Rev 3:3). But Paul does spell out some things that will happen at the *parousia*, mainly to comfort his readers, who worry about their departed loved ones. He reassures them that those believers will be seen again: at his return, Jesus will "bring with him those who have died [literally 'fallen asleep']" (4:14). Jesus, with an archangel, will oversee the resurrection of believers: "For the Lord himself, with a cry of command, with the archangel's call and with the sound of God's

4. NIV, NRSV, NEB, and NASB reflect this option.
5. Abraham J. Malherbe, *Paul and the Thessalonians: The Philosophical Tradition of Pastoral Care* (Philadelphia: Fortress Press, 1987), 76–77.

trumpet, will descend from heaven, and the dead in Christ will rise first" (4:16).

Everything will be utterly changed, even for believers who are alive at the time of this climactic event: "Then we who are alive, who are left, will be caught up in the clouds together with them to meet the Lord in the air" (4:17). This is the event that many evangelical Christians today call the "Rapture."

Paul wants to relieve the Thessalonians' anxiety and confusion about the afterlife and the *parousia*. He feels the need to build up their confidence. They need to know "that whether we are awake or asleep we may live with him" (5:10). He builds up the Thessalonians: "you are all children of light and children of the day" (5:5). "You became an example to all the believers in Macedonia" (1:7). They turned away from idols, and now they are famous for their love (1:9; 4:9-10).

Still, there is plenty of exhortation to balance out the compliments: "let us be sober, and put on the breastplate of faith and love, and for a helmet the hope of salvation" (5:8). Paul wants his flock to be ready for judgment day, which will be a frightening scenario for those who are not ready. However, "God has destined us not for wrath but for obtaining salvation through our Lord Jesus Christ, who died for us, so that whether we are awake or asleep we may live with him" (5:9-10). Paul is as certain about God's judgment on sinners as he is about believers being exempt from this "wrath." Although not prominent in the body of the letter, God's wrath looms at the end, as it did near the beginning where he spoke of "Jesus, who rescues us from the wrath that is coming" (1:10).[6] God makes the believer "[sanctified] entirely . . . kept sound and blameless at the coming of our Lord Jesus Christ" (5:23).

The lordship of Jesus is a central teaching in this letter. Five times Paul uses the phrase "Lord Jesus Christ" (1:1, 3; 5:9, 23, 28). Of course, any kind of leader—a patron, a parent—can be called "lord," or the title can be used of a king or god. In Judaism it usually refers to the one God. But for Paul (and the other apostles as well),[7] "Lord" is applied to Jesus not because he is the Messiah, but because he is divine. In distinction from the contemporary messianic ideas we see in the Dead Sea Scrolls and

6. God's "wrath" is a common term for God's judgment, but "the absence of the vengeance motif" distinguishes Paul's apocalyptic from standard Jewish apocalyptic, such as is seen in the Book of Revelation (Johan Christiaan Beker, *Paul the Apostle: The Triumph of God in Life and Thought* [Philadelphia: Fortress Press, 1980], 192).

7. See Matt 14:30; 25:44; Luke 10:41; John 11:2; 20:28; Acts 7:59, etc.

elsewhere, the Messiah Jesus is not just a mortal used by God, but is a divine figure, the "one Lord . . . through whom are all things" (1 Cor 8:6), who is "from heaven" (1 Cor 15:47), who is equal to God but emptied himself to come to earth (Phil 2:6-7), and is destined to be acknowledged by all (Phil 2:10-11). This is a remarkable modification of Jewish monotheism. New Testament authors affirm both monotheism and the divinity of Christ.[8] We come to "knowledge of the glory of God in the face of Jesus Christ" (2 Cor 4:6).

Once this insight is firmly recognized it is neither remarkable nor surprising that acknowledgment of the lordship of Jesus represents a statement of dissent from the deification of the emperor. It may be that Paul is even mocking one of the slogans of the emperor cult when he refers to "peace and security"[9]: "When they say, 'There is peace and security,' then sudden destruction will come upon them" (1 Thess 5:3). Even "gospel" (*euangelion*) itself is a term used (though usually in the plural) to signify the "good news" that the emperor brings to the empire. *Euangelion* occurs in the famous Priene inscription celebrating "the god Augustus."[10] "Savior" (*sotēr*) is another term used in the emperor cult, particularly in Asia Minor. To some degree at least, Christianity is deliberately appropriating the terminology of the emperor cult, thus rejecting the emperor's deification claims.

Faith, Love, and Hope: Ethical Advice: 5:8-28

In 5:8 we saw Paul use breastplate/helmet imagery to speak of faith, love, and hope. This triad of spiritual virtues seems to be central to his teaching. He had begun the letter "remembering . . . your work of faith and labor of love and steadfastness of hope in our Lord Jesus Christ" (1:3), and in later letters he will say "faith, hope, and love abide" (1 Cor 13:13), and will speak of faith-access to God, boasting in hope, and

8. Christian devotion is not a departure from monotheism but "a new 'binitarian' form of *monotheism*" (Larry W. Hurtado, *How on Earth Did Jesus Become a God? Historical Questions about Earliest Devotion to Jesus* [Grand Rapids: Eerdmans, 2005], 51). It affirms Jewish monotheism (ibid., 136). Paul shows "complete disdain for pagan worship" (ibid., 44).

9. This is the understanding of Neil Elliott, *Liberating Paul: The Justice of God and the Politics of the Apostle* (Maryknoll, NY: Orbis, 1994), 189. Instead of the imperial "golden age," Paul speaks of "the present evil age" (Gal 1:4), a time of perversity and stupor (Phil 2:15; 1 Thess 5:7).

10. Frances Young, *The Theology of the Pastoral Letters*. NT Theology (Cambridge: Cambridge University Press, 1994), 64.

receiving love in the heart (Rom 5:2-5). These are the virtues to be practiced in the congregation: "encourage one another and build up each
other, as indeed you are doing" (1 Thess 5:11). Even in this command
Paul practices what he preaches, building up. He wants them to respect
and even love their ministerial leaders (5:12-13), but he also wants them
to help each other: "Be at peace among yourselves. . . . encourage the
fainthearted, help the weak, be patient with all of them" (5:13-14).

He echoes the Sermon on the Mount when he says, "see that none of
you repays evil for evil; but always seek to do good" (5:15; cf. Matt
5:39-46). Even his advice to "rejoice always" (5:16) echoes Jesus' advice
to "Rejoice and be glad, for your reward is great in heaven" (Matt 5:12).
"Pray without ceasing" (5:17) recalls the lesson of one of the parables:
"their need to pray always" (Luke 18:1). Although in his letters Paul
never discusses passages from the gospels, he does occasionally draw
on gospel traditions, and we simply do not know whether he preached
on any written gospels. In his letters he focuses intensely on certain
central points. In 1 Thessalonians his focus is on practicing love in the
congregation, standing firm in faith, hoping (trusting) in the future general resurrection, and believing in the lordship of Jesus.

Near the end of this letter we see a hint of the charismatic life of the
congregation: "Do not quench the Spirit. Do not despise the words of
prophets" (5:19-20). They are to exercise judgment regarding such utterances: "test everything; hold fast to what is good" (5:21). We get a glimpse
of a customary practice in the churches: "Greet all the brothers and sisters
with a holy kiss" (5:26). Such a greeting was a way of honoring the other
person; the language of honor and welcome is frequent at the end of
Paul's letters.

Paul's Use of Hellenistic Philosophy and Religion

Scholars debate the extent and manner in which Paul makes use of
techniques and concepts of the popular Hellenistic philosophers, the
Cynics and Stoics. It has long been observed that Paul's letters resemble
in many ways the Cynic epistles, which vigorously express advice, condemnation, and spiritual principle. Abraham Malherbe finds that Paul's
approach resembles that of the "mild Cynic" who criticizes the harshness
of the rigorous Cynic.[11]

11. Abraham J. Malherbe, *Paul and the Popular Philosophers* (Minneapolis: Fortress Press, 1989), 21, 115.

More than one scholar has noted similarities between the Cynic letters and the letters of Paul, occasionally with similar teachings. The Cynic Heraclitus wrote: "Evil alone makes one a slave; virtue alone frees . . . . You yourselves are slaves on account of your desire."[12] Paul said, "I am of the flesh, sold into slavery under sin. . . . you, having once been slaves of sin . . . [have] been set free from sin . . ." (Rom 7:14; 6:17-18).

Paul's call to repentance, transformation of mind, and dedication to a new way of living reminds some scholars of the widely-influential preaching of the Stoics. Stoicism was by far the most influential philosophy in the Greco-Roman world. Stoics taught that all people had "an innate capacity to know God"[13] or to live in harmony with Nature (all Stoics) or the divine (some Stoics). This required a decisive life-change, a reorientation toward Nature or God—what we would call a conversion experience. Of course, there are huge differences between Paul's theology and Stoic teaching. But Paul may be suggesting a recognized pattern of experience[14] when he speaks of "turn[ing] to God" (1 Thess 1:9) or being "transformed" in mind (Rom 12:2). After all, he was "apostle to the Gentiles" (Rom 11:13), and we should not be surprised that he used techniques that would appeal to Gentiles.[15] Frank Hughes finds that Paul's use of recognizable rhetorical structure "suggest[s] that Paul either learned rhetoric in school or had . . . a gift for . . . grasp[ing] rhetorical precepts."[16]

No one is arguing that Paul was a Cynic or Stoic, but many contend that Paul does indeed draw on the rhetorical methods, and occasionally the thought, of Cynics and Stoics,[17] or on such thought as it had already been "transmitted or developed in Jewish theological circles."[18]

---

12. Heraclitus, *Epistle 9*, lines 32-35 (tr., Worley), in Abraham A. Malherbe, *The Cynic Epistles: A Study Edition.* SBLSBS 12 (Missoula, MT: Scholars Press, 1979), 213.

13. Malherbe, *Paul and the Thessalonians,* 31.

14. Ibid., 68–72, 81; Troels Engberg-Pedersen, *Paul and the Stoics* (Louisville: Westminster John Knox, 2000).

15. Murphy-O'Connor disagrees, saying Paul would only oppose pagan philosophy (*Paul: A Critical Life,* 120). He does not seem to see that Paul's use of philosophical terms and techniques does not make Paul an advocate of those philosophies.

16. Frank W. Hughes, "The Social Situations Implied by Rhetoric," in Karl P. Donfried and Johannes Beutler, eds., *The Thessalonians Debate: Methodological Discord or Methodological Synthesis?* (Grand Rapids: Eerdmans, 2000), 251.

17. Engberg-Pedersen, *Paul and the Stoics;* Malherbe, *Paul and the Popular Philosophers.*

18. Will Deming, "Paul and Indifferent Things," in J. Paul Sampley, ed., *Paul in the Greco-Roman World: A Handbook* (Harrisburg, PA: Trinity Press International, 2003), 393.

There seem also to be places where Paul is using terminology of the local mystery cults, something that is not surprising if he is trying to reassure recent converts that what he teaches are really "God's mysteries" (1 Cor 4:1). He uses words that have echoes in the popular Dionysian mysteries ("nurse" and "care for you," 1 Thess 2:7-8).[19] Of course, this does not mean that Paul had anything to do with the mysteries, only that he was willing to appropriate their terminology, to steal their thunder. Monotheism remains central: "you turned to God from idols" (1:9), and there may be an anti-Dionysian message in his advice to take a wife "not with lustful passion, like the Gentiles who do not know God" (4:5).

SECOND THESSALONIANS

For centuries the church took for granted the Pauline authorship of this letter, but scholarship has exposed many difficulties in this assumption, and it is no longer considered among the "undisputed letters" of Paul.[20]

The letter deals with the same eschatological concerns as 1 Thessalonians. Its stated authors are the same ("Paul, Silvanus, and Timothy," 1:1). In fact, aside from the addition of one word ("our"), the first twenty Greek words in 2 Thessalonians are identical to the first nineteen in 1 Thessalonians, and it continues with a nearly identical thanksgiving for the Thessalonians' faith and love (1:3 in both letters), enduring through "persecutions and the afflictions" (2 Thess 1:4) or "in spite of persecution" (1 Thess 1:6). Unbelievers will be punished, but believers delivered, at the coming of the Lord (1 Thess 1:10; 2 Thess 1:6-10). This high degree of parallelism raises scholarly suspicion; it appears to be a conscious attempt to mimic the style while adding to the content of the earlier letter. It looks like someone in a teaching position trying to justify his expansion of Paul's eschatological teachings.

Besides a considerable heightening of divine vengeance, the second letter contains ideas never found in the more trusted Pauline letters: "when the Lord Jesus is revealed from heaven with his mighty angels

---

19. Karl P. Donfried, *Paul, Thessalonica, and Early Christianity* (Grand Rapids: Eerdmans, 2002), 23–30; idem, *The Theology of the Shorter Pauline Letters* (Cambridge: Cambridge University Press, 1993), 14.

20. The issue of pseudepigraphy in 2 Thessalonians is discussed in four articles in Thomas L. Brodie, Dennis MacDonald, and Stanley E. Porter, eds., *The Intertextuality of the Epistles: Explorations of Theory and Practice* (Sheffield; Sheffield Academic Press, 2006).

in flaming fire, inflicting vengeance" (2 Thess 1:7-8), and the unusual phrase "eternal destruction" (v. 9). This pattern will repeat itself throughout the epistle: a repetition of the structure and phraseology of 1 Thessalonians with the addition of considerable eschatological detail never found in Paul's own letters. Unique to 2 Thessalonians is the intriguing picture of "the lawless one" (2:3) who "takes his seat in the temple of God, declaring himself to be God" (2:4), which may describe the pride of Nero or some other emperor and has some echoes in NT mentions of "the beast" and "the antichrist" (Rev 13:5-8; 1 John 2:18; 4:3), but not in Paul's writings. Something or someone is currently restraining the lawless one (2:6-7), after which this evil one will "be revealed," but then Jesus himself "will destroy" this lawless one "with the breath of his mouth" (2:8). Jesus as the agent of revenge is certainly unlike anything Paul said. Rather, it resonates with the most violent of biblical apocalyptic scenarios: the lawless one in the temple echoes Daniel 8:11-12; 11:31-36, and Jesus as violent avenger occurs in Revelation 2:16; 19:15, 21.

The intention in this eschatology is "to defuse apocalyptic expectation, not to stimulate and prepare for it as Paul does in 1 Thess 4:13–5:11."[21] The first letter is telling believers to be prepared for the end (1 Thess 5:2-8); the second letter is telling the reader "not to be . . . shaken" or think that "the day of the Lord is already here" (2 Thess 2:2); the reader is not to worry, for certain things will be revealed in due time (2:3-7).

The theme of imitation of the apostle, which we saw in 1 Thessalonians, is also present in the later letter "in order to give you an example to imitate" (3:9). As before, the exhortation to imitation is an assumption of authority, in this case setting out to silence certain "idle" people (3:11) who, if they do not obey what is "in this letter," should "be ashamed" (3:14). But this one is probably not from Paul's hand, despite the heavy-handed claim, at the end, that he writes "this greeting with my own hand" (3:17).

Second Thessalonians builds on a letter tradition: its recipients are to "hold fast to the traditions that you were taught by us, either by word of mouth or by our letter" (2:15), and not be distracted by a "letter purporting to be from us" (2:2 RSV). This remark acknowledges that pseudepigraphy[22] is already taking place! The allegation of Pauline

---

21. Mark Harding, "Disputed and Undisputed Letters of Paul," in Stanley E. Porter, ed., *The Pauline Canon.* Pauline Studies 1 (Leiden: Brill, 2004), 159.

22. Pseudepigraphy was the practice, common in those times, of creating literary works and attributing them to revered sages or prophets, and thus, in Christianity, to apostles.

pseudepigraphy places the letter in the deutero-Pauline period, since no one would have wanted to forge a Pauline letter during his lifetime, when everyone argued with him. Paul became an iconic authority figure only after he had died a martyr's death. Second Thessalonians 2:2 lets the cat out of the bag—this letter is allegedly from Paul.

The author of Second Thessalonians wants to add to the Pauline tradition; he wishes to strengthen the influence of "tradition . . . received from us" (3:6) and hold up the image of Paul "as an example to imitate" (3:9). He threatens punishment for "those who do not obey what we say in this letter" (3:14). Spiritual concepts from the first letter that are echoed in the second include the need for love and endurance (1:3-4; 2:13; 3:5; cf. 1 Thess 1:3; 3:6, 12; 5:13) and a strong Jesus-centered eschatological hope (1:7; 2:14-16; cf. 1 Thess 1:3; 4:13-16; 5:8).

Hope is a major purpose for 2 Thessalonians, to "comfort your hearts and strengthen them" (2:17); the Lord "will strengthen you and guard you from the evil one" (3:3), "giv[ing] you peace" (3:16). Violence is promised for unbelievers, but there is nothing but "peace" (1:2; 3:16) and "grace" (1:2; 3:18) for believers, at the beginning and end of the letter. "Grace" also appears in the body of the letter, showing the kindliness of God and Christ toward believers (1:12; 2:16).

There is no subtlety here, nor any emphasis on steady progress or aspiration as in 1 Thessalonians 3:12 (increasing in love); 4:10-11 ("love all the brothers and sisters . . . more and more"). In 2 Thessalonians, one is either *in* (destined for peace) or *out* (destined for fire). When people add to Paul, they oversimplify him as well.

Chapter 4

First Corinthians

Acts 17 and 18 tell of Paul's traveling through northern Greece, founding churches at Thessalonica and Philippi, continuing down to the cities of Achaia, including Athens, and founding the church at Corinth, staying there for over a year. Scholars are divided regarding the dating of this visit. The traditional school of thought placed it somewhere between 49 and 52 CE, but a more recent suggestion puts it from 41 to 44 CE.[1]

We have names of a number of the leaders in the Corinthian church, including Priscilla and Aquila, who were among those expelled from Rome by the emperor Claudius. Crispus, whom Paul baptized (1:14), was a leader in the Corinthian synagogue (Acts 18:8), as was Sosthenes (Acts 18:17). Another person Paul baptized, a certain Gaius, became his host (1:14; Rom 16:23). The Corinthian church seems to have included people from all classes, from those with big homes to Erastus, "the city treasurer" (Rom 16:23), to tentmakers, artisans, and recently redeemed slaves.[2]

Corinth was a proud and important city, made the capital of the Greek province by the emperor Augustus in 27 BCE. It was a thriving port city with all the pleasures and enticements one might expect, and was infamous for its libertine practices. Aphrodite, after all, was the patron goddess

---

1. David G. Horrell, *The Social Ethos of the Corinthian Correspondence: Interests and Ideology from 1 Corinthians to 1 Clement* (Edinburgh: T&T Clark, 1996), 73–74, based on a redating of Claudius' expulsion of Jews from Rome.

2. See Wayne A. Meeks, *The First Urban Christians: The Social World of the Apostle Paul* (New Haven: Yale University Press, 1983).

of the city. There was also a strong tradition of philosophy, or "wisdom," among the Corinthians. Paul's problems with this congregation concern sexual behavior, class attitudes on the part of the richer members, and the perspective of those who considered themselves possessed of superior wisdom.

Where Is the Wise One? Chapters 1–4

The letter claims to be from Paul and a certain Sosthenes, but the latter appears again only at Acts 18:17, where he is said to be an official of the synagogue. That is enough to tell us that he was a prominent and respected individual in a sizable Jewish community in an important Greek city. His mention does not really indicate that he was a coauthor. Rather, Paul is being both polite and sagacious, sending greetings from a powerful backer.

Paul raises the themes of wisdom and knowledge right away, though in a disarming manner. His words later in the letter will be anything but disarming; he will be picking a fight with the Corinthians who consider themselves wise. At the beginning, though, he acknowledges that, through Christ, "in every way you have been enriched . . . in speech and knowledge of every kind" (1:5). Even here the reader might detect mockery: they are enriched in *every* way, with knowledge of *every* kind—and "you are not lacking in any spiritual gift" (1:7)! In light of what comes later, these excessive compliments seem to be dripping with sarcasm.

What concerns Paul most about the Corinthians is that "there are quarrels among you" (1:11). The Corinthian congregation is torn by factionalism: "each of you says, 'I belong to Paul,' or 'I belong to Apollos,' or 'I belong to Cephas'³" (1:12). It is so bad that Paul is grateful he only baptized a few members of that congregation (1:14-16). He will take up the theme of divisiveness again in the third chapter; he is not done with his wisdom theme, or rather, his anti-wisdom theme. Paul rejects what passes for wisdom in that group. He says, "The message about the cross is foolishness to those who are perishing, but to us who are being saved it is the power of God. For it is written, 'I will destroy the wisdom of the wise'" (1:18-19). Clearly, the Gospel undermines worldly concepts of status and wisdom. Paul presses this point: "Where is the one who is wise? . . . . Where is the debater of this age? Has not God made foolish

3. We know him as Peter. Cephas is the nickname Jesus gave to Simon; it means "rock" in Aramaic. The corresponding Greek word is "Petros," the source of our "Peter."

the wisdom of the world?" (1:20). The supposed wisdom of certain Corinthians is a false (a worldly) wisdom. God gives a different, a spiritual, kind of honor. As Robert Jewett says, "Christ crucified grants honor to the lowly and brings shame to the boastful."[4]

To those who think in common ways, even to the Greeks who "desire wisdom" (1:22), the Christian "proclamation" (Greek *kerygma*) is "foolishness" (1:21). Paul is clear: "we proclaim Christ crucified, a stumbling block to Jews and foolishness to Gentiles" (1:23). Most of the occurrences of "wisdom" and "foolishness" thus far are ironic. But he is not being ironic when he proclaims "Christ the power of God and the wisdom of God" (1:24). This is *real* power and wisdom, and it will continue to shock and dismay those who think in worldly ways. The world is really foolish, and unable to recognize true wisdom: "God chose what is foolish in the world to shame the wise" (1:27). The world, after all, dishonored the Messiah.

The Corinthian Christians need to know where real wisdom is centered, and salvation as well; it is Christ who "became for us wisdom from God, and righteousness and sanctification and redemption" (1:30). Unless the Corinthians learn to recognize the true righteousness of Christ, their "wisdom" is just self-deception and pride.[5]

Paul is engaged in a fierce but carefully waged battle with those in the Corinthian congregation who consider themselves to be "spiritual" persons. He is parodying their own sayings when he allows that "those who are spiritual discern all things" (2:15), and when he says that he is "interpreting spiritual things to those who are spiritual" (2:13). He openly insults them when he calls them "infants" (3:1; 14:20). He rubs it in, saying they had to be fed milk, not solid food; they are not spiritual, but "still of the flesh" (3:3). He mocks their slogans when he calls them "rich" and "kings" (4:8), having "knowledge," "liberty" (8:1, 9), and "wisdom" (1:20). No! God will refute the wise (1:19); God has used the "foolish . . . to shame the wise" (1:27). They consider themselves "spiritual people," but they are "people of the flesh" (3:1) who manifest "jealousy and quarreling" (3:3). Paul could probably name the individuals he considers guilty, but he prefers to say "some . . . have become arrogant" (4:18). They know who they are.

---

4. Robert Jewett, "Paul, Shame, and Honor," in J. Paul Sampley, ed., *Paul in the Greco-Roman World: A Handbook* (Harrisburg, PA: Trinity Press International, 2003), 558.

5. Bruce W. Winter sees Paul reacting against the self-promoting ethic of the sophists (*Philo and Paul among the Sophists.* SNTSMS 96 [Cambridge: Cambridge University Press, 1997], 116–76).

Paul claims to lack "eloquent wisdom" or "lofty words" (1:17; 2:1), but he reminds them that when he proclaimed the Gospel among them, it happened "with a demonstration of the Spirit and of power" (2:4). (Presumably he alludes to healings, prophetic utterances, and transformed lives.) If Paul did not speak with cleverness and recognizable "wisdom," with what *did* he speak? It was with the cross-centered *kerygma:* "I decided to know nothing among you except Jesus Christ, and him crucified" (2:2). It does involve wisdom, but only the spiritually mature can recognize it (2:6). It is revealed by the Spirit; the Spirit knows "the depths of God" (2:10). Paul stands for the wisdom that comes only from the Spirit and is opposed to the self-congratulatory "wisdom" of the world. He stands for the power of God, which is opposed to the violence of human power; God will even submit to the cross, yet God's power is not diminished by suffering violence. This, of course, is baffling to the natural human mind, but with spiritual wisdom it can begin to make sense. For this to happen, one must truly rely on the Spirit and on the mind of Christ, which believers can really have: "we have the mind of Christ" (2:16).

Paul speaks God's hidden wisdom, which "none of the rulers of this age understood . . . for if they had, they would not have crucified the Lord of glory" (2:8). The identity of the "rulers" is frequently debated. Some think the reference is to worldly political powers; others think it means the invisible cosmic powers whose loyalty is questionable, but who will someday bend the knee to Christ (Phil 2:10). Nor is it clear *why* they would not have crucified him. Would they hold back out of cautious fear, out of genuine respectfulness, or out of pure malice (not wanting good to come from crucifying the Lord of glory)? Paul does not make it clear.

Since believers have the mind of Christ, they should know better than to allow divisiveness. "[A]s long as there is jealousy and quarreling among you, are you not of the flesh . . . ?" Paul asks (3:3). They are divided into factions, as "one says, 'I belong to Paul,' and another, 'I belong to Apollos'" (3:4). These are just human ministers, but "God gave the growth" (3:6). Paul and Apollos are "God's servants" (3:9). Paul changes metaphors here, in order to say that he laid the foundation while another (Apollos) built on it, but the foundation is Jesus Christ (3:10-11), without whom there is nothing. In "the Day," the worth of each "builder" or worker "will be revealed with fire" (3:13), and some workers will only be saved through a correcting fire (3:15).

Having made his point about factionalism and the true foundation, Paul utters this powerful saying: "Do you not know that you are God's temple, and that God's Spirit dwells in you?" (3:16). The "you" here (and at the end of 3:17) is plural, and the temple is the congregation, but this does not negate the significance of this metaphor for the individual. Later, while talking about individual behavior, Paul will say: "your body is a temple of the holy Spirit" (6:19). "Your" is plural, but "body" and "temple" are singular. The image covers both individual and congregation—the Spirit indwells both. Again Paul repeats his disgust with pride in wisdom: God fools the "wise" (3:19-20), and people should not "boast about human leaders" (v. 21). They all belong to Christ, "and Christ belongs to God" (3:23).

Some scholars see Apollos as Paul's main target in 1 Corinthians. According to Niels Hyldahl, Paul saw Apollos' teaching as Hellenistic philosophy and not really the Gospel at all. Apollos divided people into the spiritual people, the mental people, and the physical people ("the pneumatic, the psychic, and the sarcic"), Hyldahl says, but Paul uses Apollos' terminology to say they are all "sarcic (1 Cor 3.1-3)!"[6] Paul does seem to be mocking this division when he says, "I could not speak to you as spiritual people, but rather as people of the flesh" (3:1), but the theory that Apollos is the main target is unconvincing. It is true that, right after his attack on false wisdom in 3:18-20, Paul mentions Apollos, but "Paul" and "Cephas" as well (v. 22). These can hardly be Paul's enemies! Rather, the problem is pride and boasting. There may be some rivalry between Paul and Apollos, perhaps even a Paul faction and an Apollos faction (3:4-5), but Paul stresses that they are ministers of the *same* Lord (v. 5), planting and watering the *same* garden (v. 6), whose growth is caused by God alone (v. 7). Paul does put Apollos in his place, as a latecoming minister, but Apollos is not labeled an enemy. Paul attacks his outright enemies, but he never names them. Apollos—and Cephas, and *Paul*—are all taken down a peg, but not condemned.

Apostles are just "servants of Christ and stewards of the mysteries of God," and they need to be trustworthy (4:1-2). Of course, it is God's judgment on this, not human judgment, that matters (4:3-6). One should not boast in anything that is conferred on one (4:7). Paul mocks the Corinthians' wisdom slogan: "you have become kings" (4:8), which is just more boasting. Christlike leadership is not pompous; apostles are "the last of all, as though sentenced to death" (4:9). Paul hopes to embarrass the

---

6. Niels Hyldahl, "Paul and Hellenistic Judaism in Corinth," in Peder Borgen and Søren Giversen, eds., *The New Testament and Hellenistic Judaism* (Peabody, MA: Hendrickson, 1995), 216.

"wise" in Corinth when he writes, "We are fools for the sake of Christ, but you are wise in Christ" (4:10). They need to reverse their selfish values and experience what he has experienced: "We are weak, but you are strong. You are held in honor, but we in disrepute. . . . we are poorly clothed and beaten and homeless" (4:10-11). The point is the Christlike response: "When reviled, we bless; when persecuted, we endure" (4:12). In embodying Christlike behavior, it may be that Paul is also filling a role that was common in mime and plays: the fool or lower-class buffoon who turns the tables on his supposed social betters.[7] Thus Paul would be using a recognizable Greco-Roman cultural symbol.

Of course, Paul's critique is serious, not frivolous. He is saying that the apostolic pattern, like the Christ-pattern, is that one will be abused by the world and vindicated later. "We have become like the rubbish [*perikatharmata*] of the world, the dregs [*peripsēma*] of all things" (4:13). Those Greek terms were sometimes used to designate the human scapegoats, the *pharmakoi,* of Greek culture.[8] If Jesus was the supreme scapegoat, apostles must be little scapegoats in this evil age. Proud spirituality (4:18) is wrongheaded in every way, and the Corinthians are like "children," to be ignorant of this (4:14), but Paul has become their father, and they need to imitate him (4:15-16). He is sending Timothy as his surrogate to teach them, and he hopes to be able to come to them himself soon (4:17, 19). The roles of patronage are quite visible here: Paul is concerned for his clients, but is quite willing to discipline them, and there is a clear threat: "What would you prefer? Am I to come to you with a stick, or with love in a spirit of gentleness?" (4:21).

Sexual Boundaries;
Images of Sacrifice and Redemption: Chapters 5–6

Paul is horrified that a member of the congregation is sleeping with his stepmother, his father's second wife, a clear violation of Jewish law (Lev 18:8; 20:11). But Paul says it is equally horrifying to any decent Gentile, "immorality . . . of a kind that is not found even among pagans . . . a man living with his father's wife" (5:1). He urges that this man be "removed from among you" (5:2).

---

7. L. L. Welborn, *Paul, the Fool of Christ: A Study of 1 Corinthians 1–4 in the Comic Philosophic Tradition* (London: T&T Clark, 2005), 117–247.

8. Gustav Stählin, "περίψημα," *TDNT* 6:84–87, 90–91; Anthony Tyrrell Hanson, *The Paradox of the Cross in the Thought of St. Paul* (Sheffield: JSOT Press, 1987), 32–34.

This passage reveals the nature of the relationship between this church and its founder, or at least the relationship Paul wants. He expects (or hopes) to have the authority, as their founder, to be able to tell them "I have already pronounced judgment . . . on the man who has done such a thing" (5:3-4). Paul hopes that the expulsion will work for the man's own good; this is the probable meaning of "hand this man over to Satan for the destruction of the flesh, so that his spirit may be saved in the day of the Lord" (5:5).

Although he is focusing some of his judgment on this one individual, Paul largely holds the congregation responsible, and it is the whole group he is scolding when he says, "Your boasting is not a good thing" (5:6). Now he uses a metaphor from the cultic (ritual) system, telling them to "clean out the old yeast" (5:7), a practice families performed as part of their preparation for the Passover festival. This is a rich metaphor for Paul because it gives him the opportunity to make a connection between the slain Passover lambs and Jesus as a slain victim: "our paschal lamb, Christ, has been sacrificed" (5:7). This is the first, but not the last time in our sequential reading through Paul that we encounter a sacrificial metaphor. We do not know how far he wants his hearers to take the metaphor, whether he wants to suggest that Christ's death caused the wrath of God to "pass over" believers, just as "the LORD" or "the destroyer" passed over the blood-smeared doorposts of the Israelites "to strike down the Egyptians" (Exod 12:23). This would be a vivid, but troubling, theological image.

The sacrificial metaphor will be discussed later in this section. For now we note that Paul is focusing less on the sacrificial aspect than on the banishing of the yeast, since he wants the congregation to banish its smugness and moral laziness, "the yeast of malice and evil," and to embrace instead "the unleavened bread of sincerity and truth" (5:8). But he very much wants them to impose judgment, and he uses a line that occurs repeatedly in Deuteronomy in connection with imposing the death penalty: "Drive out the wicked person from among you" (1 Cor 5:13; Deut 13:6 [English v. 5]; 17:7; 21:21; 22:22). Is he allowing Torah still to apply when it comes to sexual crimes? Actually, he had begun by saying this immorality was offensive to pagans as well (5:1). Thus he begins with an appeal to natural law but makes use of Torah phraseology as well.

We should probably not use this passage to draw any firm conclusions about Paul's theology of the Law. He just wants the Corinthians to prohibit this kind of sexual immorality; he does not care whether they use Torah principles or natural law reasoning, as long as they do the right thing. Paul has a visceral moral reaction against what the man is doing, and indeed, Paul's own moral training is in Torah, but he is not seeking to enforce Torah observance, just a moral principle that any honest Gentile would also recognize. He is not imposing a legal structure in this letter that he refuses to impose in any of his other letters. His approach is moral and practical—and emotional!

In the next chapter[9] Paul discusses another ethical concern: the lodging of lawsuits by one believer against another. How can believers submit their cases to the courts of unbelievers, he wants to know, when believers are destined to "judge the world" (6:1-2)? This is absurd; there ought to be enough wise and trustworthy members of the congregation who can arbitrate the disputes (6:4-5). It is outrageous that believers seem to be wanting to cheat fellow-believers (6:8); this threatens their very salvation: "Do you not know that wrongdoers will not inherit the kingdom of God?" (6:9).

But it is not just economic crimes to which Paul refers; he attaches a long list of people who will not inherit the kingdom of God, and about half of the items are of a sexual nature: "Fornicators . . . adulterers, male prostitutes,[10] sodomites,[11] . . . drunkards, revilers, robbers—none of these will inherit the kingdom of God" (6:9-10). This is similar to lists that can be found in other moralists of the ancient world, particularly Stoics, but also Jewish writers like Philo of Alexandria. Paul insists that the baptized, the "washed," should be above such behavior (6:11). And here is where Paul mockingly quotes back at the Corinthians their slogan: "All things are lawful for me" (6:12). The Corinthians should not engage in selfish bodily living, but look ahead to their resurrection (6:14), for their bodies are "members of Christ" (6:15). This participation in Christ, even *inclusion* in Christ, is what makes it imperative that believers not participate in improper sex. "Do you not know that whoever is united to a prostitute becomes one body with her?" (6:16). There is no such thing as casual sex for Paul. Sexual mingling is deep participation in the other person. Believers participate in Christ, so they should not participate in any improper commingling. "Do you not know that your body is a temple of the holy Spirit within you . . . ?" (6:19). The believer belongs to Christ; all things are most definitely *not* permitted. "For you were

9. Chapter and verse divisions are not in the original, but were added hundreds of years later.
10. *Malakoi,* "soft, effeminate," BAGD.
11. *Arsenokoitai,* literally "man-couplers."

bought with a price; therefore glorify God in your body" (6:20). We will see later that Paul does not prohibit sex within marriage; but he wants believers to know that loose sexual behavior is a betrayal of the one to whom they are permanently betrothed: to Christ.

The first half of verse 20 involves a redemption metaphor, so this is the appropriate place to look at the subject of Paul's soteriological (salvation) metaphors, of which redemption is one. Redemption is the practice of purchasing the freedom of slaves or captives;[12] Christ is the source of believers' redemption (1 Cor 1:30; Rom 3:24; Col 1:14—passages that use the noun *apolytrōsis*). In 1 Corinthians 6:20 Paul uses the verb *agorazō*, derived from *agora,* or marketplace, meaning to buy anything, either things or persons. Under that last meaning it can refer either to the outright purchase of a slave or to making the manumission payment that secures a slave's freedom.[13] Slaves could often save enough money to pay their own manumission price. The implication in Paul's metaphor is that believers were like slaves or captives of sin, and the death of Christ somehow *bought* their freedom. Paul prefers metaphors to explanations. Here he is saying that the Messiah's death had some cosmic power capable of winning ("purchasing") the freedom of the captives of sin.

We can mention some of the other metaphors for the death of Christ that Paul uses. We have seen one instance of the sacrificial metaphor. In 1 Corinthians 5:7, Paul calls Christ our paschal lamb. Paul does not use the sacrificial metaphor for the death of Christ very many times, but he applies it at key moments in his narrative, at least in the Corinthian, Roman, and Galatian letters, sometimes called the "main letters" (German *Hauptbriefe*). It was an intense metaphor. Judaism, at least in the Palestinian region, was a temple-based religion, but the sacrificial rituals were symbolically important even for Diaspora Jews who may never have been able to make the trip to Jerusalem. Nor is sacrifice the only "cultic" metaphor Paul uses; he also seems to compare Christ to the scapegoat or expulsion victim in a few places (2 Cor 5:21; Gal 3:13; Rom 7:4; 8:3). The effectiveness of a metaphor is in its ability to provoke thought and to make comparisons. There need only be one point of contact between metaphor and object for the metaphor to be effective. Scapegoat has at least two points of contact (between Jesus and the scapegoat): rejection

---

12. James D. G. Dunn, *The Theology of Paul the Apostle* (Grand Rapids: Eerdmans, 1998), 227–28.

13. BAGD lists several examples of slave redemption with *agorazō*. One is in POxy. 1149, 5-6.

and death. With sacrifice there is the concept of sacred dedication and death. Sacrifice and scapegoat were the ritual means for cleansing the community of impurity and sin. These cultic metaphors are powerful because they suggest that the death of Jesus was sacred and that it cleansed the community of impurity. (See the chapter on Romans for more explanation of impurity and purification rituals. Another metaphor, justification, will be discussed in the Galatians and Romans chapters.)

In 1 Corinthians 6:20 we see a metaphor of redemption, the process whereby slaves were freed through payment of a price. Paul's metaphors are pictures that show the death of Christ having a beneficial and saving effect the way the sacrifice purges impurity, or the scapegoat banishes sin, or a manumission payment buys someone's freedom. However, it is important that we not take Paul's metaphors overly literally. The fact that he can use such diverse metaphors means that there is more than one way to describe what the Messiah's death accomplished. The Messiah was not *literally* a sacrificed bull, a banished goat, or a sum of money. Rather, Paul is using vivid metaphors with a religious history and (therefore) emotional depth. There is evocative power, for a Scripture-loving people, in drawing out new meanings from scriptural passages. Additionally, the redemption metaphor would have evoked a strong reaction in Paul's addressees because many of them were slaves who were seeking to be manumitted (redeemed) or who had already been manumitted. This was a crucial event in their lives, and Paul wants them to see the death of Jesus as having the same life-changing, rescuing power.

More Sex, Food, and Sensitivity: Chapters 7–9

In case one's concept of the Corinthian congregation is too simplistic, chapter 7 should banish such innocence, for it starts out by responding to Corinthians who favor celibacy. Here Paul explicitly says that he is responding to what "you wrote: 'It is well for a man not to touch a woman'" (7:1). Paul himself is a celibate, but his views differ from those of the Corinthian celibates. Because of the human tendency toward immorality (*porneia*), Paul feels it is better for most men and women to be married (7:2). Further, it is an opportunity for each partner to be devoted to the other, which he expresses as handing over one's authority over one's body to the loved one (7:4). In fact, it is not proper to withhold sex from each other, "except perhaps by agreement for a set time, to devote yourselves to prayer" (7:5), but then they should resume sexual activity. Paul is making a concession to the needs of sinful humans (7:6). He admits that he would prefer that everyone were "as I myself am" [celibate] (7:7), but does not think this is realistic. Regarding unmarried people, "if they are not practicing self-control, they should marry. For it is better to marry than to be aflame with passion" (7:9). Clearly, then, there are three available levels: the highest is celibacy (see 7:38), unattainable for most people; next is devoted married life; last is the level of fornication, which is contemptible and sinful. Thus Paul's practicality is never divorced from morality, but his morality seeks also to be practical.

People should not divorce on the basis of the religious conversion of one partner. For the unbeliever might be "made holy" by the Christian spouse, might be saved (7:14, 16). Nor should men alter their circumcision status as a result of the salvation experience; the circumcised should not seek to undo their circumcision (something that was actually undergone by some Jews who sought to fit into Hellenistic society), nor should the uncircumcised get circumcised (7:18), for "circumcision is nothing, and uncircumcision is nothing; but obeying the commandments of God is everything" (7:19).

People should not actively seek to change their politico-social status (7:17, 20), including slaves, yet if slaves have an opportunity to become free, they should take it (7:21; this is the meaning given in RSV and NIV, and is an alternative in NAB and NRSV). What matters is that no one should be inwardly and spiritually enslaved—except to God. Those who are slaves should consider themselves free, while the free should consider themselves slaves of Christ (7:22). Paul repeats the redemption saying from 6:20, but makes a different point: "You were bought with a price; do not become slaves of human masters" (7:23). It is a spiritual point: do not be inwardly enslaved to "human masters." Paul is advocating spiritual transformation. This will have an effect on socialization in the world outside the church, but it must derive entirely from the Spirit. Paul never treats social change as an end in itself. Instead, "It is well for you to remain as you are" (7:26). Thus Paul's advice is profoundly radical in a spiritual sense, but generally conservative in an outward social sense. If a man is married, "do not seek to be free"; if single, "do not seek a wife" (7:27); married people tend to be preoccupied with their spouses instead of with the Lord (7:33-34). But even here, Paul is not rigid: "But if you marry, you do not sin . . . . Let them marry" (7:28, 36). A widow *may* remarry, though to remain a widow is better (7:39-40).

All this moral advice to the Corinthians does not mean that Paul's eschatological teaching has been forgotten. He anticipates Christ's imminent return: "the appointed time has grown short; . . . the present form of this world is passing away" (7:29, 31). Christ will return and there will be a general resurrection (14:21-23). But first he must deal with more practical concerns.

One tricky problem is the issue of food dedicated to idols. It was a common practice in Gentile cities for butchers to have their meat formally "dedicated" to the local god or gods, and to let their buyers know that this had been done. Paul begins his discussion of this subject by once again putting "knowledge" (*gnōsis*) in its place: "Knowledge puffs up, but love builds up" (8:1). He follows this with a point that anyone familiar with the teachings of Socrates would have to accept: "Anyone who claims to know something does not yet have the necessary knowledge" (8:2). It is becoming clear that Paul has a real conflict with the "knowers" in the congregation. These knowers were saying that it mattered not at all that the meat was ostensibly dedicated to idols, since idols are unreal; the knowers know better. In such a city one would have to become vegetarian to avoid idol-dedicated meat. Paul actually agrees with them in principle, but not in practice, because he wants the knowers to be more sensitive to the scruples of those (who could include both Jews and former pagans) who are offended by even the appearance of participation in idolatry.

Once again Paul makes a profoundly important theological statement in the middle of a discussion of another subject. He says, "there is one God, the Father, from whom are all things and for whom we exist, and one Lord, Jesus Christ, through whom are all things and through whom we exist" (8:6). This simultaneously affirms Jewish monotheism (one God) and the uniquely Christian recognition of a divine Messiah (one Lord) who is actually the creator or cocreator of the world. It is a statement of monumental importance in understanding Paul's theology and christology. He does retain the monotheistic view, but it is what we should call "inclusive monotheism," since the lordship of Jesus is included in deity. Jesus is both human and divine, even playing a role in the creation of the world. There had been other Jews who held an inclusive monotheist view, including within the Deity an emanation of Godly Wisdom (*sophia* in Greek) or Word (*memra* in Aramaic and *logos* in Greek).[14] But there were many other Jews who held to an "exclusive

14. See Emil Schürer, *The History of the Jewish People in the Age of Jesus Christ (175 B.C. – A.D. 134)* rev. Geza Vermes and Fergus Millar (Edinburgh: T&T Clark, 1973; originally 1901–9); Martin McNamara, *Targum and Testament; Aramaic Paraphrases of the Hebrew Bible: A Light on the New Testament* (Shannon, Ire.: Irish University Press, 1972); William Horbury, *Jewish*

monotheism," that God is one and alone, and this became the standard view for rabbinic Judaism in the centuries after Christ as it distanced itself from all messianic and apocalyptic forms of Judaism.

Among world religions today there are three main exemplars of exclusive monotheism—rabbinic Judaism, Islam, and Sikhism—and three major advocates of inclusive monotheism—Zoroastrianism, certain forms of Vedantic Hindu philosophy, and Christianity. Obviously this goes beyond the scope of this book, but this point must be made: Inclusive monotheism is not polytheism. It is monotheistic because it posits *absolute unity* on the divine level. Divine beings work with absolute harmony and connectedness; Father, Son, and Spirit work together and through each other; in Zoroastrianism the divine "Immortals" (Wisdom, Good Mind, Law, Devotion, Divine Kingdom, Health, Immortality) work through and with each other. This is not the case in polytheism. Socrates manifests a monotheistic instinct when he makes fun of the popular idea of gods fighting among themselves (Plato's *Euthyphro* 8A–9A), which is what happens in polytheism.

Paul shares with his audience the conviction that there is only one God (and one Lord, connected with God), and that idols are not real. But because some of the converts did quite recently believe idols to be real (8:7) they are offended by the knowers' carefree approach to idol-offered meat. Therefore, the knowers should beware lest their "liberty" become "a stumbling block to the weak" (8:9). Paul's point is not "theological" (concerning actual gods) but ethical. He concedes that these "weak" pagan converts lack the understanding of the knowers, but what good is "knowledge" that is used insensitively, causing harm to the weak (8:11-13)? The "strong" and "wise" seem to be the more educated and upper-class members, while the "weak" are lower-class pagan converts who had "difficulty in seeing meat independent of its ritual setting."[15]

We find another theological point lodged in the middle of this argument: In the second half of verse 11 Paul refers to "those weak believers [lit. 'brothers'] for whom Christ died." This shows his atonement theology: Christ died for all sinners, which means for all people. A brother or sister is anyone who has accepted Christ. But his main point is still

---

Messianism and the Cult of Christ (London: SCM, 1998); John J. Collins, *The Scepter and the Star: The Messiahs of the Dead Sea Scrolls and Other Ancient Literature* (New York: Doubleday, 1995); Larry Hurtado, *How on Earth Did Jesus Become a God?*.

15. William W. Meissner, *The Cultic Origins of Christianity: The Dynamics of Religious Development* (Collegeville, MN: Liturgical Press, 2000), 123.

ethical: every brother or sister should be sensitive to every other's needs. Instead of asserting one's rights, one should seek to edify.[16]

This does not mean that one has lost one's freedom (9:1), nor does the argument of the preceding chapters mean that one has no right to take "a believing wife, as do the other apostles and the brothers of the Lord and Cephas" (9:5). (Actually the Greek would be more accurately rendered "sister-wife.") Paul moves on seamlessly into another point: that apostles have the right to receive support (food and shelter) from their flock (9:6-7). In 9:9-10 he derives the latter meaning from Deuteronomy 25:4, a passage about not muzzling oxen while they are treading grain; in effect Paul is saying "do not muzzle the apostle." He is trying to get the Corinthians to concede his right to instruct them. "If others share this rightful claim on you, do not we still more?" (9:12). In the same way, the Levites had a right to "share in the sacrificial offerings" (9:13; citing Lev 6:11 [English 6:18]). Paul claims that he has not yet exercised his right to support (9:12, 15, 18). His goal is to make the Corinthians aware of their obligation to be kind and devoted to others, even those below themselves. Paul is obligated to God (9:16-17), so he goes to great lengths to reach people with the Gospel, even making himself a slave for others, becoming like one under the Law in order to reach Jews and like one who is Law-free to reach Gentiles (9:19-22). "I have become all things to all people, that I might by all means save some" (9:22).

Paul is undermining the traditional concept of the leader as a patron with high worldly status.[17] He is showing that a true leader is a servant, even a slave; there is no differentiation between "servant" and "slave" in Greek; both are *doulos*. Paul wishes to inspire his readers, especially the knowers, with the same urgent desire to serve; they should even compete, like athletes, to excel at this, and to win an imperishable crown (9:24-25). Paul "runs" and "punish[es]" himself hard in this contest (9:26-27). This is a not-very-subtle hint to the knowers that they ought to drive themselves harder, to be more sensitive to the needs of the "weak." They need to be interested in building up, as God is: "Love builds up" (8:1).

---

16. See Michael J. Gorman, *Apostle of the Crucified Lord: A Theological Introduction to Paul and His Letters* (Grand Rapids: Eerdmans, 2004), 257.

17. Dale B. Martin, *Slavery as Salvation: The Metaphor of Slavery in Pauline Christology* (New Haven: Yale University Press, 1990), 134–35.

The Typology and Ethics of Communion: Chapters 10–11

Even when Paul moves to the subject of the ritual or sacramental practice of the church, ethics and sensitivity to others are still foremost. This is most obvious in chapter 11, where he wants the wealthy to be more sensitive to the poor, and not to be frivolous about the Eucharist.

First, however, he gives them a lesson in Bible interpretation. He describes the Israelites' passage through the sea as a "baptism" and (drawing on an extra-biblical tradition) identifies the rock that followed them as "Christ" (10:2, 4). This is what we now refer to as typological interpretation. The Greek work *typos* means, literally "stamp." When discussing Scripture or other literary classics one could identify a story, person, or events as a *type,* meaning that it prefigured something occurring later. Paul does not use the word *typos* here, but he seems to be saying that the "sea" was a type—a prefiguration—of baptism. He goes even further when he says "the rock was Christ" (10:4); this is actual *identification* of the rock with Christ. We could still call this typology, however: the identifying of something in an older text with something in a newer text. Typology involves different degrees of identification. In verse 6 Paul uses *typoi,* the plural of *typos,* translated "examples" by NRSV: "Now these things occurred as examples for us, so that we might not desire evil as they did." He had spoken in 10:5 of God striking down the disobedient Israelites; this amounts to a warning to "us," Paul is telling the Corinthians. Their reveling, their indulging, their testing God, their grumbling (10:7-10) got them into trouble. The punishments they suffered happened "to serve as an example [*typikōs*]," and were "written down to instruct us, on whom the ends of the ages have come" (10:11). *Scripture seems to be inherently prophetic.* What Paul is most interested in finding in the Scriptures are not prophecies of the Messiah, but prophecies of the church.[18]

What is happening in the Corinthian congregation is a serious trial, but God "will not let you be tested beyond your strength" (10:13). The knowers, the strong, the weak should all be able to embody Christ in their shared living. The unworthy behavior of the Israelites was "idolatry," and so is that of some of the Corinthians (10:14).

After such a confrontational remark Paul becomes diplomatic, saying that he is speaking to "sensible people" who can understand him (10:15).

18. Richard B. Hays, *Echoes of Scripture in the Letters of Paul* (New Haven: Yale University Press, 1989), 121. On 1 Cor 10:1-11, see pp. 99–104. Among his numerous comments on promise and fulfillment (and the mind of the interpreter) are those on 24, 106–7, 154–56, 189, 215 n. 87.

Now he makes his point about ritual and sacrament: "The cup of blessing that we bless, is it not a sharing in the blood of Christ?" (10:16). Jews also, through their sacrificial rituals and meals, become "partners in the altar" (10:18). Does this, then, mean "that food sacrificed to idols is anything, or that an idol is anything?" (10:19). No, but pagans are sacrificing "to demons," and the members of Christ's body should not become "partners with demons" (v. 20). It may seem that Paul is contradicting his purely ethical, non-metaphysical advice in chapter 8, giving now a metaphysical reason. But in chapter 8 he was talking to people who (correctly) did not take the idolatrous rituals seriously; he is now talking about the *reality* of communion rituals and what one is contacting through them. One needs to take communion seriously, and avoid pagan rituals or mysteries: "You cannot drink the cup of the Lord and the cup of demons" (10:21). This is a real danger; it was common in the big cities to receive invitations to "dine with Serapis, or to dine with Anubis, or some other god."[19]

We should not be surprised by the vehemence of Paul's teaching or the sharpness of his sarcasm. Paul ironically quotes the Corinthians' slogan "All things are lawful," only to respond, "but not all things are beneficial. 'All things are lawful,' but not all things build up" (10:23). If one takes on the "mind of Christ" (2:16) one thinks of others more than of oneself; one does not "seek [one's] own advantage" (10:24).

Paul summarizes this line of argument by saying one can eat whatever is sold in the market, and if one is a guest, one should eat whatever is placed before one (10:26-27), but if the host says, "This has been offered in sacrifice," then one should not eat it, for the sake of the *other's* conscience (10:28-29), so he or she does not draw the incorrect conclusion that pagan gods are to be respected. It is important to be sensitive to others, to "give no offense to Jews or to Greeks" (10:32); some of the "weak" who object to eating idol-offered food are undoubtedly Jews. Paul wants others to follow his example; he is devoted to the salvation of others, "not seeking my own advantage" (10:33).

Paul makes bold to command the Corinthians: "Be imitators of me, as I am of Christ" (11:1). This is not out of place in the ancient world. Since Paul brought the Corinthians to Christ and founded their church, he has a certain authority over them. To put it in terms of the social obligations understood in that day and age, they are the clients and he is the patron. Further, he can exercise some influence on their behalf with

19. Morton Scott Enslin, *The Ethics of Paul* (Nashville: Abingdon, 1957), 140–41.

his patron, Christ. This may sound shocking and crude to our ears, and it *would* be crude if Paul were asking them to believe that he could obtain favors for them from Christ that Christ was not otherwise willing to give. Paul claims no such thing. Christ is not a harsh and distant lord. The patronage metaphor is not to be taken so literally. But Paul is indeed drawing on common concepts of patronage in order to get his listeners to understand the hierarchical relationships, with God and Christ at the top. In that sense, and with sensitivity to Paul's values, one can cautiously say that Paul is using a political metaphor, that is, a patronage metaphor, for relationship to God and for his role as a lesser patron. He certainly seeks to exercise instructional authority over what he considers to be his flock, and this is a form of "political" authority.

Some of the Corinthians are willing and eager to learn from their spiritual patron, and he speaks to them, perhaps, when he says, "I commend you because you remember me in everything and maintain the traditions just as I handed them on to you" (11:2). He does appear to be a bit over-optimistic here. If they were so loyal to him, why would he need to write this letter; why would he need to say, "when you come together it is not for the better but for the worse" (11:17)? Perhaps he is like the stern parent who mingles affection with criticism.

Paul is not done spelling out the hierarchy of human relationships. He makes it clear that "Christ is the head of every man, and the husband is the head of his wife" (11:3). This would not have been considered controversial in his day. Centuries earlier Aristotle had thought it necessary to explain male superiority, which indicates that some Greek women were more assertive than he thought they should be. This may also be Paul's perception of certain Corinthian women. His instructions in this chapter, however, apply to both men and women, and they are simultaneously social and metaphysical. He insists that women in church should have their heads veiled (11:13), which means a hair-covering. It may be that female hair is sexually provocative (11:15), and so should be reined in. Long hair identifies female gender. A man with long hair is acting effeminately (11:14).

Sociological study suggests that Paul's concern about hairdos stands for a defense of social roles and boundaries. "Unbound hair suggests . . . freedom, loss of control, and blurring of clear sexual roles. Loose hair suggests loose morals . . . a danger to the social order."[20]

20. Jerome H. Neyrey, *Paul, in Other Words: A Cultural Reading of His Letters* (Louisville: Westminster John Knox, 1990), 132.

These social-structural meanings have metaphysical corollaries. Paul says the man is the image and reflection of God, while "woman is the reflection of man" (11:7). This means that the man is patterned after God, while the woman is patterned after man. It is a statement about origins, about primacy. The Genesis statement that "the rib that the LORD God had taken from the man he made into a woman" (2:22) lies behind Paul's statement: "Indeed, man was not made from woman, but woman from man. Neither was man created for the sake of woman, but woman for the sake of man. For this reason a woman ought to have a symbol of authority on her head, because of the angels" (11:8-10). And yet, men and women are interdependent, and both depend on God (11:11-12).

What of the angels? One theory is that all worship is performed in front of the angels, so proper decorum in worship is proper decorum before the angels.[21] Another theory (favored by the church father Tertullian)[22] is that Paul is warning against provoking the lustful Nephilim, the "sons of God [who] went in to the daughters of humans" (Gen 6:4), referred to as "the Watchers" by later Jewish writers.[23] The Watchers brought witchcraft and other evils to the earth (*1 Enoch* 7-8, 15). Despite the lurid details, this is actually similar to the other theory because it involves decorum in front of invisible observers, only not all the observers are good.

Decorum and order involve hierarchy. The husband as "head of his wife" (11:3) uses body-language to convey a social concept. Paul's strong concerns about what is "proper," what is "degrading," what is "not for the better but for the worse" (vv. 13, 14, 17) seems to stand for a "classification system that clarifies precise roles and statuses" for the genders.[24] Paul has no tolerance for "immorality" (*porneia*) (5:1; 6:13, 18) or "impurity" (*akatharsia*) (1 Thess 4:7) in the church; we must "cleanse ourselves from every defilement" (2 Cor 7:1); believers must be "blameless" (1 Cor 1:8).

Paul reiterates that "there are divisions among you; . . . factions" (1 Cor 11:18-19). In this case he means divisions of social class manifested during the Lord's Supper. The ritual of the Lord's Supper took place

---

21. Neyrey, *Paul, in Other Words,* 133; Raymond F. Collins, *First Corinthians.* SP 7 (Collegeville, MN: Liturgical Press, 1999), 412.

22. *On the Veiling of Virgins* 7; David E. Garland, *First Corinthians.* BECNT (Grand Rapids: Baker Academic, 2003), 526.

23. *1 Enoch* chs. 6, 12, 16; *Jub.* 5:1-2; *T. Reub.* 5:5-6; see Garland, *First Corinthians,* 527.

24. Neyrey, *Paul, in Other Words,* 137.

within the setting of a real supper, a shared meal. Some of the wealthier members have plenty to eat, and some are actually getting drunk, while poorer members are going hungry; this shames the poor (1 Cor 11:21-22). Now Paul takes the opportunity to give them the eucharistic wording he approves, and backs it up with a claim of direct revelation from Christ: "For I received from the Lord what I also handed on to you" (11:23), which obviously would make Paul's version superior to the other versions of the Eucharist that are being practiced,[25] two of which did not involve any mention of blood.[26] Paul makes the sacrificial idea foremost: "This is my body that is for you. . . . This cup is the new covenant in my blood" (11:24-25). It is to be done "in remembrance of me" (occurring in both of those verses). Remembering is again foremost in what looks like the conclusion of the ritual: "For as often as you eat this bread and drink the cup, you proclaim the Lord's death until he comes" (11:26).

The "death" itself has so much significance that it is proclaimed. This was not the case in all the churches. We do not know if it was so in Corinth *before* Paul wrote this letter. It seems *not* to have been the case in the churches that used the *Didachē* or the shorter text of Luke, which make no mention of a "covenant in my blood." *Christ* was central to all Christian churches, but *the death* was not always the central focus. Christology was always central, but sacrificial atonement was not, though for Paul it was.

Even when Paul turns to an ethical point the "body and blood" have divine power: "Whoever, therefore, eats the bread or drinks the cup of the Lord in an unworthy manner will be answerable for the body and blood of the Lord" (11:27). One needs to question whether one is worthy, one needs to be "discerning the body," or one will fall under judgment (11:28-29). That is why there are many illnesses and deaths in the Corin-

---

25. As evidenced by the different eucharistic wording in Mark, Matthew, and Luke, and in the eucharistic prayer in the *Didachē* (roughly 100 CE), which speaks of the wine as a messianic symbol ("the vine of David," 9:2) and the bread as symbolizing the diverse origin of Christians (gathered from many hills into one loaf). The *Didachē* does not equate the wine with blood or the bread with a broken body.

26. The *Didachē* (previous note) and the shorter text of Luke, found in the oldest Western manuscript Greek (D) and in the oldest Latin and Syriac translations. In these manuscripts the sacrificial verses 22:19b-20 ("given for you. . . . covenant in my blood") are not present (Bart D. Ehrman, *Misquoting Jesus: The Story Behind Who Changed the Bible and Why* [HarperSan Francisco, 2005], 166–67). Even in manuscripts with the longer text the verse ordering varies greatly at this point, giving evidence of an intense debate about liturgical wording.

thian congregation (v. 30). They are being disciplined and are in danger of being condemned (v. 32). Therefore, "when you come together to eat, wait for one another" (v. 33); if one is famished, one should eat at home (v. 34). This last remark probably contributed to the eventual reality that the Lord's Supper ceased to be a real supper, becoming solely a ritual.

Love and Cooperation: Chapters 12–14

Paul begins chapter 12 with a remark about the motivation of certain statements; no one who is Spirit-motivated would ever say "Let Jesus be cursed!" and no one can say "'Jesus is Lord,' except by the Holy Spirit" (12:3). Some scholars think there were unorthodox teachers who were actually saying, "Let Jesus be cursed," or "Jesus is accursed," but we cannot confirm this, much less discover whether the statement was some kind of paradoxical Gnostic axiom or simply an anti-Christian remark. One might speculate, however, that Paul would hardly need to go to the trouble here of refuting an anti-Christian sentiment; he might, however, need to counter some twisted Gnostic saying. He does not follow up on this thread, but goes on to talk about spiritual gifts.

His point in chapter 12 is that the spiritual gifts are all to be valued; they all come from the same Spirit (12:4), and legitimate *gnōsis* is a gift of the Spirit. To one comes "the utterance of wisdom [*sophia*], and to another the utterance of knowledge [*gnōsis*] according to the same Spirit," to others the gifts of faith, of healing, of prophecy, discernment of spirits, speaking in tongues, and the interpretation of tongues (12:8-10). The Corinthians seem to be valuing more dramatic gifts like speaking in tongues more highly than the teaching gifts. They are all necessary; one does not expect the foot to be a hand or the ear to function like an eye; each part has its legitimate function (12:12-18). Paul shows his consideration for the less-respected members when he says, "the members of the body that seem to be weaker are indispensable, and those members of the body that we think less honorable we clothe with greater honor, and our less respectable members are treated with greater respect" (12:22-23). God has constructed the body this way so that there may be no pride of place, "but the members may have the same care for one another" (v. 25).

This is how Paul makes his point to the proud among the Corinthians, the ones who value their "greater" gifts of wisdom. He wants them rather to be considerate of all the other "members," especially the weaker ones. And what is the greatest gift? On that subject he crafts one of the greatest short sermons ever given: what we now call 1 Corinthians 13.

The "love chapter," though often cited apart from its context, fits well within its position in the letter. It continues Paul's emphasis on ethics, and it fills out the challenge of 12:31 to strive for the greatest gift. Paul gives a poetic structure to the chapter. Verses 1 to 3 have the structure "if I do X, but do not have love, I am nothing." Verses 4 to 9 have the structure "love is A, B, and C; it is not D, E, and F. Love does such-and-such, and it endures." He also makes his point about the gifts the Corinthians overrate:

> [Love] bears all things, believes all things, hopes all things, endures all things. Love never ends. But as for prophecies, they will come to an end; as for tongues, they will cease; as for knowledge, it will come to an end. For we know [*ginōskomen*] only in part, and we prophesy only in part; but when the complete comes, the partial will come to an end. (1 Cor 13:7-10)

He tells the Corinthians to stop being spiritually childish; we now see hazily, as in a cloudy mirror, but "then . . . face to face. Now I know only in part; then I will know fully" (13:11-12). He repeats the spiritual triad we saw in 1 Thessalonians: "And now faith, hope, and love abide, these three; and the greatest of these is love" (13:13). *That* is real knowledge. This chapter's message (*Love!*) heightens the message of the preceding chapters (*Be considerate! Be ethical!*).

Michael Gorman calls this "cruciform love," which Paul is recommending for the church: "giving special attention to its poorer and weaker members . . . love that is patient and kind . . . bearing and enduring all things."[27] This does not mean that the other gifts are irrelevant. In fact, Paul says, "strive for the spiritual gifts, and especially that you may prophesy,"[28] for those who speak in tongues "are speaking mysteries in the Spirit" (14:1-2). But it is better to prophesy, to proclaim a message in the common language (Greek) that everyone can understand. "Those who speak in a tongue build up themselves, but those who prophesy build up the church. Now I would like all of you to speak in tongues, but even more to prophesy" (14:4-5).

There was not much sitting still in a Pauline church! There was plenty of charismatic experience and enthusiastic (which means God-filled)

---

27. Gorman, *Apostle of the Crucified*, 277.

28. Note that the verb is "prophesy," which will always rhyme with "try" in all of its conjugated forms. There is no such word as "prophesize." The noun form is "prophecy," rhyming with "see."

expression. Paul does not suppress these experiences, but he wants them to be as beneficial for newcomers as they are for the regulars. That is why it is necessary that there be "interpretation of tongues" (also a Spirit-filled activity), in which someone interprets what has just been spoken in the angelic tongues. Any speaking is useful only if it is comprehensible to others, if it builds up the church, if newcomers can understand it (14:9-12, 23-24). Paul goes so far as to say, "I speak in tongues more than all of you; nevertheless, in church I would rather speak five words with my mind, in order to instruct others also, than ten thousand words in a tongue" (vv. 18-19). He repeats his point: "do not be children in your thinking . . . be adults [*teleion*, which can also be translated "perfect"]" (v. 20). Newcomers will be put off by mere babbling in tongues, but will be convinced by prophecy (vv. 23-24)

Anyone attempting to visualize a Pauline worship service will find 1 Corinthians to be Paul's richest letter. "When you come together, each one has a hymn, a lesson, a revelation, a tongue, or an interpretation" (v. 26). Paul wants to limit the number of tongues-messages: "If anyone speaks in a tongue, let there be only two or at most three," and each should always be followed by an interpretation (v. 27), nor should they try to speak at once (vv. 30-31). Evidently these sensible things are not happening currently, or Paul would not have to call for them. Some who engage in ecstatic experience think they cannot help themselves, but Paul soberly brings them back to earth by saying, "the spirits of prophets are subject to the prophets" (14:32). This has many implications, not just for responsible control over one's ecstatic experience but for recognition of the fact that all religious experience is interpreted. All divine messages are interpreted and shaped by the human recipient.

Another, even more controversial, subject is opened up by the following verses: "women should be silent in the churches. For they are not permitted to speak, but should be subordinate, as the law also says. If there is anything they desire to know, let them ask their husbands at home. For it is shameful for a woman to speak in church" (14:34-35). This is very unexpected, and it is inconsistent with Paul's immediately preceding remark that "you can all prophesy" (14:31), with his referring to women as coworkers, with his calling the woman Junia "prominent among the apostles" (Rom 16:7), and with his mention of other women as leaders (1 Cor 1:11), benefactors, and hosts of churches (1 Cor 16:19; Rom 16:1-2, 5). For this and for text-critical (manuscript-related) reasons, a number of scholars consider these verses to be a scribal interpolation, not written by Paul.[29] Evidently someone early in the Pauline tradition thought it was a proper understanding of what Paul meant when he said "all things should be done decently and in order" (14:40). But we have no other reliably Pauline passage forbidding female participation in the prophesying and interpretation going on in the churches. In fact, women prophets seem to have had a very important role in the life of the Corinthian church.[30] Women patrons and hosts were important in the Pauline churches.[31]

The Resurrection of Christ and of Believers: Chapter 15

First Corinthians 15 begins with the centrality of the substitutionary death of Christ and moves on to discuss the resurrection of believers. First Paul wants to identify the source of his teaching and the centrality of the crucifixion in his Gospel: "For I handed on to you as of first importance what I in turn had received: that Christ died for our sins in accordance with the scriptures" (15:3). Believers and scholars have spent twenty centuries trying to identify which scriptures he intends; many believers today point to the suffering servant figure in Isaiah 53, but this figure does not appear in any major way in the NT, though it does seem to lie behind Romans 4:25 (cf. Isa 53:5). Isaiah 53 is probably one of the scriptures Paul has in mind here; others could be Wisdom 2–3; Zechariah 11:13; 12:10; 13:7; Psalms 22, 35, and 69, about a suffering innocent one; and possibly Hosea 6:2 and Jonah 2:1, which speak of revival on the third day. Paul's letters probably give us only a fraction of what he said in his sermons.

There is also the complicated question of exactly what is meant by "Christ died for our sins." Many Christians today assume that it means he died a substitutionary death, standing in for all human beings, who deserve death (that is, damnation), literally "paying the price" for sin, enduring and thus removing the sentence of eternal damnation that every

29. This insertion occurs at different locations in different ancient manuscripts, and its final position, at vv. 34-35, interrupts Paul's remarks about prophets in the church (Horrell, *Social Ethos*, 190–91; Bart D. Ehrman, *Lost Christianities: The Battles for Scripture and the Faiths We Never Knew* [Oxford: Oxford University Press, 2003], 38).

30. Antoinette Clark Wire, *The Corinthian Women Prophets: A Reconstruction through Paul's Rhetoric* (Minneapolis: Fortress Press, 1990).

31. Carolyn Osiek and Margaret Y. MacDonald, with Janet H. Tulloch, *A Woman's Place: House Churches in Earliest Christianity* (Minneapolis: Fortress Press, 2006).

person who has ever lived would otherwise suffer. Some of this theology seems to be present in Paul's thinking, but not all of it. For one thing, there is no indication that Paul believed in a hell of perpetual punishment; rather, he seems to hold to the quite widespread idea that sinners will simply be destroyed and not resurrected; "for the wages of sin is death, but the free gift of God is eternal life in Christ Jesus our Lord" (Rom 6:23); "If you sow to your own flesh, you will reap corruption from the flesh; but if you sow to the Spirit, you will reap eternal life from the Spirit" (Gal 6:8). Paul does use the metaphor of Christ paying for our sins ("you were bought with a price," 1 Cor 6:20; 7:23). He does speak of sin being "condemned" in his flesh (Rom 8:3), of Christ "becoming a curse for us" (Gal 3:13), and that God "made him to be sin" for our sake (2 Cor 5:21). So, although later theologians and preachers have taken Paul too literally and crudely, creating harsh doctrines of rescue from retribution through sacrificial purchase, they have not created these out of whole cloth; Paul does teach some kind of substitutionary death: "He died for all" (2 Cor 5:15); he "was handed over to death for our trespasses" (Rom 4:25).

But the rest of the story is resurrection, and that is crucial. The rest of Romans 4:25 reads "and was raised for our justification." And resurrection is the main subject of 1 Corinthians 15, first Christ's, and then believers'. Still recounting the tradition that he received and handed on, Paul speaks of Christ's burial and resurrection, his appearance to Cephas and the Twelve, then "to more than five hundred brothers at once" (15:5-6). After this the resurrected Christ appeared to James (almost certainly Paul means the Lord's brother), then to the other apostles, and "last of all, as to one untimely born, he appeared also to me" (15:7-8). Paul practices a bit of rhetorical humility here as he recounts his personal story: "For I am the least of the apostles, unfit to be called an apostle, because I persecuted the church of God"; but he was saved and called, by the grace of God (vv. 9-10).

Christ's resurrection is linked to the truth of the future resurrection of believers. Paul's concern is that "some of you say there is no resurrection of the dead" (15:12). But "if there is no resurrection of the dead, then Christ has not been raised" (v. 13), and everything Paul has said would be a lie (v. 15). The resurrection of believers is as essential to Christian belief as is the resurrection of Christ! These are truths, not metaphors. Further, the resurrection is linked to the atonement, the cleansing from sin: "If Christ has not been raised, your faith is futile and you are still in your sins" (v. 17). If there is no resurrection then Christians, with their great hopes, "are of all people most to be pitied" (v. 19).

But in fact, Christ *is* "raised from the dead, the first fruits of those who have died" (15:20). One person (Adam) brought death to all; now one person brings life to the human race (v. 22). At Christ's coming he will raise those who belong to him, and then, when he has subdued every ruler and authority and power, he will hand over his kingdom to the Father (vv. 23-24). Scholars debate whether the authorities and powers are heavenly or earthly ones. I think he means both; we can take "every" quite literally here. And the last enemy to be defeated is death (v. 26). When he has subjected everything to himself, then the Son will hand it all over to God, "so that God may be all in all" (v. 28). This will be the climactic perfection of the time-space universe, accomplished by Christ's spiritual power. Philosophers such as Pierre Teilhard de Chardin have seen this as the revelation of the purpose of life itself: the "spiritual renovation of the earth" or the "Christogenesis" of reality.[32]

Paul makes reference to people who were being baptized for the dead, but not to either support or oppose the practice; he refers to it in order to support his point: why would people bother doing it unless there really is a resurrection? (v. 29). Furthermore, why would Paul allow himself to face so much danger if there were no resurrection? (vv. 30-32).

The Corinthians had evidently asked a question: "How are the dead raised? With what kind of body do they come?" (15:35). Paul uses an agricultural comparison: a seed must die to be brought back to life, and different seeds produce different bodies (vv. 36-38). There is "one flesh for human beings, another for animals, another for birds," and so on; he is stressing that "not all flesh is alike" (v. 39). Many readers have had a hard time understanding such remarks as "there are both heavenly bodies and earthly bodies, but the glory of the heavenly is one thing, and that of the earthly is another" (v. 40). In case the complete *difference* of these levels was not comprehended, Paul points out that the brightness, the "glory" of the sun differs from the moon's and from the stars'; so also will our new body be different from our earthly one (vv. 41-42). "What is sown is perishable; what is raised is imperishable" (v. 42). In the course of this chapter Paul makes twenty sharp contrasts between the earthly body and the heavenly one. He distinguishes the dishonorable, weak, natural, earthly body from the glorious, powerful, spiritual, heavenly body (vv. 43-44, 47). The natural man came first, then the

32. Pierre Teilhard de Chardin, *The Phenomenon of Man* (New York: Harper & Row, 1959) 245, 297; "to fulfill . . . the world is, for God, to unify it by uniting it organically with himself" (pp. 293–94).

heavenly man (v. 47). The first Adam was a living being, but "the last Adam" is "a life-giving spirit" (v. 45). The *form of life*, the bodily vehicle, will be different in the heavenly life: "flesh and blood cannot inherit the kingdom of God, nor does the perishable inherit the imperishable" (v. 50). The spiritual (*pneumatikos*) body will not be subject to corruption; obviously that is completely different from the bodies we have here. Its basic life-force is not fading; its source and home are in heaven, not on earth. Evidently it is made of a different *substance* than we can understand, yet it is a body (*sōma*), a life-vehicle, and not a disembodied spirit.

Because of the difficulty of imagining a *spiritual body*, many readers (then and now) strongly resist the central point of this chapter, that there will be a completely different kind of body in the next life. Paul was dealing with a congregation full of people who grew up with the Greek viewpoint that the body is a tomb of the soul, that immortality of the soul is to be desired and expected but the body must be left behind, since the soul needs no body. Paul gives no ground to this point of view. Perhaps he expected the Corinthians, by now, to have moved toward the Jewish viewpoint. Most of these Greeks either had been to synagogue or had heard in other ways the Jewish view that all life, even in the afterlife, is *embodied*. Paul accepts this, but he wants believers to recognize that the heavenly body is of a different kind than the earthly one. He does not waver on this subject; he possesses reliable knowledge about the afterlife. He had, after all, seen the resurrected and glorious form of Christ on the Damascus road. He seems also to have received specific instruction on this. He proceeds to impart his knowledge.

"We will all be changed, in an instant, in the blink of an eye, at the last trumpet" (15:51-52). The dead will be "raised imperishable" (v. 52). The mortal must become immortal, the corruptible become incorruptible, and *that* will fulfill the prophecy (vv. 53-54), "death has been swallowed up in victory" (probably Isa 25:8). Christ's resurrection fulfills the hopes of the prophets: "Where, O death, is your sting?" (v. 55; citing Hos 13:14). Paul will return to the theme of how we will be "clothed" in 2 Corinthians (5:1-6), while making a different point. Here in 1 Corinthians 15:35-54 his point is to convince the Corinthians that they really will be raised but will receive a new and completely different kind of body. Thus they can retain some of their "spiritual" ideas, but they also need to move toward a more realistic Jewish idea: people need bodies, both here and there. Paul is trying to explain something that has never been clearly described: a new and spiritual body that is nevertheless really a *body*, neither a disembodied spirit nor a reanimated corpse.

A Necessary Charity—the Collection: Chapter 16

The subject of the final chapter is the collection Paul is organizing for the poor believers (the "saints") in Jerusalem. He has also "ordered" the churches in Galatia to contribute to this cause, and he does the same to the Corinthians, even specifying on what day of the week it should occur (16:1-2). He orders that some people be selected to carry the collection to Jerusalem, but it is Paul himself who will dispatch them (16:3). This collection is a very serious matter, and Paul's leadership is intimately wrapped up in it. One could express this with a stress on love and duty (Paul is concerned for the poor and will do everything he can to help them) or with emphasis on patronage (Paul, as the spiritual leader, has the *right,* as well as the obligation, to help his poorest clients).

Paul discusses his travel plans; he will approach Corinth by land, coming down from Macedonia; he hopes to stay with them for a while; Timothy may arrive before him (16:5-10). But for now Paul will stay in Ephesus until Pentecost (16:8, which tells us that 1 Corinthians is written from Ephesus in the early spring). As earlier in the letter, Paul makes some cautious and respectful remarks about his fellow apostle Apollos that contain a hint of criticism: Apollos did not take Paul's advice on something (16:12). As "an eloquent man" from Alexandria (Acts 18:24), Apollos may offer interpretations that differ from Paul's, but not enough to evoke a denunciation.

Paul sends greetings from a number of his coworkers, including Aquila and Prisca (cf. Rom 16:3-4; undoubtedly the same as Aquila and *Priscilla* in Acts 18:2, 18), who have a church in their house (1 Cor 16:19). The holy kiss makes its reappearance (v. 20; cf. 1 Thess 5:26; 2 Cor 13:12). A fascinating line is this one: "Let anyone be accursed who has no love for the Lord. Our Lord, come [*Maranatha*]" (16:22). Perhaps there are loiterers on the edges of the congregation who have not made a commitment to Christ. They need to respond to the message or depart; there is no neutral position.

Chapter 5

Second Corinthians

The composition history of 2 Corinthians is much discussed, with the most common view being that it was really two different letters, and also that 1 Corinthians was preceded by a now lost letter. One scholar speculates that, while based in Ephesus, Paul wrote an initial letter to the Corinthians (mentioned in 1 Cor 5:9). Then, hearing disturbing news from his allies in Corinth, he wrote 1 Corinthians in response and sent Timothy to Corinth with it. In 55 CE Timothy returned without accomplishing Paul's will in the congregation. Paul made a short visit to Corinth, where he was rebuffed. He returned to Ephesus and wrote the stern or "tearful" letter (see 2 Cor 7:8-12),[1] which may be what we now know as 2 Corinthians 10–13.[2] Titus took it to Corinth, and apparently Paul's advice was followed by the church. After being imprisoned from fall 55 to spring 56, Paul heard good news from Titus and then wrote a fourth letter to Corinth, probably preserved as 2 Corinthians 1–9.[3] However, I will consider the chapters in canonical order here.

Sacrificial Suffering: Chapters 1–2

After a standard greeting comes a blessing, in which Paul emphasizes certain qualities of God: "the Father of mercies and the God of all con-

---

1. Calvin Roetzel, *Paul: The Man and the Myth* (Edinburgh: T&T Clark, 1999), 106–7.
2. Ibid., 114.
3. Ibid., 107.

58

solation, who consoles us in all our affliction, so that we may be able to console" others who are afflicted (1:3-4). Here is one of the key meanings of the suffering of Christ, for Paul: to empower us to suffer for others: "For just as the sufferings of Christ are abundant for us, so also our consolation is abundant through Christ" (1:5).[4] His affliction is "for your consolation and salvation" (1:6). Evidently some members of the Corinthian congregation are also suffering, and Paul reminds them that this gives them a share in God's consolation (1:7).

Paul's own suffering will be mentioned again and again (1:8; 4:8-11), partly to remind the readers that a true apostle must experience Christlike suffering, and partly to actually verify his apostleship. Paul also seeks to validate his apostleship by reminding his readers of his "frankness and godly sincerity"; he did not seek to overawe them through a show of human wisdom (1:12).

"Boasting" is a major theme in this epistle. More than just the *fact* of human pride, it is meant to draw attention to the content and justification of one's pride. Paul seems to assume that humans *will* boast, so the crucial question becomes: *in what* are they boasting? Paul wants to boast that he has conducted himself rightly toward the Corinthians, operating with sincerity and "by the grace of God" (1:12), not saying "yes" and "no" at the same time (1:17). He wants his—and *their*—sincerity and spirituality to be such as to enable them to boast in him, and him to boast in them, on judgment day, "on the day of the Lord Jesus" (1:14). He wants the Corinthians to look forward to two visits from him, one while he is en route to Macedonia and one when he returns from there (1:16).

Sometimes Paul seems to interrupt himself. After his remarks about not contradicting himself with "yes and no" (1:17-18), he then affirms that "yes" is in Jesus (1:19); "For in him every one of God's promises is a 'Yes,'" and the "Amen" ("so be it," in Hebrew) is also in him (1:20). This statement about Christ leads directly into a statement about Paul's commissioning: Paul is anointed by God (1:21), sealed by God, and has received God's Spirit (1:22). In 2 Corinthians, Paul seems particularly concerned to establish, or at least strengthen, the legitimacy of his claim to be an apostle. But it is at least equally true that Paul is anxious to establish or strengthen the Corinthians as disciples, not boasting in their own spirituality and wisdom but wholly focused on loyalty to God and Christ.

---

4. On Paul's sufferings as part of Christ's own sufferings see the comments on Col 1:24 in chapter 9.

Despite his concern about opposition to him at Corinth, Paul knows that he still has authority as founder of the community, and he would show them some mercy. His decision not to visit them in the near future is in order "to spare you" (1:23); he will not make "another painful visit" to them (2:1) like a previous visit when they had a conflict. He is their patron, but a kindly patron: "we are workers with you for your joy" (1:24). He would not want to "cause you pain" (2:2), but he might have to if he were to visit Corinth now. For in a previous letter, "I wrote you out of much distress and anguish of heart and with many tears, not to cause you pain, but to let you know the abundant love that I have for you" (2:4). We can surmise that the letter was quite confrontational. In 2 Corinthians 7:8, Paul admits that the letter saddened his readers. A particular enemy of Paul's in the congregation seems to have been the subject of the confrontation: ". . . if anyone has caused pain, he has caused it not to me, but . . . to all of you. This punishment by the majority is enough for such a person" (2:5-6). Evidently Paul prevailed in this conflict and can afford now to recommend mercy: "forgive and console him . . . I urge you to reaffirm your love for him" (2:7-8), but he still points out that the person's motivations were those of Satan (2:11). We will say more about this person when he is brought up again in 7:12.

A sophisticated metaphor of sacrificial suffering follows (2:14-17). Paul uses several words that were part of ordinary speech but were also technical terms in sacrificial rituals, both Jewish and Hellenistic. In 2:14 he refers to himself as a "fragrance" (*osmē*) and believers as "the aroma [*euōdia*] of Christ" to those who are being saved (2:15), but "a fragrance of death" to those who are choosing death (2:16). These Greek words are frequently paired in the LXX to refer to the "sweet-smelling" aroma of the burning flesh of sacrificial offerings (Lev 1:9, 13, 17; 3:5, 11, etc.); if he accepts the offering, God enjoys the aroma.

Another metaphor is operating in these verses. Paul uses a verb (*thriambeuō*, "lead in triumph") that refers to what the victor does in a military victory parade.[5] Paul describes himself as a prisoner led around in Christ's victory parade: God "in Christ always leads us in triumphal procession, and through us spreads in every place the fragrance that comes from knowing him" (2:14). The fragrance may correspond to the scent of the incense that is burned during these parades. A master of irony, Paul is boasting in being Christ's prisoner; his greatest victory is

5. Jerry W. McCant, *2 Corinthians* (Sheffield: Sheffield Academic Press, 1999), 34.

that he has been conquered by Christ, the most magnanimous of conquerors, who now uses him to spread the Christly aroma to those who are being saved. The fragrance does double duty, functioning as victory-parade odor and then (after the mention of "aroma" in 2:15) suggesting a sacrifice pleasing to God.

Finally, in case the metaphor is not complicated enough, Paul adds the image of greedy economic motivation: some people are "peddlers of God's word," like salesmen out for personal profit, but Paul speaks out of "sincerity, as [one] sent from God" (2:17).

The Letter and the Spirit; Reflecting the Image of God: Chapters 3–4

Paul poses the question: does he need letters of recommendation, either *to* or *from* the Corinthians? No, the Corinthians themselves "are our letter . . . a letter of Christ, prepared by us, written not with ink but with the Spirit of the living God, not on tablets of stone but on tablets of human hearts" (3:1-3). Here Paul is using the velvet glove approach to establish his authority. He will not "claim anything as coming from us; our competence is from God, who has made us competent to be ministers of a new covenant ["new testament," KJV], not of letter but of spirit; for the letter kills, but the Spirit gives life" (3:6). Paul is contrasting a dead and inflexible written "letter" with a living and inwardly-operating Spirit.

He is probably saying much more; he may be providing the key to his whole interpretive approach to Scripture as well as to his social idea. "Spirit" stands for Paul's symbolic or allegorical reading of the Jewish law, while "letter" stands for a more literalizing reading, perhaps that of the Pharisees. There seems to be a Platonizing approach here: seeing an underlying and more *real* meaning to a text than its literal meaning. The spiritual interpretation is true; "the physical is but a shadow of this truth."[6] Underlying this interpretive strategy is a universalizing social strategy; "the spirit is universal,"[7] not specific to Israel. It is the *spiritual* meaning, not the *literal* meaning of any text or practice, that really matters. In his longest letter he spells this out: "a person is not a Jew who is

---

6. Daniel Boyarin, *A Radical Jew: Paul and the Politics of Identity* (Berkeley: University of California Press: 1994), 86.

7. Ibid., 7; cf. 55–59, 105–6. But Paul is "not quite a platonist"; he does not believe in "immaterial existence of souls" (p. 61).

one outwardly"; rather, "real circumcision is a matter of the heart" (Rom 2:28-29). For Paul the real (or "new") covenant with God is not restricted to a genetic line, but belongs to all who have faith in the Messiah (Rom 3:30; 4:11; 9:8). This subject will be explored at greater length in the chapters on Galatians and Romans, but we see indications of this issue in the Corinthian correspondence, both in the irrelevance of the markers of ethnic identity ("circumcision is nothing, and uncircumcision is nothing," 1 Cor 7:19) and the importance of spiritual interpretation ("the Spirit gives life," 2 Cor 3:6).

Next, Paul compares the "deadly" aspects of the Mosaic law and an ethnically isolated community with the "lively" aspects of the Spirit and a potentially universal community. He recalls to readers' minds the story of how, when Moses descended from Mount Sinai with the ten commandments, his face was shining with such glory that people could not bear to look upon him (Exod 34:29-30). "Now if the ministry of death . . . came in glory . . . how much more will the ministry of the Spirit come in glory?" (3:7-8). It is so much greater that the old glory seems, in comparison, to have "lost its glory" (3:10).

Paul *does* acknowledge the old covenant's glory even while pointing out that its glory is fading (3:11, 13) and it is unable to liberate (3:14, 17). But even its fading glory seems to anticipate another and permanent glory. To call the old covenant a "ministry of death" (v. 7) is to call it helpless, not inherently evil. The Law is powerless against sin and death. Further, it is largely negative in nature, a "ministry of condemnation," but the "ministry of justification" abounds in glory (v. 9) and brings freedom and transformation (vv. 17-18). Paul can preach it with boldness, unlike the veil-covered Moses (vv. 12-13; Exod 34:34-35).

Paul then uses the image of the veil to symbolize the hindered vision, the dull-mindedness, of contemporary Jews "when they hear the reading of the old covenant," since "only in Christ is it set aside" (v. 14). Messiah-recognition is the key to an unveiled comprehension of the OT, since its deeper meanings concern the Messiah. There is a linkage between Messiah-identification, reading comprehension, and one's spiritual condition. One's reading needs to be Spirit-illuminated. "Now the Lord is the Spirit, and where the Spirit of the Lord is, there is freedom" (v. 17).

This leads to the great saying: "all of us, with unveiled faces, seeing the glory of the Lord as though reflected in a mirror, are being transformed into the same image from one degree of glory to another; for this comes from the Lord, the Spirit" (3:18). "One degree of glory to another" indicates progressive development from stage to stage of spiritual maturation. Spiritual growth is a matter of reflecting and of taking on the divine nature through a process of step-by-step transformation. This process of gradual divinization or deification was later called *theōsis*. It was an important theme in the first five hundred years of Christian thought, but it came to be neglected in the Western churches.[8]

Paul brings up his own reputation and mission again. He does not hide things or falsify the word of God, but declares the truth openly (4:2). His message is "veiled" (perhaps meaning "confusing") only "to those who are perishing" (4:3), who are rejecting it, whose minds are blinded by "the god of this world" and so are unable to see "the light of the gospel of the glory" of Christ (4:4). Christ's glory *is* the Gospel!

The rest of 4:4 shows Christ's uniqueness: "Christ, who is the image (*eikōn*) of God." This is a statement of high christology. No one else, no lawgiver, no prophet, no apostle, can be called the image of God. Christ is "Lord" (*kyrios*) (4:5), one of the two principal names of God in the Old Testament. Just as the Creator God said "let there be light" (Gen 1:3), so he shines "in our hearts to give the light of the knowledge of the glory of God in the face of [Jesus] Christ" (4:6). ("Jesus" is absent from some manuscripts.) It is precisely the "face," that is, the *person*, of Jesus Christ that transmits God's glory to us. God is the ultimate source, but Jesus the *immediate* source, of glory. There is no divinization without Jesus, the transmitter of divinity and the embodiment of glory.

The transmission is from God to Christ to believers, but it really is *God's* power that is held "in clay jars" (4:7). Even though afflicted, limited, struck down, believers are not despairing, not destroyed (4:8-9). But a true believer is "always carrying in the body the death of Jesus," always replicating the suffering of Christ, "always being given up to death for Jesus' sake" (4:10-11). For Paul this suffering brings "life in you" (4:12); an apostle's life is a life for others. Believers, especially apostles, suffer now, but they will be raised up as Jesus was raised (v. 14), "so that grace, as it extends to more and more people, may increase thanksgiving, to the glory of God" (v. 15).

This sequence leads to a slogan by which one can live and be happy: "So we do not lose heart. Even though our outer nature is wasting away,

---

8. Recent collections on the subject are Stephen Finlan and Vladimir Kharlamov, eds., *Theōsis: Deification in Christian Tradition*. PTMS 52 (Eugene, OR: Wipf & Stock, 2006); Michael J. Christensen and Jeffrey A. Wittung, eds., *Partakers of the Divine Nature: The History and Development of Deification in the Christian Traditions* (Madison, NJ: Fairleigh Dickinson University Press, 2007).

our inner nature is being renewed day by day" (4:16). Renew (*anakainoō*), renewal (*anakainōsis*), and new covenant (*kainē diathēkē*) are central to Paul's theology of transformation: "be transformed by the renewing of your mind" (Rom 12:2); "walk in newness of life" (Rom 6:4); "you . . . have clothed yourselves with the new self, which is being renewed" (Col 3:10). He may be drawing on promises of renewal in Psalm 103:5 ("your youth is renewed like the eagle's") and Lamentations 5:21 ("renew our days as of old"). All of Paul's hope depends on the promise of spiritual completion: "the one who began a good work among you will bring it to completion" (Phil 1:6). Here in 2 Corinthians he speaks of daily renewal of the self, promising "an eternal weight of glory" (4:16-17). Believers live by the promise of eternity and not by what is seen, "for what can be seen is temporary, but what cannot be seen is eternal" (4:18).

The New Creation; Becoming Righteousness: Chapter 5

Paul continues the newness theme. With much greater brevity than in 1 Corinthians 15:35-54 he speaks of the resurrection body, using the analogy of a new tent or dwelling, "a house not made with hands, eternal in the heavens" (5:1). In the earthly "tent we groan, longing to be clothed with our heavenly dwelling" (5:2). The Spirit is "a guarantee" on this promise of a heavenly body (5:5). This is enough for now; it gives hope and enables endurance; believers "walk by faith" (5:7). The believer would willingly "be away from the body," but "we make it our aim to please" God whether "at home with the Lord" or "away" (in the body) (5:8-9).

Next comes something unexpected in the Pauline literature: "all of us must appear before the judgment seat of Christ" (5:10). Although Paul does expect to be judged when "the Lord comes" (1 Cor 4:4-5), we do not consider the view of Christ as judge to be characteristic of Paul; in Romans 2:5-8 it is clearly God who will judge.[9] So 2 Corinthians 5:10 is somewhat unexpected. But there are other things to notice in this sentence, namely the basis on which judgment is made: "so that each may receive recompense for what has been done in the body, whether good or evil" (5:10). People will be judged by their *works*![10] For those who are familiar with the usual summary of Paul's soteriology (salvation by faith, not works), this may be hard to understand. That simple summary, however, does

9. The idea of Christ as judge is more at home at Revelation (2:23; 22:12) or Matthew (25:31-33).
10. Also in Rom 2:6-7; 1 Cor 3:13-15; Gal 6:7-8.

not tell all. The notion that faith is the path to salvation does not negate the idea that evil works will be punished. Works matter, especially on the negative end of the judgment spectrum. On the positive end one is saved by faith, but faith has *enabled* one to do good works,[11] and it may be that those good works are a factor in salvation (Rom 2:7, 10).

Next comes another self-appraisal by Paul. He hopes that his motives are apparent to the Corinthians; he is "giving you an opportunity to boast about us . . . For if we are beside ourselves, it is for God; if we are in our right mind, it is for you" (5:11-13). This may support the allegation that Paul's self-defense is actually a parody.[12] Boasting is mentioned so many times in this letter, and from so many different angles, that it is clearly a major topic in the letter. Is Paul really trying to get the Corin-thians to engage in *correct* boasting, as 1:14; 5:12; and 10:17 imply, or to defend his own correct boasting (as in 1:12; 7:4; 8:24; 9:2; 10:8, 16; 11:16-18, 30; 12:1, 5-6, 9), or is he (perhaps in 7:4, 14; 10:8, 13, 15; 11:10, 12, 16-18, 21) ridiculing the human tendency toward selfish boasting and more specifically ridiculing the Corinthians' spiritual pride? One can sense sarcasm in such a remark as this: "let no one think that I am a fool; but if you do, then accept me as a fool, so that I too may boast a little" (11:16). This comes in the middle of a passage (10:12–12:6) where "boasting" (the verb is *kauchaomai*) and "commending" (the verb is *synistēmi*) are men-tioned twenty times. This dense repetition either means that Paul lacks literary imagination or that he has more of it than most of his readers have appreciated.

In 2 Corinthians 5:14-21 Paul returns to his central soteriological teach-ings. It is no coincidence that he moves from a mockery of human boast-ing to a recounting of salvation. The divine solution answers the human problem. He reminds his readers that "one has died for all; therefore all have died" (5:14). Humanity symbolically died when the Son of God died in our place, or as our representative.[13] In any case "he died for all," and this means that we are obligated to him and should live for him

11. As the poor Christians of Macedonia had "overflowed in . . . generosity" (2 Cor 8:2), and as the Spirit empowers one with "love . . . kindness, generosity" to "work for the good of all" (Gal 5:22-23; 6:10).

12. It parodies the common misinterpretation of religious ecstasy as drunkenness (Mc-Cant, *2 Corinthians,* 52).

13. Morna D. Hooker insists that "therefore all have died" shows that Christ died as a *representative* of humanity, not as a *substitute* (*From Adam to Christ: Essays on Paul* [Cam-bridge: Cambridge University Press, 1990], 51).

(5:15). This is a spiritual loyalty and is more important than any fleshly claims, even those of the apostles who knew Christ in the flesh: "even though we once knew Christ from a human point of view, we know him no longer in that way" (5:16).[14] *Spiritual* knowledge is what matters. Because of the Messiah everything has changed: "So if anyone is in Christ, there is a new creation: everything old has passed away; see, everything has become new!" (5:17). (NASB has "he is a new creature"; *ktisis* can be either creature or creation.) Just as the "inner nature" is daily renewed (4:16), so believers experience a new creation or become a new creature. What is new is that they have been reconciled to God. Through Christ, God "reconciled us to himself" (which changes *us*) and has "given us the ministry of reconciliation" (5:18)—Paul's assignment.

Importantly, Paul clarifies the fact that God did this. God was not induced or persuaded, but did the reconciling himself: "in Christ God was reconciling the world to himself, not counting their trespasses against them" (5:19). Many readers of other Pauline passages have concluded that the death of Jesus was a kind of sacrificial payment that persuaded God, and in some of those passages Paul does not eliminate this as a possible interpretation, but here he *does* eliminate it: God was not persuaded or conciliated; rather, God did the reconciling.

The culminating image in this passage seems to be the Levitical scapegoat:[15] "For our sake he made him to be sin who knew no sin" (5:21). This is not a sacrificial image; a sacrificial animal is pure and a gift to God. It is the scapegoat that is "made" sin—that is, takes it on, becomes impure, and bears away sin; its "task is confined to transport."[16] The scapegoat carries corruption and is identified with what it carries.

Scapegoating seems to be a much more primitive ritual than sacrifice. Quite literally "all the iniquities of the people of Israel" are put "on the head of the goat" and "the goat shall bear on itself all their iniquities to a barren region" (Lev 16:21-22). The sacrificial victim, on the other hand, is killed either purely as a gift to God, or in order to obtain its life-carrying

---

14. This is yet another instance in which "flesh" is inferior to "spirit" (Boyarin, *A Radical Jew*, 29–31).

15. James D. G. Dunn, *The Theology of Paul the Apostle* (Grand Rapids: Eerdmans, 1998), 217; B. Hudson McLean, *The Cursed Christ: Mediterranean Expulsion Rituals and Pauline Soteriology*. JSNTSup 126 (Sheffield: Sheffield Academic Press, 1996), 109–10, 144.

16. Translating Adrian Schenker, *Versöhnung und Sühne: Wege gewaltfreier Konfliktlösung im Alten Testament mit einem Ausblick auf das Neue Testament*. Biblische Beiträge 15 (Fribourg: Verlag Schweizerisches Katholisches Bibelwerk, 1981), 116.

blood, which is used to purify the temple. There is complicated symbolism here. The temple symbolizes the nation; the priests stand for the people; impurity stands for impropriety; blood stands for life. The scapegoat ritual has none of this, only the crude deportation of sin.

For ease of communication I have used the word "scapegoating" here, but I intend it to include the tradition of expulsion rituals in Greek and Ancient Near Eastern cultures, which often involved human victims.[17] Even Athens had such a ritual; during the Thargelia festival two human *pharmakoi* were selected, garlanded, led in procession around the city, and then banished in order to purify the city.[18] Paul would know that those Gentiles who were unfamiliar with the Jewish scapegoat would at least have heard of other rituals of transfer and expulsion.

Expulsion rituals involved a *sudden* change of status between victim and community. The innocent animal takes on the community's sin or disease while the guilty community takes on the animal's innocence or purity. It is a magical reversal of conditions, and it held an important place in the imagination even after its actual practice declined.

Such a sudden exchange is seen in the astounding image that culminates 2 Corinthians 5:21—"so that in him we might become the righteousness of God." Just as Christ was "made" sin, so now the community is *made righteousness!* We are still within the cultic metaphor, with the community benefiting from the reversal ritual. Although Paul's Gospel involves more than just an interpretation of what took place at the cross, he does attach his soteriology to notions of a great transaction, even a ritual event, happening there. The cross functions as a reversal ritual; humanity experiences a reversal of conditions because the innocent Messiah took on human sin, while sinful humans can take on innocence—but only if they believe. Thus the crude substitutionary theologies of later times—in which Christ literally paid the price of sin and received God's wrath—are indeed based on some key passages in Paul,[19] but these theologies distort Paul by isolating certain sayings and taking them literally while underrating others such as 2 Corinthians 5:19 and Romans

17. For a description of the Greek *pharmakos* rituals, as well as of expulsion rituals in Hittite culture, see Stephen Finlan, *The Background and Content of Paul's Cultic Atonement Metaphors.* AcBib 19 (Atlanta: SBL/Brill, 2004), 77–83.

18. Walter Burkert, *Structure and History in Greek Mythology and Ritual* (Berkeley: University of California Press, 1979), 65; McLean, *Cursed Christ,* 210, citing Hipponax fragment 4.

19. 1 Thess 5:9-10; Rom 3:24-25; 4:25; 5:9-10; 8:1-4; 1 Cor 5:7; 6:20; 2 Cor 5:21; Gal 3:13.

5:8, which work against the idea of the death as any kind of payoff. But we have already seen that 1 Corinthians 6:20; 7:23 use commercial trans- actional language to picture the Messiah's death as a payment, and we will see that Romans 3:24 and Galatians 3:13 do the same. Paul clearly did think of some kind of transaction taking place on the cross, one that could be pictured with commercial, sacrificial, and scapegoat terminol- ogy. He mixes these metaphors, apparently not wanting any one to domi- nate the others, yet repeatedly using images that describe *some* kind of transaction that temporarily changed the Messiah's status ("made . . . sin," 5:21) while permanently changing the status of believers (becoming the righteousness of God). This certainly looks like a reversal ritual.

Paul did not worry about the difficulty of fully harmonizing his vari- ous images. He was a preacher and his mission was to win souls. Any effective metaphor was fair game: "To the weak I became weak, so that I might win the weak. I have become all things to all people, that I might by all means save some" (1 Cor 9:22). Evidently, for those who believed in the power of sacrifice and scapegoat rituals Paul would use ritual imagery to picture how the death of Christ had a sin-cleansing or sin- banishing effect.

Apostolic Defense and Authority; Patronage: Chapters 6–7

Paul appeals to his readers to understand that he is working for their good (6:1-3), persevering through "afflictions, hardships, calamities, beatings, imprisonments, riots, labors, sleepless nights, hunger" (6:4-5), always in "holiness of spirit, genuine love, truthful speech" (6:6-7), al- though slandered, misunderstood (vv. 8-9), and suffering (vv. 9-10). This apostolic self-defense seems in earnest, not parodic. He needs the Cor- inthians to believe that "our heart is wide open" (6:11),[20] and his goal is to get them to "open wide your hearts also" (v. 13). If they are open- hearted they will have a better attitude toward Paul, who is open toward them. Then they will allow themselves to be taught by their founding apostle.

There is jarring change of tone and message in 6:14-17, shifting from a call for openness to a call for strictness. The command, "Do not be

---

20. This is probably an "epistolary plural," purely rhetorical. But other plurals in the first nine chapters of the letter *do* reflect the plural authorship of Paul and Timothy accord- ing to Jerome Murphy-O'Connor, *Paul the Letter-Writer: His World, His Options, His Skills* (Collegeville, MN: Liturgical Press, 1995), 28–31.

mismatched with unbelievers" (6:14) seems to contradict the advice against divorcing unbelieving husbands or wives in 1 Corinthians 7:10-14. The question "What agreement does Christ have with Beliar?"[21] (2 Cor 6:15) contradicts Paul's idea that a spouse can work for the salvation of the unbelieving partner. It seems that someone with apocalyptic beliefs and a strong separatist strategy ("come out from them, and be separate from them," 2 Cor 6:17) inserted these verses into the text. The different content, the unusual vocabulary, and the fact that 7:2 picks up right where 6:13 left off, with a plea for openness, are enough to convince many scholars that this is a later interpolation, not written by Paul.[22]

The thought resumes at 2 Corinthians 7:2 with a plea to "make room in your hearts for us," and a defense, "we have wronged no one." Paul works his audience carefully, praising them ("I have great pride in you," 7:4), noting their loyalty ("your mourning, your zeal for me," 7:7), but also gently commanding (7:2), and reminding them that "we were afflicted in every way" (7:5).

Paul refers to a previous letter (2 Cor 10–13?) when he says "even if I made you sorry with my letter, I do not regret it" (7:8), and the reason is "because your grief led to repentance" (7:9). Ever the pastor, Paul counsels "godly sorrow produces a repentance that leads to salvation" (7:10). He had written regarding a particular person, "the one who did the wrong" (7:12), and many have concluded that he is referring to the adulterous individual of 1 Corinthians 5:1-11.[23] In 2 Corinthians 7:12 he goes on to speak of "the one who was wronged," which may mean the stepmother in the adulterous relationship. Whatever the concern, Paul seems to have triumphed in the matter, so that he can say, "I was not disgraced," and he was right to boast to Titus about the Corinthians (7:14). They have made their spiritual patron proud. Further, they were properly obedient to Titus when he visited them (7:15), so it may be that Paul sent Titus to see that the adulterer was cast out of the congregation (1 Cor 5:2, 7). Although he is a great critic of the worldly patron-client relationship, Paul perpetuates a different kind of patron-client pattern

---

21. The demonic figure Beliar (or Belial) occurs in the Dead Sea Scrolls and in *T. Levi* 18.

22. Luke Timothy Johnson, *The Writings of the New Testament: An Interpretation* (Philadelphia: Fortress Press, 1986), 292; Roetzel, *Paul: The Man and the Myth,* 114.

23. Colin G. Kruse agrees with this view, which has prevailed since the time of the early church ("The Offender and the Offence in 2 Corinthians 2:5 and 7:12," *Evangelical Quarterly* 60 [1988]: 131–33).

in which believers are obedient to apostles (their spiritual patrons) and everyone, *especially* apostles, are clients, even slaves, of Christ. As with the worldly relationship, so the spiritual one is characterized by attitudes of submission, obedience, concern, and boasting. The degree to which this reproduces earthly power structures and the extent to which it replaces or spiritualizes them is a complex subject. One could certainly say that Paul goes against patronage when he demands that the strong accommodate themselves to the weak.[24] Or one could say that Paul is "anti-structural" in his opposition to society's hierarchy, but that he introduces new "hierarchical structures within the anti-structural church."[25] It may be that believers are the only ones able to recognize that everyone experiences some shame, but that God gives a new kind of honor that is spiritual. Believers could even be called "the community of the shamed made right by the death and resurrection of Christ."[26]

The Collection for the Saints: Chapters 8–9

Paul is now going to exercise his apostolic authority to persuade the Corinthians to give generously to the collection for the poor saints in Jerusalem. He starts by holding up the churches of Macedonia, who *have* so given, even "beyond their means" (8:3). They begged to be able to take part in this service (8:4). After such a narrative, how could the Corinthians not give generously? They would feel ashamed. This also is how patronage works. (Look how loyal my other clients were!) Even when the praising begins ("Now as you excel in everything—in faith, in speech,

---

24. Dale B. Martin, *Slavery as Salvation: The Metaphor of Slavery in Pauline Christology* (New Haven: Yale University Press, 1990), 141–42; similarly, Paul opposed exploitive structures (Neil Elliott, *Liberating Paul: The Justice of God and the Politics of the Apostle* The Bible and Liberation [Maryknoll, NY: Orbis, 1994], 202–10). See the section below on Philippians 2, regarding Paul's reversal of Roman values.

25. Norman R. Petersen, *Rediscovering Paul: Philemon and the Sociology of Paul's Narrative World* (Philadelphia: Fortress Press, 1985), 157–58; similarly, Paul's is an "anti-imperial gospel" but "he 'reinscribed' imperial images and relations within his arguments" (Richard A. Horsley, "Rhetoric and Empire—and 1 Corinthians," in idem, ed., *Paul and Politics: Ekklesia, Israel, Imperium, Interpretation* [Harrisburg, PA: Trinity Press International, 2000], 92–93). Petersen says something Horsley does not: it may be "that once anti-structural groups emerge, it is necessary for them to develop their own internal structures" (*Rediscovering Paul,* 153).

26. Robert Jewett, "Paul, Shame, and Honor," in J. Paul Sampley, ed., *Paul in the Greco-Roman World: A Handbook* (Harrisburg, PA: Trinity Press International, 2003), 551–74, at 561.

in knowledge," 8:7), we wonder if there is not a hint of sarcasm, and thus of shaming, in it. But it is all for a good end: "I am testing the genuineness of your love" (8:8). As Christ became "poor" so that we might become "rich," so the Corinthians ought to become poor for others (8:9). Apparently they began to contribute "last year" (8:10), and now need to "finish doing it" (8:11). Paul has sent Titus to Corinth, carrying *this* letter (8:17); Titus seems to be held in high esteem by the Corinthians and Paul tries to raise his own standing by a continuous reminder that Titus "has . . . been appointed by the churches to travel with us"; he is "my partner and co-worker" (8:19, 23).

Paul takes very seriously "this generous undertaking for the glory of the Lord" (8:19). His reputation among other church leaders might to some degree depend on the success of this collection. He wishes "that no one should blame us about this generous gift that we are administering" (8:20). In case anyone has failed to perceive the importance of the collection, he pleads his case. He has already boasted about them to the Macedonians (9:2), and it will prove an empty boast if they do not give, and "bountifully" (9:3-6). There is a spiritual law operative here: giving sparingly will mean receiving sparingly, but "the one who sows bountifully will also reap bountifully" (9:6). One should do it "not reluctantly or under compulsion, for God loves a cheerful giver" (9:7). The reward will be everlasting; giving will "increase the harvest of your righteousness" (9:10); it enriches *them* while also glorifying God (9:11, 13). This grace-filled work (cf. 9:14) may serve the "symbolic function" of creating "reconciliation between his gentile communities and the Jerusalem church."[27] Although there is no benediction and closing, this may be the end of one of Paul's letters to the Corinthians: "Thanks be to God for his indescribable gift!" (v. 15).

What Is to Be Praised? The Self-Defense of Chapters 10–13

These chapters are widely considered by scholars to be a separate letter from the chapters that precede. The discussion no longer concerns the collection, but is all about apostleship, particularly *Paul's* apostleship. These chapters, however, seem to lack the confident tone and the clever irony of 2 Corinthians 1–2, 6–7. Paul does not seem relaxed when he has to "appeal to" or "ask" the Corinthians (10:1-2), or when he threatens to "show boldness" in opposing some of them on his next visit (10:2). He

---

27. Johnson, *Writings of the New Testament*, 298.

will "wage war" (10:3-4) and "punish every disobedience" (10:6), in order to "take every thought captive to obey Christ" (10:5). The matter is deadly serious: *every thought* must be made captive to Christ; there is no neutral subject matter.

This passage tends to support the view that Paul is fighting against specific opponents who have made concrete arguments against him: "We destroy arguments and every proud obstacle raised up against the knowledge of God" (10:4-5). There will be no compromise; his enemies are arguing against God! Paul admits he may "boast a little too much of our authority," but it is for the purpose of building up the believers (v. 8). He also admits that his letters may seem a bit severe, but they communicate the same thing that he had when he was personally present (10:11).

Paul is responding to some very personal criticism, which says that "his bodily presence is weak, and his speech contemptible" (10:10). He handles this with sarcasm: "We do not dare to classify or compare ourselves with some of those who commend themselves," but he is in dead earnest when he says that "when they measure themselves by one another . . . they do not show good sense" (10:12). There is no place for self-assertion in the Lord. Paul himself "will not boast beyond limits, but will keep within the field that God has assigned to us" (10:13). This seems to indicate that a limited "boasting" or self-defense is proper and altogether different from disproportionate boasting. It is crucial not to "overstep" (v. 14). He wants to be able to "proclaim the good news in lands beyond you" (v. 16), and it is to *that* end that his "boasting" (his assertiveness) is directed. This can be called boasting in the Lord (v. 17). Paul is one "whom the Lord commends" (v. 18).

In chapter 11 some of Paul's irony and sharp humor reappears. At least twice he signals to the reader that he is speaking parodically: "What I am saying in regard to this boastful confidence, I am saying not with the Lord's authority, but as a fool; . . . I am talking like a madman" (11:17, 23). Parody helps ease the communication of a serious message. Paul asks the Corinthians to "bear with me in a little foolishness!" (11:1). He is jealous for the Corinthians like a husband for his virgin bride (11:2), but he is worried that she has been corrupted by the "cunning" serpent, as Eve was (11:3). This is a very suggestive analogy. He laments the fact that the Corinthians are susceptible to listening to "a different gospel" and hearing about "another Jesus," which is being presented by the "super-apostles" (11:4-5).

It may be that these super-apostles are known for their eloquence. Paul says, "I may be untrained in speech, but not in knowledge" (11:6).

He wonders if he made a mistake by being so unselfish toward the Corinthians. When he was with them he asked for nothing; he was supported by other churches (11:7-9). His enemies have used this to claim that Paul does not love the Corinthians (11:11-12). Now his anger overflows: these people are "false apostles . . . disguising themselves as apostles of Christ. And no wonder! Even Satan disguises himself as an angel of light" (11:13-14).

Disgust with the Corinthians moves Paul to parody. I'll boast like a fool, he says, since you only accept fools (11:16-18): "you gladly put up with fools, being wise yourselves! For you put up with it when someone makes slaves of you, or preys upon you . . . or gives you a slap in the face" (11:19-20). Presumably the Corinthians will recognize the actions of some of their leaders in these remarks. Paul has all the qualifications they might have, and more, because he has endured "far greater labors, far more imprisonments, with countless floggings" (11:23) than his foes.[28] "Five times I have received from the Jews the forty lashes minus one. Three times I was beaten with rods. Once I received a stoning. Three times I was shipwrecked" (11:24-25). In Paul's understanding, one of the marks of a true apostle is this replication of the sufferings of the Messiah. This catalog of suffering from verses 23 to 33 goes on for 143 Greek words. He endured being "often without food, cold and naked," suffered many physical attacks, and was "under daily pressure because of my anxiety for all the churches" (11:26-28). In a rare instance of confirmation of a story from Acts, he alludes to his escape from Damascus in a basket, although Paul mentions only the enmity of the governor under King Aretas (11:32), while Luke speaks of the hostility of the local Jews, who resented Paul's effective preaching (Acts 9:22-24).

His enemies, the "super-apostles," are probably not boasting of their sufferings, but of their wisdom and their visions. Therefore Paul will boast of a vision he had, although he only talks about it in the third person. "I know a person in Christ who . . . was caught up to the third heaven," and was even "caught up into Paradise and heard things that are not to be told, that no mortal is permitted to repeat" (12:2, 4). Despite Paul's rhetorical distancing of himself from this story (especially in v. 5), most scholars believe he is describing his own visionary experience. It adds to the preceding argument only if it is autobiographical. He lets

---

28. This section can be considered an encomium, which formally enunciates his praiseworthy deeds and virtues (Bruce J. Malina and Jerome H. Neyrey, *Portraits of Paul: An Archaeology of Ancient Personality* [Louisville: Westminster John Knox, 1996], 55–61).

the cat out of the bag when he says that he refrains from saying any more, "so that no one may think better of me than what is seen in me . . . even considering the exceptional character of the revelations" (12:6-7). Evidently Paul has quite a bit to brag about in this area! In fact, "a thorn was given me in the flesh" in order to keep him from becoming elated (12:7).

Who or what is this "thorn," this "messenger of Satan" (12:7)? Believers and scholars have offered many theories, from the idea of a literal demon sent to afflict him to the medically-based explanations that enjoy much support today: that Paul had an eye disease[29] or epilepsy. It triggered an important religious experience for Paul; three times he prayed and begged for it to be removed, but the Lord "said to me, 'My grace is sufficient for you, for power is made perfect in weakness.' So, I will boast all the more gladly of my weaknesses, so that that the power of Christ may dwell in me" (12:9). Now we begin to realize that Paul's continuing play with "boasting" is meant to undermine boasting; it makes no worldly sense to boast in weakness; boasting is an attempt to deny weakness. But God became weak on the cross; God became humble in the earthly Jesus; God's way is not the way of self-assertion. Thus Paul's rhetoric of boasting is ironic, meant to undermine the whole life of self-assertion and the things that accompany it, like deception and exploitation.

This reversal of worldly ways of looking at things needs to affect the individual believer so that she or he can say, with Paul, "I am content with weaknesses, insults . . . calamities for the sake of Christ; for whenever I am weak, then I am strong" (12:10). Paul is defining not only what is necessary for an apostle but also what is necessary for a believer. This represents a value system different from the world's. Paul identifies the false apostles with worldly values. Only if one perceives the different values can one understand what he means: "I am not at all inferior to these super-apostles, even though I am nothing" (12:11). Evidently, when he was among them many of the "signs and wonders" associated with apostleship were visible (12:12), but he wants them to recognize this other set of apostolic signs: "hardships, persecutions" (12:10).

---

29. This is the most likely theory, in my view. After his call experience he was temporarily blinded, and scales later fell from his eyes (Acts 9:9, 18). When he praises the kindness of the Galatians he says they would have torn out their own eyes and given them to him if they could (Gal 4:15). He hand-writes the end of that letter, saying "See what large letters I make when I am writing in my own hand" (Gal 6:11), something characteristic of poor-sighted individuals.

Paul is saving up for the Corinthians as a parent saves up for his or her children (12:14), "I will most gladly spend and be spent for you" (12:15). He is tugging on their heartstrings here, but he will soon move over to the sterner side of parenting. He resorts to irony, parroting his opponents' view that he, Paul, "took you in by deceit" (12:16), and then straightforwardly asks them if Titus or any of his other representatives took advantage of them (12:17-18), knowing full well that even his enemies would not assert that. Paul insists that everything he has done has been "for the sake of building you up" (12:19). Paul's exasperation starts to show: "For I fear that when I come, I may find you not as I wish, and that you may find me not as you wish," and he will attack their rivalries and jealousies (12:20). He may have to mourn over those who did not repent after he scolded them for their immorality (12:21) on his previous visit.

His next visit will be his third, and he had warned them before "that if I come again, I will not be lenient" (13:1-2). Again Paul plays on the theme of strength in weakness. Christ, too, was weak when he was crucified, "but lives by the power of God" (13:4). The same is true of believers: they "are weak in him," but they will "live with him by the power of God" (13:5).

His final admonitions include "examine yourselves" (13:5); watch out for wrongdoing (13:7), and realize that no one can actually "do anything against the truth, but only for the truth" (13:8). God's providence rules. In the end Paul hopes he will not have to be severe when he visits them (13:10). Finally he exhorts them to "put things in order, encourage one another [or: listen to my appeal], agree with one another, live in peace" (13:11). We get a glimpse of a charming social practice in the Pauline churches: "Greet one another with a holy kiss" (13:12). Of course, all these noble sentiments have a tough side. Such a close sharing of spiritual life means that there is strong group pressure on the individual, a pressure for unanimity.

Finally Paul gives what could be interpreted as a Trinitarian teaching, mentioning each of the three divine persons and a divine quality associated with each: "The grace of the Lord Jesus Christ, the love of God, and the communion of the Holy Spirit be with all of you" (13:13).

Chapter 6

Galatians

Something that was not an issue at Thessalonica or Corinth was of central importance in the churches of Galatia (central Asia Minor): the question whether Gentile converts needed to accept the marks, and undergo the rituals, of conversion to Judaism. This was simultaneously an intensely social and a deeply theological issue, and one that threatened the Gospel itself, in Paul's view.

We need to recognize certain continuities and discontinuities: we must distinguish the Jewish makeup of the Jesus movement from the predominantly Gentile makeup of the Pauline churches, but also recognize that Jews who had been part of the Jesus movement were now Christian apostles and leaders. Some of these leaders thought of Gentiles as foreigners who needed to undergo conversion to Judaism if they were to enter the covenant with God. Judaism had a procedure for conversion of proselytes involving a prolonged period of instruction, as well as, for males, the painful and dangerous rite of circumcision. For some generations many Gentiles had been attending synagogue and listening to the teachings. They were drawn to "the Jewish philosophy," but most of the men did not choose to undergo circumcision, nor did the majority of Gentiles thus attracted follow the highly detailed food laws of the Jews. If formal proselyte conversion were required, most of these Gentiles would never convert, and the spread of Christianity would be greatly hindered. Further, Paul could not tolerate a class structure in the church, with converts being seen as inferior to those who were born Jews.

Paul's foes in Galatia, those who were trying to require Gentile men to be circumcised, were supported by some of the Jewish Christian leaders of the Jerusalem church, and Paul was faced with the difficult task of validating the Jesus tradition while opposing the stance of some of those who could claim the strongest roots in the Jesus tradition. Such a quandary could, theoretically, lead to a cautious and diplomatic strategy, but that was not Paul's choice, at least not in Galatians. He decided to attack those who were "Judaizing" (*ioudaizein*, "to live like Jews," Gal 2:14), even though it meant taking issue with those who enjoyed more prestige within the wider church than he did. Paul was taking a stand on principle, trusting that the truth of his argument, the strength of his influence over the churches he founded, and the activity of the Spirit working with the Galatians, would be enough to persuade them of the truth of his position.

Apostleship from God, Not Humans: Chapters 1–2

Since his confrontational path will set him at odds with some Jerusalem leaders, Paul goes out of his way to repudiate the usual ways of establishing one's credentials by naming one's teachers and allies. Right from the beginning Paul identifies himself as an apostle "sent neither by human commission nor from human authorities, but through Jesus Christ and God the Father" (Gal 1:1). His apostleship was conferred directly by Jesus. Paul is not "seeking human approval"; he is "a slave of Christ" (1:10). The apparently low status of a slave becomes the highest status possible when one is a slave of Christ.

Paul sees himself involved in a sharp conflict between God and the forces of evil that would corrupt the Gospel. There is no room for compromise. Even in his opening greeting Paul sets out to define the sides in this conflict: he wishes grace and peace from "the Lord Jesus Christ, who gave himself for our sins to set us free from the present evil age" (Gal 1:3-4). We must remember, of course, that "Christ" means "Messiah" (anointed one), and that "Lord" was the name of the God of Israel. So who is Jesus? He is *Kyrios Iēsous Christos,* Lord Jesus Messiah. The Messiah is both *divine* ("Lord") and *human* ("Jesus"). Already this differs from the messianic concepts of most Jews, for whom the Messiah was just human.

Paul knows that the messianic way will not fit within the existing framework of Judaism, but his foes in Galatia do not. With such a limited viewpoint they are (wittingly or unwittingly) servants of this "evil age," and what they teach is really a false Gospel. Paul confronts his readers/auditors with this: "I am astonished that you are so quickly deserting the one who called you in [the] grace [of Christ] and are turning to a different gospel" (1:6), although he quickly adds "not that there is another gospel" (1:7). But those "who are confusing you" with the Judaizing teaching "want to pervert the gospel of Christ" (1:7). Do not listen to anyone who does that, Paul demands. Even if an angel, or even Paul himself were to preach a different Gospel from "what we proclaimed to you, let that one be accursed!" (1:8). The word for "accursed" is *anathema*. Besides the usual meaning of being under a curse, it can also signify something that is under a religious ban of destruction or death; this was the meaning of the Hebrew *herem*, for which *anathema* is the translation. It is thus a word with a dire and violent background.

Paul reiterates: "I want you to know, brothers and sisters, that the gospel that was proclaimed by me is not of human origin. . . . I received it through a revelation of Jesus Christ" (1:11-12). This is one of Paul's few references to what is sometimes called his conversion experience. He admits that in his "earlier life in Judaism" he "was violently persecuting the church of God and was trying to destroy it" (1:13). Paul was, indeed, a successful and leading Pharisee; he "advanced in Judaism beyond many among my people of the same age" (1:14). He gives almost no details of his Damascus road experience, only the spiritual essentials: God "was pleased to reveal his Son to[1] me, so that I might proclaim him among the Gentiles" (1:15-16). It is highly likely that his readers already knew the particulars of this experience, both from his own lips and from oral tradition in their community. Thus Paul is able to focus on the *source* of his apostleship.

After God revealed his Son to Paul, "I did not confer with any human being, nor did I go up to Jerusalem to those who were already apostles before me, but I went away at once into Arabia, and afterwards I returned to Damascus. Then after three years I did go up to Jerusalem to visit Cephas[2] and stayed with him fifteen days" (1:16-18). Further, he met none of the other apostles except "James the Lord's brother" (1:19). He is almost bragging that he was not trained by the Jerusalem apostles! Only after three years did he meet them *at all*, and even then he spent only fifteen days with them. He then departed for "Syria and Cilicia" (1:21), the latter being the region where lay Tarsus, the city in which he grew up. Acts 9 seems to coordinate well with this narrative; Barnabas took Paul to meet the apostles (Acts 9:27); he then went to Caesarea and on to Tarsus (Acts 9:30).

---

1. A more accurate translation is "*in* me," as given in KJV, NASB, NJB, and NIV.

2. Paul wants to show his knowledge of Peter's nickname in both Aramaic and Greek (2:7-9).

Paul wants to emphasize how little connection he has with the Jerusalem apostles. "Then after fourteen years I went up again to Jerusalem with Barnabas" (2:1). It is unclear whether these fourteen years include the three mentioned in 1:18 or whether they should be added to the three years. In any case, a long time elapsed before Paul ever made a lengthy visit to Jerusalem. Even at this time he was following a message from God, not a human being: "I went up in response to a revelation" (2:2). So, fourteen or seventeen years after his encounter with the risen Christ, Paul introduces the Jerusalem apostles to "the gospel that I proclaim among the Gentiles"; he also circumcises the "Greek" Titus, but no one has compelled him to do this (2:2-3). However, "false believers [literally "brothers"] . . . slipped in to spy on the freedom we have in Christ Jesus" in order to "enslave us" (2:4). We can only guess that these people were making the same demand: trying to persuade Gentile men that they needed to be circumcised, to become Jews before they could become full-fledged Christians. All Paul says is: "we did not submit to them even for a moment" (2:5).

These agitators are connected to the Jerusalem church but they are more rigid than the Jerusalem apostles themselves. Still, Paul makes some shockingly rude remarks about the latter, calling them "those who were supposed to be acknowledged leaders" (2:6) or "acknowledged pillars" (2:9), but he never calls them "false" or Satanic. He certainly dispels any aura of saintliness they might have in people's minds, but he does not picture them as enemies. They had extended some respect to him; they had listened to him explain his Gospel, and "those leaders contributed nothing" to his teaching or ministry (2:6). In fact, they realized that he "had been entrusted with the gospel for the uncircumcised, just as Peter had been entrusted with the gospel for the circumcised," and that the same one who worked through Peter "also worked through me" (2:7-8). When they recognized the grace in him, then "James and Cephas and John, who were acknowledged pillars . . . gave to Barnabas and me the right hand of fellowship, agreeing that we should go to the Gentiles and they to the circumcised" (2:9). Paul may be talking about the famed Apostolic Council (Acts 15) here, though from his unique viewpoint, avoiding any mention of the Council's Torah-derived ruling against idolatry, incest, and bloody meat. Some scholars strongly object to the suggestion that Paul is describing the same event. Richard Longenecker finds it "inconceivable" that, if the Council had already taken place, Paul would not tell the Galatians about the Council's decision against requiring circumcision.[3] But Longenecker may be underrating how harmful to Paul's argument it would be to mention a decree that *did* impose a few Torah rules. *Any* submission to Torah is fatal to Paul's argument in Galatians.

In any case, when Paul finally names the apostles he demotes them ("*acknowledged* pillars"), yet also claims their approval. In his teaching and ministry he owes them nothing, but he will mention that they have endorsed his mission to the Gentiles. In terms of the honor-shame paradigm, Paul occupies the honorable high ground. He owes nothing to any human; he is God's agent, and the other apostles had to acknowledge that.

It is not just a matter of pride and power; there is more at stake here, as Paul makes clear in the story of his confronting Peter over the issue of "Judaizing." When Cephas visited Antioch, Paul "opposed him to his face" (2:11), for he used to eat with Gentiles "until certain people came from James" and persuaded him to withdraw from the (non-kosher) table of the Gentiles (2:12). This creates a social barrier, even a class structure, within the church, and Paul will not tolerate it for a moment. Others also "joined him in this hypocrisy,"[4] "even Barnabas" (2:13), so Paul confronts "Cephas before them all, 'If you, though a Jew, live like a Gentile and not like a Jew, how can you compel the Gentiles to live like Jews?'" (2:14). The verb for "live like Jews" is *ioudaizō* ("to judaize"). Paul makes one of his great summarizing statements of his Gospel: "we know that a person is justified not by the works of the law but through faith in Jesus Christ. And we have come to believe in Christ Jesus, so that we might be justified by *faith in Christ* [*pistis Christou*] and not by doing the works of the law, because no one will be justified by the works of the law" (2:16).

There is a heated debate about whether the italicized phrase signifies belief *in* Christ (an *objective genitive*) or the faith or faithfulness of Christ himself (a *subjective genitive*). The first was the traditional interpretation, but many scholars have come to support the second.[5] Sam Williams sees the phrase as referring to the faithful obedience of Christ; it does not mean belief *in* Christ because "the person of Christ is not faith's object. *God* is . . . [P]istis Christou . . . indicat[es] means or basis . . . the means

---

3. Richard N. Longenecker, *Galatians.* WBC 41 (Dallas: Word Books, 1990), lxxix.

4. Our word "hypocrisy" comes from the Greek *hypokrisis,* which Paul uses here.

5. Richard B. Hays, Luke Timothy Johnson, Sam Williams, Stanley Stowers, Morna D. Hooker, Douglas Campbell, Thomas F. Torrance, Leander Keck.

by which *God* effects salvation."[6] Opposing this view is the argument of James D. G. Dunn that if one turns all these passages into references to the faithfulness of Jesus himself, one is left without any noun phrase for the believer's faith,[7] which is central to Paul's message: "those who believe are blessed" (Gal 3:9). Not work, but "faith is reckoned as righteousness" (Rom 4:5), and we saw the same works/faith opposition in Galatians 2:16. It may be that Dunn's argument looks stronger when the focus is on Galatians, where there is an intense faith-works dichotomy, while the view of Williams and others may be more persuasive when the focus is on Romans, where the beneficial effects of Christ's "obedience" are stressed and there is a possible equivalence between "faith" and "obedience." Therefore further discussion of the *pistis Christou* debate will be postponed to the Romans chapter.

At the end of Galatians 2, Paul spells out the essentials of his Gospel. While under the Law one experiences condemnation, but by participation in Christ one gets new life: "For through the law I died to the law, so that I might live to God. I have been crucified with Christ; and it is no longer I who live, but it is Christ who lives in me" (Gal 2:19-20). Faith is the source of true living: "and the life I now live in the flesh I live by faith in the Son of God, who loved me and gave himself for me" (Gal 2:20), and we see again that the climactic act was the death of the Son. What is spelled out here is not the logic, but the *result* of the saving death—life for believers. Did Christ die as a warrior dies to save his comrades? Did he die like a scapegoat, who is burdened with the community's sins? Or was he comparable to a sacrificial animal whose death provides the means for the cleansing of impurity? We would have to look elsewhere in Paul to get a clue; here we find only the saving fact. It seems, in fact, that the logic of how the death brought salvation changes from passage to passage, from metaphor to metaphor, suggesting that the logic was not the important thing. The logic is merely derived from the metaphors, and Paul will use any metaphor that seems to be vivid and compelling. What matters is salvation, and Paul links it to the death of Christ, and to having faith in Christ and in the efficacy of his death and resurrection. This is simultaneously faith in the *person* of Christ and in the *work* of Christ on the cross. None of that has anything to do with following the Jewish law, "for if justification comes through the law, then Christ died for nothing" (2:21).

6. Sam K. Williams, "Again *Pistis Christou*," *CBQ* 49 (1987): 434, 443.
7. James D. G. Dunn, "Once More: *PISTIS CHRISTOU*," in Eugene H. Lovering, Jr., ed., *SBL Seminar Papers, 1991*. SBLSP 30 (Atlanta: Scholars Press, 1991), 736.

Removing the Curse, Extending the Promise: 3:1-18

In this chapter, besides using specifically Jewish images, Paul will use religious language that has meaning for the Gentiles of Galatia. In the first verse he assaults them: "You foolish Galatians! Who has bewitched you? It was before your eyes that Jesus Christ was publicly exhibited as crucified?" (3:1). The word for "bewitch," or using the evil eye (*baskainō*), was known both in ordinary daily speech and in learned circles because of a well-known passage[8] in which Plato attacks those who deceitfully charm or bully weak-minded people into changing their opinions[9]— exactly what Paul sees as happening in Galatia. Plato equates it with bewitching: "all which deceives, bewitches."[10] Even if Paul never read *The Republic*, he could have encountered this equation in many other writers, since the remark was frequently cited. Apart from any possible literary connection, "bewitching" would carry a certain sting for the Galatian Gentiles, who were trying to turn away from their pagan superstitions, which included ideas of bewitching and cursing.

What of the second half of that verse? The "public" part of Jesus crucified could refer either to the public nature of crucifixion itself or, more likely, to Paul's preaching about the cross, which was plainly presented *to them*. Paul reminds the Galatians that they received the Spirit in response to Paul's preaching and not "by doing the works of the law . . . Are you so foolish? Having started with the Spirit, are you now ending with the flesh?" (3:2-3). Turning to the Law is a form of turning to the flesh. It was not "by your doing the works of the law" that they experienced "miracles" (3:4-5) right after their conversion.

Paul uses the faith of Abraham to support the truth about salvation by faith. It was because Abraham *believed* that he was considered righteous, and now "those who believe are children of Abraham" (3:6-7). First we must observe that the Greek verb for "believe" (*pisteuō*) and the noun for "faith" (*pistis*) are cognate, something that is lost in English, not only because "believe" and "faith" are not cognate but because we tend to think of doctrines when we speak of believing, whereas *pisteuō* primarily refers to *trusting*. A helpful exercise is occasionally to insert the word "trust" into some familiar "faith" or "belief" passages in order to recover that meaning: "daughter, your [trust] has saved you" (Luke

---

8. Sam K. Williams, *Galatians* (Nashville: Abingdon Press, 1997), 83.

9. Plato, *The Republic* 413C-E, in *The Great Dialogues of Plato,* trans. W. H. D. Rouse (New York: Mentor, 1956).

10. Ibid., 413D, p. 213.

8:48); "Abraham [trusted] God, and it was reckoned to him as righteousness" (Gal 3:6). The other important point to note from these verses is Paul's redefinition of "children of Abraham." People in the ancient world identified themselves by their family lines, and to be a child of Abraham was a source of great pride for Jews. Paul makes this no longer a genetic but a spiritual category. Trust-faith makes one a child of Abraham. Scholars sometimes call this "fictive kinship." It was important both for feelings of prestige and for theological reflection in the Pauline churches.

But this is no fiction for Paul. All of it was promised beforehand, in Genesis: "the scripture, foreseeing that God would justify the Gentiles by faith, declared the gospel beforehand to Abraham, saying, 'All the Gentiles shall be blessed in you'" (3:8). Among the promises to Abraham (that he would have a son who would give rise to numerous offspring, a great nation that would possess the land) was this promise: "all the nations of the earth shall be blessed in him"; "all the nations of the earth shall gain blessing for themselves through your offspring" (Gen 18:18; 26:4; cf. 12:3; 22:18; 28:14). This received less attention in the interpretive tradition than the other promises, but for Paul this five-times-repeated promise is the pre-gospel: Abraham's faith-induced blessing will be passed on to all peoples. Isaac and his descendants were not an end in themselves, but were to be the means for spreading a blessing to all peoples. This, and not the ethnically-specific Torah, is the means of salvation.

Pauline studies were given a wake-up call by E. P. Sanders, who attacked the simplistic contrast of a Judaism interested in earning salvation by outward obedience to the Law with Paul's proclamation of unearned salvation by faith. Sanders argued that the pattern of Jewish religion was "covenantal nomism," in which works of the Law were not a way of earning salvation, but were the proof of obedience after one was *already* in the covenant.[11] James D. G. Dunn builds on Sanders but heightens one aspect, the Jewish "sense of special privilege and prerogative over against others peoples . . . Paul's chief target is a covenantal nomism understood in restrictively nationalistic terms—'works of the law' as maintaining Jewish identity . . . exclud[ing] Gentiles as such from the covenant promise."[12] But the problem for Paul is not *just* national exclusivity; the

11. E. P. Sanders, *Paul and Palestinian Judaism* (Philadelphia: Fortress Press, 1977), 75–76, 182, 204, 235.

12. James D. G. Dunn, "The Theology of Galatians: The Issue of Covenantal Nomism," in Jouette M. Bassler, ed., *Pauline Theology, Vol. I: Thessalonians, Philippians, Galatians, Philemon* (Minneapolis: Fortress Press, 1991), 126, 137.

curse on those *within* the Law-covenant is also a problem, as is the fact that the Law is not based on faith but on "doing" (3:12). *Anything* that is not based on faith is a problem (Rom 14:23). Paul contrasts "faith" and "doing" in Galatians 3:10 and again in 3:12. Let us explore the problems of "curse" and of "doing."

"Cursed is everyone who does not observe and obey all the things written in the book of the law" (3:10, citing Deut 11:28). This refers to the curse (that is, the threat) that is part of YHWH's covenant with Israel. Dunn wants the curse to refer to the exclusion of Gentiles,[13] but in fact the curse applies only to those who are under the Law (Deut 26:18). It is for *Israel* that God "set[s] before you . . . a blessing and a curse: the blessing, if you obey the commandments of the LORD your God that I am commanding you today; and the curse, if you do not obey the commandments of the LORD your God" (Deut 11:26-28). Paul is saying that anyone who voluntarily comes under Torah also comes under this curse (threat). Even for Gentiles, then, "all who rely on the works of the law are under a curse" (Gal 3:10). And they will not, apparently, be able to fulfill those works and avoid that curse: "Now it is evident that no one is justified before God by the law; for 'The one who is righteous will live by faith'" (3:11)—citing Habakkuk 2:4, Paul's strongest proof-text from the prophets for salvation by faith. For Paul, salvation had always *really* been by faith (3:9 and elsewhere), but the Jewish obsession with works of Torah had obscured this truth.

Paul does what the OT does not do: he makes a sharp contrast between living by faith (which brings justification) and living by diligent attention to the Law (which cannot make one just). The Law is not based on faith, but on a regime of *doing:* "the law does not rest on faith; on the contrary, 'Whoever does the works of the law will live by them'" (3:12; Lev 18:5).

This much is clear and comprehensible. Paul complicates the picture when he brings in a metaphor for the saving death of Jesus. To do this he draws on another kind of curse, the metaphysical curse of sin that, in Leviticus 16, is laid upon the scapegoat. Paul conflates (combines) the non-transferable curse of Deuteronomy with the transferable curse of Leviticus when he says: "Christ redeemed us from the curse of the law by becoming a curse for us—for it is written, 'Cursed is everyone who hangs on a tree'" (3:13). The quote from Deuteronomy 21:23 is enlisted to show that the cruci-

---

13. James D. G. Dunn, *Jesus, Paul, and the Law: Studies in Mark and Galatians* (Louisville: Westminster John Knox, 1990), 229; idem, "Theology of Galatians," 137; but partially corrected in his *The Theology of Paul the Apostle* (Grand Rapids: Eerdmans, 1998), 226–27.

fied Christ was "cursed," which indeed was the public's perception of all victims of crucifixion: one is publicly humiliated; it is a "cursed" fate—but it is good for the community. The scapegoat is also accursed. It is treated as repulsive, is spat upon, stabbed, and cursed[14] before being driven out of the community, carrying away with it the community's sin or curse. This is a very primitive ritual involving a magical transference of metaphysical qualities (sin or curse) onto a body that will carry them away.

Paul combines several metaphors. In 3:13 Christ saves in three different ways: (1) he *purchases* our freedom ("redeemed us"), (2) he becomes a curse-bearer, like the scapegoat ("becoming a curse" is exaggerated language for taking on a curse), and (3) he takes on the legal penalty (in a legal setting the "curse" is the penalty). The rescue or salvation is accomplished vicariously by Christ paying for others, bearing others' curse, enduring others' penalty.

The Messiah's death accomplishes several things: it removes the Torah's curse-threat and deports the community's weight of sin. Christ thus both fulfills and resolves the Torah. He fulfills or replaces the scapegoat ritual and resolves or removes the Law's threat. He does what Torah was unable to do: remove sin permanently (not annually). Fulfillment is an aspect of *typology*: the belief that certain stories, characters, and rituals in the OT are impressions (or *types*) pointing ahead to their fulfillment in Christ (see the discussion of 1 Corinthians 10). Although he does not say *typos* and does not use the word for "goat," Paul is using scapegoat typology here,[15] with the familiar pattern of a victim bearing away a curse and bringing about a reversal of status between victim and community. Paul sees Deuteronomy's threat against covenant-breakers—which could not be removed by ritual means—as erased by the typological fulfillment of a primitive expulsion ritual in Leviticus. So it is not just Christ who removes the Law's threat; it is christological typology.

Conflation is a key factor in this form of interpretation. The scapegoat metaphor is conflated with the redemption-purchase image. Christ's death redeemed or purchased (*exagorazō*) those who were slaves of sin and the Law.[16] There is no getting around the economic meaning of this word. *Exagorazō* and *agorazō* (1 Cor 6:20) were common marketplace terms for

---

14. According to *Barnabas* 7:7-9; Tertullian, *Adv. Marcion* 3.7.7; *Mishnah Yoma* 6.4; B. Hudson McLean, *The Cursed Christ: Mediterranean Expulsion Rituals and Pauline Soteriology.* JSNTSup 126 (Sheffield: Sheffield Academic Pres, 1996), 83–84.

15. McLean, *Cursed Christ*, 124–27.

16. McLean, *Cursed Christ*, 130–31; Dunn, *Theology of Paul*, 228.

purchasing goods, including slaves.[17] Paul's conflation of metaphors constructs a new theology, heightening the element of *exchange*. In this new metaphorical theology the scapegoat takes on a kind of purchasing power, while ransoming or redeeming takes on an atmosphere of cultic holiness. The death of Christ becomes a holy payment. Of course, this creates philosophical problems for us, since slave redemption and expulsion ritual are no longer current practices or meaningful images, and if we take these metaphors too literally we develop the strange notion of God using a ritual murder in order to dismiss legal charges against humanity. God begins to seem violent, arbitrary, and more payment-exacting than forgiving. These problems are inherent in the primitive metaphors Paul chose to use. We can ameliorate, but not eliminate, this problem if we refuse to take Paul's metaphors too literally, and if we prefer the whole of his teaching (in which God's salvation is not purchased but is freely given) to the image created by the cultic and purchase metaphors. But the problem will persist, since Paul did link salvation to the crucifixion as a bloody cultic event that purchases/redeems people (Gal 3:13; 1 Cor 7:23; Rom 3:24-25).

Christian atonement doctrine descends from Paul's synthesis of the sacrificial, scapegoat, and redemption metaphors for the saving death of Christ, although Christians have largely forgotten that Paul is stringing together *different* metaphorical images, which speaks of Paul's creativity and ought to warn us against being overly literal-minded. When we analyze Paul's reshaping of scriptural images we have just *begun* to understand him. Besides reinterpreting Jewish theology, Paul uses Gentile religious themes that would have been very meaningful to the Galatians. Curses and curse-expulsion were important in the ancestral Hittite[18] and Phrygian[19] cultures, and curses had spiritual and legal force in the blended culture of Paul's Galatia. Curse inscriptions protected buildings; curse scepters were raised to protect tombs; violators were threatened with judicial consequences before the gods; curse tablets appealed to the gods when violations did occur.[20] Lawsuits were framed

---

17. See the examples in Friedrich Büchsel, ἀγοράζω, ἐξαγοράζω, *TDNT* 1:124–26.

18. David P. Wright, *The Disposal of Impurity: Elimination Rites in the Bible and in Hittite and Mesopotamian Literature.* SBLDS 101 (Atlanta: Scholars Press, 1987).

19. Susan M. Elliott, *Cutting Too Close for Comfort: Paul's Letter to the Galatians in Its Anatolian Cultic Context.* JSNTSup 248 (London: T&T Clark, 2003), 59, 62–67, 75–77, 118–20.

20. Susan M. Elliott, "The Rhetorical Strategy of Paul's Letter to the Galatians in Its Anatolian Cultic Context: Circumcision and the Castration of the *Galli* of the Mother of the Gods." Ph.D. dissertation, Loyola University Chicago (1997), 160–68, 187–90.

as curses, and the defendant could be "redeemed" from the curse by setting up a pillar with an inscription admitting guilt and listing the penalty.[21] "The curse of the law" has an additional resonance for *this* audience, alongside Deuteronomy's threat against covenant-breakers. We can hardly comprehend Paul unless we take note of his clever use of local color in his allusions.

What is the outcome of this curse-removal? It is the fulfillment of God's promise to Abraham, the extension of blessing to the Gentiles in the form of "the promise of the Spirit through faith" to everyone (3:14). One cannot annul a will[22] once it has been written, and God's promises to Abraham had the legal force of such a will (3:15-16). But for Paul the promise is not the favoring of Israel; it is the coming of the Messiah. The promise was "to his offspring [*sperma*]; it does not say, 'And to offsprings,' as of many; but it says, 'And to your offspring,' that is, to one person, who is Christ" (3:16). Paul is taking advantage of the fact that *sperma* is grammatically singular (though it often signifies "descendants"). He sees it as testifying to a *particular* descendant of Abraham: the Messiah.

For Paul the blessing of the Gentiles is central to the Gospel. When God promised this to Abraham, God "pre-evangelized" (a literal translation of *proeuēngelisato* in Galatians 3:8, rendered "declared the gospel beforehand" in NRSV). This pre-gospel is called a covenant (3:17). The later, nationally-specific, Mosaic law was just a temporary measure: "the law . . . does not annul a covenant previously ratified by God" (3:17). The promise and the "inheritance" (being offspring of God) are what matter: "For if the inheritance comes from the law, it no longer comes from the promise; but God granted it to Abraham through the promise" (3:18). The Law was just a measure to spell out what behaviors were disapproved during the long period of waiting for the Messiah: "It was added because of transgressions, until the offspring would come to whom the promise had been made" (3:19).

---

21. Franz Cumont, *The Oriental Religions in Roman Paganism* (New York: Dover, 1956, from the 1911 translation), 40; Elliott, "Rhetorical Strategy,"176–86, 639–42. The analogy, for the Galatians, is that Christ functions like a curse tablet that removes a curse-accusation (ibid., 644)

22. Most translators use context here in choosing "will" over "covenant" for *diathēkē* for this sentence.

The Age of Faith: 3:19-29

Paul makes a remark that has proved baffling: the Law "was ordained through angels by a mediator" (3:19). The point seems to be that the Law came through sub-divine beings—angels and a human mediator (Moses). That the Law was either written or shaped by angels, and not by God, does not mean that the Law is opposed to God, but that it came from an imperfect source (angels).[23] Law itself seems to be limited; no law is life-giving or righteousness-conferring (3:21). Again Paul stresses the temporary nature of the Torah, a kind of sin-confining function awaiting the time when "what was promised through faith in Jesus Christ might be given to those who believe" (3:22). Both the faithfulness of Jesus and the faith of believers are essential, and both could be involved in the odd expressions "before faith came" and "now that faith has come" (3:23, 25). These speak of *an age of faith,* initiated by Jesus but needing the faith of believers to become real in the present world.

It is important to understand Paul's teaching about the temporary nature of the Torah: "Now before faith came, we were imprisoned and guarded under the law until faith would be revealed. Therefore the law was our disciplinarian until Christ came" (3:23-24). In Hellenistic societies the disciplinarian (*paidagōgos*) or pedagogue was a sort of stern chaperone for older boys to keep them out of trouble for the few years preceding their emergence into legal manhood. Jewish families were not known for having these disciplinarians; the image is a Gentile one, and yet Paul is using it to stand for the Torah! As ever, we need to keep Paul's dual audience (Jewish and Gentile) in mind, and be always ready for a clever and shocking metaphor.

The disciplinarian analogy is an excellent one: these disciplinarians were reputed to be strict and demanding, and they were temporary, for the period just preceding adulthood. Coming out from under the disciplinarian was a much-desired event. In the same way, coming out from under the domineering Torah and into the age of faith was a real coming of the age, in Paul's view: "But now that faith has come, we are no longer subject to a disciplinarian" (3:25). One comes into the status of a child of God: "for in Christ Jesus you are all children of God through faith" (3:26).

---

23. James D. G. Dunn claims that "the reference is much more positive than has often been assumed," citing Deut 33:3; *Jub.* 1.29, Philo, *Som.* 1.143 (*Theology of Paul*, 140). But Paul is much more law-critical than these sources. Acts 7:53 and Heb 2:2 also mention an angel-mediated law, but Acts 7:48 and Heb 10:1-11 marginalize Torah or Temple, so they tend to work against Dunn's theory.

The Gospel is a breakthrough into freedom, not only a coming-of-age but a raise in status. Believers are baptized into, and clothed with, Christ (3:27), eliminating the distinctions that were so important in the sinful world: "There is no longer Jew or Greek, there is no longer slave or free, there is no longer male and female; for all of you are one in Christ Jesus" (3:28). Torah-abiding Jews have no superiority to "Greeks" (Gentiles); aristocrats and freedpersons have no superiority to slaves; men have no superiority to women in the church. Believers receive the status of heirs: "And if you belong to Christ, then you are Abraham's offspring, heirs according to the promise" (3:29). This is a noble status! Being clothed with Christ, belonging to Christ, means one is no longer under a controlling disciplinarian. One is a child and heir of God, with all the privileges and responsibilities that implies. The Gospel proclaims the adulthood of the spirit.

The social implications are almost incalculable, and we can see that the Christian tradition was unable to stay loyal to this principle, reinstituting each of the status barriers Galatians 3:28 tried to dismantle. What of the status of women in particular? This saying "runs counter to the general acceptance of male religious privileges" by Jews and Gentiles alike.[24] As Tatha Wiley observes, "This was a conflict over *membership* and he says nothing that could be remotely construed to differentiate between women and men members."[25] This seems to mean that Paul's "communities were characterized by an *absence of difference* among members in their initiation, participation, and leadership."[26] In the Corinthian and Roman correspondence Paul addresses a number of women leaders in the community, and in Romans 16:7 he speaks of one woman (Junia) as an apostle.[27]

We have spoken of the adulthood of the spirit. How does this theme of faith as a coming of age coordinate with Paul's substitutionary theology? Poorly. Clearly, Paul is yoking together two different systems of thought here. It makes sense to speak of the Messiah inaugurating an

24. Elisabeth Schüssler Fiorenza, *In Memory of Her: A Feminist Theological Reconstruction of Christian Origins* (New York: Crossroad, 1994), 217.

25. Tatha Wiley, *Paul and the Gentile Women: Reframing Galatians* (New York: Continuum, 2005), 117–18.

26. Ibid., 96.

27. Of course, there is much more to say about Paul and women in his churches. See, for instance, the articles in Elisabeth Schüssler Fiorenza, ed., *Searching the Scriptures; Volume Two: A Feminist Commentary* (New York: Crossroad, 1994).

age of faith and Spirit-guidance, replacing a domineering system of religious law, enabling Jews to emerge as mature sons instead of children under a disciplinarian, and extending sonship to Gentiles without any required period of pedagogue-control. But Paul also says that it is Christ's death as a curse-bearer that extends the blessing to the Gentiles (3:13-14). This uses the logic of an ancient national ritual to argue for something that requires a transcendence of such rituals. Thus does Paul use a ritual—really a magical—logic completely unrelated to faith or Spirit while arguing for a new community based on faith and Spirit. It is with good reason that scholars continue to generate so many theories about what Paul's central message was: He has more than one central message! One of his messages involves complete replacement of the Torah system; his other message builds on ritual and legal concepts drawn from Torah, but also from the broad arena of Gentile concepts. Paul had an instinct for the vivid and compelling metaphor.

In fact, even his way of compressing two ways of thinking into one message is persuasive. He is able to argue with equal vigor for continuity and for discontinuity between the old way and the new way. When he says "those who believe are the descendants of Abraham" (3:7) he shows the new way (faith) while affirming a connection to the old (Abraham). The idea of gaining freedom from the Law's curse through a fulfillment of the Law's provision for curse-bearing communicates the same message: believers live in a post-curse age because Christ acted out a once-and-for-all version of the Law's annual curse-expulsion ritual. While not entirely logical, this succeeds rhetorically. Not only does the old testify to the new; the Law is made to argue for deliverance from itself!

No Longer Slaves: Chapter 4

Paul seems to continue his metaphor of the disciplinarian, saying an heir is no different from a slave while he is still under the disciplinarian (4:1-2). In the same way "while we were minors, we were enslaved to the elemental spirits [*stoicheia*] of the world" (4:3). *Stoicheia* can refer either to the elements underlying all things or to personalized astrological powers revered by many Gentiles.[28] This is a stunning move. Paul seems to be equating service to the Torah (under a disciplinarian) to Gentile enslavement to the elemental powers (under the *stoicheia*). The ancient reader may have been as baffled as the modern one when Paul

---

28. David R. Bundrick, "*Ta Stoicheia tou Kosmou* (Gal 4:3)," *JETS* 34 (1991): 356–57.

draws into the story the divine Son, Torah, and adoption: "when the fullness of time had come, God sent his Son, born of a woman, born under the law, in order to redeem those who were under the law, so that we might receive adoption" (4:4-5). Who is being redeemed, and who adopted? Is God redeeming the Jews but adopting the Gentiles? That would make the sentence extremely awkward. Is it just about Jews being redeemed and adopted? But Paul's main audience is Gentile, and he is certainly talking about Gentile religion a few verses later: serving "beings that by nature are not gods" (4:8). The most logical conclusion is that God is rescuing *all* those under the Law, both Jews and Gentile proselytes, and adopting them all. After all, Gentiles do need to be rescued from the Law—in Galatia. Therefore when Paul speaks of the result he need make no distinction between Jews and Gentiles: "And because you are children, God sent the Spirit of his Son into our hearts, crying, 'Abba, Father!'" (4:6). Evidently Jews and Gentiles stand in equal need of such adoption, after which one is "no longer a slave but a child, and . . . an heir" (4:7).

For Paul no one is *naturally* a child of God, either by race or by the mere fact of being human. When Paul speaks of being a child of God he is referring to an *adoptive* sonship. This can be quite a stunning realization for the reader. Being a child of God turns out to be conditional on one's faith. It is a new status, and everyone stands in need of adoption by God. Gentiles are still Paul's main target, those who were formerly enslaved "to beings that by nature are not gods." The "beings" here are again the *stoicheia*. Turning to the Torah would be like turning "back again to the weak and beggarly elemental spirits [*stoicheia*]" (4:9). This is a bold and confrontational remark. "Observing special days, and months, and seasons, and years" (4:10) in the Jewish calendar is just a new form of enslavement to the *stoicheia*![29]

Paul moves now from insult to appeal. He wrings his hands in despair. Has he labored in vain for them (4:11)? When he was with them, they did him no wrong (4:12). He had originally tarried in their region "because of a physical infirmity," and they had treated him as though he were an angel, or Jesus Christ himself (4:13-14). In fact, "you would have torn out your eyes and given them to me" (4:15). We have already mentioned that this may be a clue that Paul's "thorn in the flesh" (2 Cor 12:7) was an eye disease.

29. Among many others, see Martinus C. deBoer, "The Meaning of the Phrase τα στοιξεια του κοσμου in Galatians," in *NTS* 53 (2007).

By reminding the Galatians of how good they had been to him before, Paul is trying to make them embarrassed about their heartbreaking foolishness now, treating him as an enemy when he tells them the truth (4:16). The agitators for Jewish observance are really just isolating the Galatians (4:17). Paul's concern for them is like birth labor, as he waits for Christ to be born in them (4:19), an awkward yet powerful metaphor.[30] Since the Galatians are interested in Jewish tradition, Paul will draw an illustration from Genesis for them. He speaks of Abraham's two sons, one born to a slave woman, one to a free woman (4:22). Only the son of the free woman was born "through the promise" (4:23), referring to God's promise of offspring to Abraham and Sarah. "Now this is an allegory" (4:24), Paul says, and he uses the Greek word "allegorizing." His allegory concerns freedom and slavery. The slave woman (Hagar, with whom Abraham had his first son) was "from Mount Sinai, bearing children for slavery" (4:24). She stands for "Mount Sinai in Arabia and corresponds to the present Jerusalem, for she is in slavery with her children" (4:25). The religious powers in Jerusalem would not be happy to be equated with Hagar, slavery, and Arabia! The church, of course, equates to Sarah, the "free woman," and "the Jerusalem above" (4:26). The church is spiritual and free; the Torah-based religion is material and unfree.

Paul then quotes a paradoxical saying from Isaiah 54, that the barren[31] woman has more children than the woman with a husband (4:27). The apparently barren Sarah proved fertile. Spiritually speaking, God's promises are more fertile than anything, and true preaching generates many "children" (converts). Those who have faith "are children of the promise" (4:28), and they should drive out the children of the slave woman (4:30)—the circumcision agitators. Believers are children "of the free woman" (4:31); the Gospel is itself a revelation of freedom, of spiritual adulthood.

The Fruits of the Spirit; Crucifying the Flesh: Chapter 5

"For freedom Christ has set us free. Stand firm, therefore, and do not submit again to a yoke of slavery" (5:1). Submitting to the Torah would be returning to slavery. There is no gray area here; if the Galatians submit

---

30. This is explored in detail in Beverly Roberts Gaventa, *Our Mother Saint Paul* (Louisville: Westminster John Knox, 2007), chapter 2.

31. Better here than NRSV's "desolate," though either is technically acceptable for *erēmos*.

to circumcision, "Christ will be of no benefit to you" (5:2). One cannot just be circumcised; one would have to submit to the entire Law (5:3). The whole project of seeking to be justified by the Law is evidence that "you have fallen away from grace" (5:4). This recalls the epistle's opening lament about "so quickly deserting the one who called you by grace" (1:6). Grace speaks of the generosity and favor of God (Ps 84:12 [NRSV v. 11]).

It is God's generosity that saves, and one's Jewish or Gentile status does not make a bit of difference: "in Christ Jesus neither circumcision nor uncircumcision counts for anything; the only thing that counts is faith working through love" (5:6). It is a major principle of Paul's that God saves the circumcised and the uncircumcised by the same method, "on the ground of faith" (Rom 3:30), yet there are a few scholars who claim that Paul's talk of "faith" was aimed only at Gentiles and "that Paul had no argument against the Jewish law in relation to Israel and the Jews,"[32] thus promoting "two ways or paths to salvation," Torah for Jews and "faith" for Gentiles.[33] This goes right against the principle that "there is no distinction between Jew and Greek" (Rom 10:12); "there is no longer Jew or Greek" (Gal 3:28).

Apparently some were claiming that Paul still preached circumcision; Paul finds it necessary to ask, "why am I still being persecuted if I am still preaching circumcision?" (5:11).[34] Paul's anger moves him to make a violent and exaggerated comment: "I wish those who unsettle you would castrate themselves!" (5:12), that the knife would slip, in other words.[35] But he probably is also making a negative allusion to the castrated priests, the *galli*, of the cult of Cybele and Attis,[36] sometimes called the Phrygian cult because of its origin in the Phrygian homeland, in Galatia. The Cybele cult was a highly successful mystery religion, and its priests occupied a unique "liminal" position, transgressing the boundaries between male and female, savage and civilized, which gave them an aura of divine power.[37] On the other hand, it undoubtedly evoked revulsion in many, who were offended by its excessive practices and its

---

32. John G. Gager, *Reinventing Paul* (Oxford: Oxford University Press, 2000), 57.

33. Ibid., 59; Lloyd Gaston, *Paul and the Torah* (Vancouver: University of British Columbia Press, 1987), 148.

34. This strongly implies that his persecutors were Jewish.

35. Only if one is overly literal is one confused by the fact that the circumcision candidate, not the wielder of the knife, would be the one castrated if there were a slip-up.

36. See Elliott, *Cutting Too Close*, 154–257. Strange as religious castration may seem, religious behavior is often provocative and transgressive of normal social behavior.

37. Ibid., 167–73.

effeminate priests. Paul's sarcastic equating of circumcision with pagan self-castration is yet another shocking attack on the circumcision party.

Paul's repeated point is that all such rituals were enslaving, but "you were called to freedom" (5:13). He seems to be relying on the Jesus tradition when he says, "for the whole law is summed up in a single commandment, 'You shall love your neighbor as yourself'" (5:14; cf. Matt 22:37-40).[38] Their continuous competition, "biting and devouring one another" (cf. 5:15), is a betrayal of the Gospel. In fact, real devotion to the Gospel requires some kind of asceticism: "live by the Spirit . . . and do not gratify the desires of the flesh" (5:16). There is no compromising: "For what the flesh desires is opposed to the Spirit, and what the Spirit desires is opposed to the flesh; for these are opposed to each other, to prevent you from doing what you want"(5:17). The flesh drives one into behaving against one's will (see Rom 7). The flesh leads us not just into the obvious sins of lust, greed, idolatry, drunkenness, and violence (Gal 5:19-21), but also the more intellectual sins of "strife, jealousy . . . factions" (5:20), conceit, envy (5:26), and religious pride such as motivates the circumcision faction ("for self-indulgence," 5:13; they are secretive, they induce fear, they boast: 2:4, 12; 6:13). Those who commit the sins of 5:19-21 "will not inherit the kingdom of God" (5:21), a rare instance of Paul using the kingdom phrase that Jesus used in his preaching.

Besides being a skilled polemicist, Paul can write masterful prose: "the fruit of the Spirit is love, joy, peace, patience, kindness, generosity, faithfulness, gentleness, and self-control" (5:22-23). But make no mistake: this requires a severe self-discipline: "those who belong to Christ Jesus have crucified the flesh with its passions and desires" (5:24). True loyalty to God, true recognition of Jesus, and true following of the Spirit require a real repudiation of the flesh. Whenever Paul spells out the way of true dedication, he also condemns fleshly desire (see Rom 8:5-13).

The Law of Christ: Chapter 6

The whole substance of the new way is to "bear one another's burdens, and in this way you will fulfill the law of Christ" (6:2). Some scholars have agonized over this last phrase, taking it so literally as to mean that Paul envisioned Christ's way as having a legal structure—that Torah should be followed, just in a new way. This is too literal-minded. Prob-

---

38. Dunn sees Paul alluding here to Jesus' own teaching (and example) of love as the principal commandment (Dunn, *Theology of Paul,* 655).

ably Paul is appropriating the terminology of his foes, here, using *nomos* ("law" or "principle") to say that if you need a law or principle, then look to the principle of Christ. Or he may be saying that love fulfills the whole Law (as in 5:14; Rom 8:4; 13:10), but this would hardly be Torah any more, without kosher and Sabbath laws, without purifying or tithing or holy days. If love was the Law's real message all along, then "neither circumcision nor uncircumcision counts for anything" (Gal 5:6), all the detailed cultic laws become a mere distraction, and one has to doubt that they were given by God at all. This goes beyond what Paul is willing to spell out in detail. He does not want to discredit Judaism, but to get people to accept that a new phase has begun, now that "faith has come." Paul has the difficult task of simultaneously trying to affirm the legitimacy and the obsolescence of the Law. The best way to do this is to speak of the Law as a legitimate but adolescent stage that has now been left behind. This works best when the focus is on humanity and faith and obedience; it is more problematic when one focuses on the actions of God. It is hard for Paul to give a direct answer to the question of whether God actually gave the Law or not; having the *angels* give it is a good compromise, attributing a *limited* legitimacy to it.

The emphasis in Galatians 6 is ethical; in verse 4 Paul asks people to question their tendency to boast, which is fleshly. Living for the "flesh . . . will reap corruption from the flesh; but if you sow to the Spirit, you will reap eternal life from the Spirit" (6:8). They should overflow with kindness toward each other and "not grow weary in doing what is right" (6:9). Obviously "works" are important. "Let us work for the good of all, and especially for those of the family of faith" (6:10).

Here at the end of the letter Paul evidently sends his secretary away and writes: "See what large letters I make when I am writing in my own hand!" (6:11), probably an indication of Paul's poor eyesight. He also launches one more attack on the circumcision party: they just "want to make a good showing in the flesh" (6:12). Their concern with reputation is flesh-motivated. The "good showing" is probably the formal recognition they get from the local Jewish community as well as protection from persecution by Roman authorities. They do it "only that they may not be persecuted for the cross of Christ" (6:12). Paul has no respect for these people; they do not "themselves obey the law," they only want to "boast about your flesh" (6:13)—gain prestige in the eyes of outsiders. But one should not seek prestige in the world's eyes; the pattern of a true disciple involves repudiation of worldly ways: "May I never boast of anything except the cross of our Lord Jesus Christ, by which the world has been crucified to me, and I to the world" (6:14). Not prestige, but suffering, shows that one is following Christ: "for I carry the marks of Jesus branded on my body" (6:17).

One of Paul's most effective summarizing statements is this: "For neither circumcision nor uncircumcision is anything; but a new creation is everything" (6:15). The whole letter has been pointing toward a new way of understanding God, a Messiah-way, a Law-free way, a Spirit-led way. Paul's teaching is truly a "new age" teaching. Now that faith has come, we are no longer under a disciplinarian. Now that the Son has come, we are offered the status of sonship, which also means we enter into brotherly and sisterly relations with others: "through love become slaves to one another" (5:13). *This* is how freedom is to be used, and it leads to a community that could be called the *true* Israel, a spiritual Israel: "peace be upon them, and mercy, and upon the Israel of God" (6:16). There still is a "rule," it is just a rule of "faith working through love" (5:6), even a "law" of love (6:2).

Chapter 7

Romans

We have seen that in the Corinthian and Galatian correspondence Paul sets out to discredit those he perceives as foes. In Romans he is considerably more diplomatic. He does not seem to be concerned with enemies, but with correcting some attitudes in the congregation. Paul did not found the congregation at Rome, so he cannot be so bold in asserting authority over its members. His argument in Romans is developed more carefully and at greater length than in the other letters. There are similarities to Galatians in that both letters concern Torah, Jews, Gentiles, the Spirit, and the significance of the death of Christ, but in Romans Paul is more concerned with *attitudes* between Jews and Gentiles, and circumcision is discussed in only a few verses, starting with 2:25.

In Romans, Paul does not call his readers "stupid" or say that they are "bewitched," or make fun of their local leaders by calling them "superapostles." The rhetoric in Romans is less focused on personalities and more on the subject matter: righteousness through faith and participation in Christ, the Law testifying to the Gospel, following the Spirit instead of the flesh.

The Righteousness of God; the Sinfulness of Humanity: Chapters 1–2

Paul is "a slave of Jesus Christ, called to be an apostle, set apart for the gospel of God" (1:1). That his apostleship is from God is one of the two points he establishes at the beginning. The other is that the Gospel fulfills what was "promised beforehand through his prophets" (1:2).

Presumably he would go into detail about particular OT passages in his sermons. Here he just wants to establish the *fact* that the Gospel was promised in Scripture, which testified to "the gospel concerning his Son, who was descended from David according to the flesh and was declared to be Son of God with power according to the spirit of holiness by resurrection from the dead" (1:3-4). It is "through" him that Paul received his "apostleship to bring about the obedience of faith among all the Gentiles" (1:5). There is not the same need that there was in Galatians to *contrast* this with the receiving of instruction from human apostles.

"The obedience of faith" has been one of the foci of the debate over whether *pistis Christou* refers to faith *in* or the faithfulness *of* Jesus. We will take up this subject at the end of our discussion of Romans 5. Under any interpretation Paul is helping to "bring about" the faith of believers. There are several choices as to the intended nuance. It could be that the *decision* to believe or trust is being highlighted—obedience as *assent* to the teaching. Believers are "called to belong to Jesus Christ" (1:6). In the same sentence Paul affirms both free will and some kind of destiny for those "called to be saints" (1:7). God and "the Lord Jesus Christ" send "grace" and "peace" (1:7), and the Roman Christians have been so receptive of these blessings that their faith is renowned "throughout the world" (1:8).

In sharp contrast to his scolding tone in Galatians, Paul is careful to praise his audience in Romans; he thinks of them constantly, praying to be able to visit them soon, to share a spiritual gift with them (1:9-11). He hopes "we may be mutually encouraged by each other's faith, both yours and mine" (1:12). He is eager to preach the Gospel to them (1:15). And what is the Gospel? With rhetorical flourish he says it "is the power of God for salvation to everyone who has faith, to the Jew first and also to the Greek" (1:16). Further, "in it the righteousness of God is revealed through faith for faith" (1:17).[1] This probably indicates a human faith-response to God's (prior) faithfulness. The Gospel proclaims the kindly and saving intention of God, fulfilled through human faith-acceptance. This was already revealed in the prophets, Paul insists: "as it is written, 'The one who is righteous will live by faith'" (1:17), citing Habakkuk 2:4 as he had done at Galatians 3:11.

---

1. On the righteousness of God (1:17) as *equivalent* to the saving power (1:16), see Ernst Käsemann, *New Testament Questions of Today* (London: SCM, 1969), 168–82; James D. G. Dunn, *Romans 1–8*. WBC 38A (Dallas: Word Books, 1988), 41–42.

Faith is not here contrasted with Law-observance, but this is where Paul will bring in the pervasive problem of sin and the judgment of God it evokes, for "the wrath of God is revealed from heaven against all ungodliness and wickedness" (1:18). Judgment day was a standard part of Jewish belief at this time, and it is as much a part of the theology of Paul the Christian as it had been of Paul the Pharisee. This is a judgment of all humanity. God is self-revealed in nature, so Gentiles are not off the hook. "For what can be known about God is plain to them . . . Ever since the creation of the world his eternal power and divine nature, invisible though they are, have been understood and seen through the things he has made" (1:19-20). They may not have met God, as Abraham did, or received a law code, as Moses did, but they surely knew of his moral attributes. In fact, "though they knew God they did not honor him as God" (1:21), and instead became vain and foolish (1:21-22).

This sounds close to the generalizing putdowns of Gentiles that many Jews would utter, but the next line concerns something quite specific: they "exchanged the glory of the immortal God for images resembling a mortal human being or birds or four-footed animals or reptiles" (1:23). It is possible, though by no means established, that this refers to the identities assumed, and the animal masks worn, by initiates into the mysteries of Mithras, a mystery cult that spread rapidly among Roman soldiers and among civilians in parts of Asia Minor such as Paul's home town, Tarsus.[2] Some of the grades through which initiates passed had animal names (raven and lion), some human (nymph, soldier, Persian, runner of the sun, father). References that would have been obscure to recipients of Paul's other letters might have been clear to his Roman audience.

In any case, the point is that there was a link between the Gentiles' irreverence and their personal misconduct, so "God gave them up in the lusts of their hearts to impurity, to the degrading of their bodies among themselves" (1:24). They chose this degradation, and God allowed them to sink into it, the probable meaning of "giving them up" to it. They revered the creature rather than the Creator (1:25), possibly a reference to the Roman emperor cult. Paul's critique of Gentiles is not much different from what one could encounter in other Jewish literature of the time.[3]

---

2. Plutarch (*Vit. Pomp.* 24.7) says that Mithras worship was introduced into the Roman army by the Cilician pirates conquered by the Romans in the 60s BCE (Franz Cumont, *The Mysteries of Mithra* [New York: Dover, 1956], 36–37).

3. Worshiping beasts and idols is seen in Wis 11:15; 12:24; 15:18; *T. Naph.* 3:3. Gentiles are drawn to evil sexual passions (*Sib. Or.* 3.185, 596-600; Philo *Abr.* 135-37).

Paul attacks homosexual activity in the following verses, both that of women who "exchanged natural intercourse for unnatural" (1:26), and of men who "were consumed with passion for one another" and who "received in their own persons the due penalty for their error" (1:27), a probable reference to venereal disease. And again, "God gave them up to a debased mind" (1:28). These Gentiles became violent, drunken, malicious, boastful, gossipy, and rebellious toward parents (1:29-30). They should have known better. "They know God's decree, that those who practice such things deserve to die" (1:32), yet they still did these things. There are certain truths about God and about right and wrong that even the Gentiles know, for God's "eternal power and divine nature" are visible in creation (1:20). This resembles the critique of Philo of Alexandria, who claimed there was a natural law that everyone knows, since the divine *logos* (reason) pervades everywhere: "the word of nature enjoins what one ought to do, and forbids what one ought not to do."[4]

Paul shifts his target at the beginning of chapter 2. Surmising that the Jewish members of his audience would, by this point, be feeling superior to the foolish Gentiles, Paul warns them: "in passing judgment on another you condemn yourself, because you, the judge, are doing the very same things" (2:1). Jews do the same things as Gentiles? Not possible! But he says it again, and then asks them if they are ready to repent (2:3-4). Judgment day awaits everyone: "by your hard and impenitent heart you are storing up wrath for yourself on the day of wrath" (2:5), and God "will repay according to each one's deeds" (2:6); "to those who by patiently doing good seek for glory and honor and immortality, he will give eternal life, while for those who are self-seeking and who obey not the truth but wickedness, there will be wrath and fury" (2:7-8). These verses are difficult for those who want Paul's message to be simply "salvation by faith, not works," without qualification. But clearly there are qualifications. He reaffirms the idea of judgment by works several times, in 2:16 (God will judge our hidden works); Galatians 6:7 (we reap what we sow; similarly in 2 Cor 5:10). Further, good as well as bad works will be repaid (Rom 2:7-8). There is "peace for everyone who does good" (2:10). Those who do not know the Torah "will also perish apart from the law," while those who *do* know the Torah "will be judged by the law" (2:12).

Paul is leading up to a conclusion that all are condemned, equally, but first it is necessary to unsettle his Jewish listeners with a few unusual

---

4. Philo, *Jos.* 29. See also *Spec. Leg.* 2.45; *Mig.* 128-29; *Plant.* 8-9; *Opif.* 36; Richard A. Horsley, "The Law of Nature in Philo and Cicero," *HTR* 71 (1978): 37, 48, 53.

statements. He says that when Gentiles "do instinctively what the law requires . . . they show that what the law requires is written on their hearts" (2:14-15). This is a shocking statement; it almost makes the Torah unnecessary, though right and wrong matter: "God, through Jesus Christ, will judge the secret thoughts of all" (2:16). How does God judge "through" Jesus Christ? Perhaps, as the truly obedient human being, he is qualified to act as a fellow judge in this court. Paul's target here is the conscience of the Jewish listener: "But if you call yourself a Jew and rely on the law and boast of your relation to God . . . and if you are sure that you are a guide to the blind . . . a teacher of children . . . will you not teach yourself? While you preach against stealing, do you steal?" (2:17, 19-21). Besides a general moral probing, there is something quite specific: "You that abhor idols, do you rob temples?" (2:22). Paul seems to be referring to some embezzlement scandal, much as a preacher today might refer to some current scandal in order to make a point. Paul is trying to awaken a guilty conscience: "You that boast in the law, do you dishonor God by breaking the law?" (2:23). Isn't an uncircumcised Gentile man who keeps the principles of the Law as though he were circumcised (2:26)? He would be able to "condemn you" (2:27). Any Jewish Christian who had enjoyed Paul's evisceration of Gentile sinfulness in the previous chapter is thoroughly chagrined by this point. Paul is using a recognizable prophetic technique, first attacking outsiders, then insiders (see Amos 1–2).

Paul spells out his view on righteousness and Jewishness: "a person is not a Jew who is one outwardly, nor is true circumcision something external and physical. Rather, a person is a Jew who is one inwardly, and real circumcision is a matter of the heart—it is spiritual and not literal" (2:28-29). Daniel Boyarin says that "spiritual" and "literal" are hermeneutical terms for Paul.[5] *Spiritual-not-literal* is analogous to *figurative-not-literal* and to *universalizing-not-nationalistic*[6] and stands for opposing cultural tendencies: "one toward a universalism which emphasized the capacity for all human beings to be saved and the other a reaction against this universalism which re-emphasized the particular privileges of the Jewish People."[7]

---

5. Daniel Boyarin, *A Radical Jew: Paul and the Politics of Identity* (Berkeley: University of California Press: 1994), 86–87.

6. Ibid., 7, 13, 56, 78.

7. Ibid., 59.

The New Mercy Seat; Supersessionism: Chapter 3

Paul can moderate his rhetoric—at least in Romans! There is an advantage to being a Jew, he says (3:1), because the Jews "were entrusted with the oracles of God" (3:2). It actually ends up being a small thing if some Jews have proven to be unfaithful; it does not change God's faithfulness (3:3-4); human wickedness does not mean that God is unjust (3:5-6). Nor should we go ahead and sin so "that good may come" (3:8), as some had evidently accused Paul of saying. Apparently some people have made a mockery of Paul's paradoxical way of speaking. He wishes now to show that he can speak straightforwardly: "Jews and Greeks alike . . . are all under the power of sin" (3:9), as the Bible has said: "there is no one who seeks God. All have turned aside" (3:11-12; Ps 53:3-4); "their throats are opened graves; they use their tongues to deceive" (3:13; Ps 5:10 [5:9, NRSV]); "Their feet are swift to shed blood" (3:15; Isa 59:7). This pattern continues through verse 20.

By Romans 3:20 the reader, presumably, feels shame at being part of this sinful collective, the human race. Paul will show the way out of this morass of sin by means of something fully separate from the Law, although prophesied in the Law:

> But now, apart from the law, the righteousness of God has been disclosed, and it is attested by the law and the prophets, the righteousness of God through faith in Jesus Christ[8] for all who believe. (3:21-22)

Finally some righteousness is in sight, after all the conviction of sin that preceded! But is there really a way out?—"all have sinned and fall short of the glory of God" (3:23). Yes, we know. Was there some *good* news?—"they are now justified by his grace as a gift, through the redemption that is in Christ Jesus, whom God put forward as a place[9] of atonement by his blood, effective through faith. He did this to show his righteousness" (3:24-25a).

Deliverance comes through this combination of redemption, justification, and atonement. "Justified" means "declared just," which, in a court setting (and one's soul *is* on trial), means acquittal or pardon. "As a gift" and "by his grace" indicate that this justification is freely given.

---

8. Or "the faith of Jesus Christ"; see "The *Pistis Christou* Debate" below.

9. NRSV's marginal translation "place of atonement" is more accurate than its reading "sacrifice of atonement." The best discussion of *hilasterion* is Daniel P. Bailey's dissertation, summarized as "Jesus as the Mercy Seat: The Semantics and Theology of Paul's Use of *Hilasterion* in Romans 3:25," in *Tyndale Bulletin* 51 (2000): 155–58.

"Redemption" (*apolytrōsis*) was an important word in the ancient world; it referred to the manumission payment that purchased a slave's freedom, but it could also signify the ransom payment that secured the freedom of hostages. For the slaves and ex-slaves in Paul's audience it would have been a powerful metaphor for release from slavery or captivity. How does God save? Like that generous patron who purchased my freedom! But there is more; actually Paul's sentence stretches from verse 22b through verse 26. This is some of his densest writing, so we need to unpack it slowly.

Paul uses a judicial metaphor, a commercial metaphor with political overtones (redemption), and a cultic (ritual) metaphor, but we need to challenge the choices "sacrifice" (NRSV) or "expiation" (NAB) to translate the Greek word *hilastērion*. In English, "expiation" means to make amends, to make up for an offense, or to cleanse. This is correct for some of the words in the *hilas-* word group, but is not a correct translation for *hilastērion,* which is the technical term for the lid of the ark of the covenant, referred to in NAB as "the propitiatory," and in RSV and NRSV as the "mercy seat." It was the peak location in Judah's whole ritual system, so we must spend a moment to convey how this important item functioned in the Jewish ritual, which will tell us what metaphorical power it has for Paul.

The main concern of the ritual system was purification, and the sacrificial rituals provided the means for purification. Impurity was a spiritual or metaphysical problem, not a hygienic one. Many kinds of actions, not only sinful ones, caused impurity to lodge in the Temple (Num 19:13-20), which was the "house of the Lord." If too much impurity accumulated in the Temple there was a danger that God would depart from it and abandon Judah.[10] Therefore there was a weekly purging of the outer furnishings of the Temple, such as the sacrificial altar and the incense altar. The substance used to cleanse the Temple furnishings was the blood of the consecrated sin sacrifices or "purification offerings," as some scholars prefer to call them. Sacrificial animals were not being *punished* in the place of humans; there is no hint of sacrifice being a judicial pantomime or a substitutionary punishment. Rather, sacrifice was simultaneously a gift (or payment) to God ("My offering . . . my pleasing odor, you shall take care to offer to me at its appointed time," Num 28:2) and a means for obtaining blood, which contains the life-force.

---

10. As seems to be happening in Ezek 10:3-4, 18.

Impurity was a kind of death-force that could only be negated by the life-force carried in the blood of consecrated animals.

The Torah says "the blood is the life" and "the life of the flesh is in the blood, and I have given it to you for making atonement" (Deut 12:23; Lev 17:11). We should understand the primary meaning of "atone" to be "cleanse" or "purge," even though "atonement" (in English) means "reconcile" or "make up." The primary meaning of the Hebrew *kipper* is impurity-cleansing, although propitiation (appeasing or making favorable) is also implied in many passages.[11] "Atonement" is a fairly complicated idea. In Hebrew the emphasis was on purification, but it was also related to propitiating or appeasing the Deity.

The emphasis was just the opposite in the Greek Bible, the LXX. When translating *kipper,* the LXX most often used words meaning propitiate (*hileōs genou,* "become favorable," or *hilaskomai,* "conciliate"),[12] but sometimes used the word for "purify," *katharizō.*

The most important purgation ceremony was the annual cleansing of the mercy seat in the innermost sanctum, the Most Holy Place, a forbidden room that was entered only once a year, on the Day of Atonement, and only by the chief priest. In the Pentateuch the Most Holy Place contained the ark of the covenant, the box built by Moses to contain the Ten Commandments. The mercy seat, called *kappōret* in Hebrew and *hilastērion* in the LXX, was the lid of the ark. The mercy seat was built according to God's instructions, made of "two cherubim of gold" with outspread wings, covering the ark (Exod 25:17-20). It was here, on the Day of Atonement, that the impurity resulting from the worst sins and the unidentified sins of the nation were cleansed, when the blood of the sin-sacrifices was sprinkled on the mercy seat by the high priest.[13] Even though the neo-Babylonians carried away the ark in the sixth century BCE and there was no ark in the Second Temple's Most Holy Place, the ritual was still followed: the high priest went into this room on the Day of Atonement and sprinkled blood in the place where the *hilastērion* would have been. For most Jews the *hilastērion* had always been a place that existed in the imagination, and it still existed there long after the literal *hilastērion* had been lost.

---

11. This involved actually changing God's mind (Exod 32:11-14; Dan 9:16-19; Num 25:11-13) or propitiating angry humans (2 Sam 21:3-9).

12. Deuteronomy 21:8 ("absolve"); 1 Kings 8:30, 34 ("hear the plea . . . hear . . . and forgive"); Amos 7:2 ("O Lord God, forgive").

13. Frank H. Gorman Jr., *The Ideology of Ritual: Space, Time and Status in the Priestly Theology.* JSOTSup 91 (Sheffield: Sheffield Academic Press, 1990), 52–58.

This provides the basis for a powerful metaphor for Paul. Jesus is the new *hilastērion,* the *place* where the impurities of the nation or the world are cleansed and good relations with God reestablished. Paul does not, here, call Christ the sacrificial animal, but the mercy seat or the place of atonement. The *hilastērion* is part of sacrificial space, but it is not the sacrificial animal. Translators should stay close to what an author actually says. Therefore, "(new) mercy seat" or "place of atonement" would be better than "expiation" (NAB) or "sacrifice" (NRSV) in Romans 3:25.

Our difficulties with this sentence are hardly over. *Hilastērion* is followed by "by his blood, effective through faith" (3:25). NRSV supplies "effective through faith," indicating that believers must exercise faith to receive the atoning result. This is a logical guess, but it adds to what is actually present in the Greek. The faith-phrase may simply be signaling that Jesus is not the literal mercy seat but the mercy seat of the new age, the age of faith.

What do we do with "by his blood"? Most translations link it to *hilastērion* to signify sacrifice, although we have seen that *hilastērion* is really the *place* of sacrifice. The most awkward attempt is the NIV's "through faith in his blood," which makes blood the *object* of faith! TNIV does away with this misleading phrase, but retains the inaccurate "sacrifice of atonement." A better translation of verse 25a would be "whom God put forward as a mercy seat of faith, through his shedding of blood." The messianic martyr is the *new* mercy seat, then, and the shedding of his blood achieves atonement. Paul combines martyrology with sacrificial typology.

I hope that with this explanation the reader can put together some concept of how this cultic metaphor works, and how it combines with two other metaphors here. The death functions as a redemption payment and a purifying sacrifice, and it results in acquittal ("justified by his grace as a gift").

And still we are not finished with this sentence. Verse 25b continues, "because in his divine forbearance he had passed over the sins previously committed." Although the preposition *dia* with the accusative is usually translated "because of," that does not seem to be the best choice here. The intention seems to be that God demonstrated his love *by* postponing punishment until the redeemer, who made punishment unnecessary, should come. This point is essentially repeated in the next verse, where God is proving his righteousness in the present because he *is* righteous and *makes* righteous (justifies) "the one who has faith in Jesus" (v. 26; or "who has the faith of Jesus"). The generosity of God is in view.

So we see that in his most theology-packed sentence (Rom 3:22b-26) Paul says that all are sinners, yet all can be made just through the redemption that is in Messiah Jesus, whom God put forward as a new *hilastērion* for the age of faith, to demonstrate his generosity and to make righteous all who believe. Justification or the making-righteous of believers is mentioned twice (3:24, 26). This is not a reward for faith but is a result of living "in Christ Jesus" (6:11; 1 Cor 1:30), "living in the faith" (2 Cor 13:5).[14] There is another expression that occurs five times in these verses, if we include Romans 3:21: "the righteousness of God." In verses 21-22 the prophesied righteousness of God occurs "apart from law" and is made available to all who believe. In verses 25-26 the righteousness of God is demonstrated by his passing over of past sins and making believers righteous.

Some scholars reject the idea that justification includes an actual making-righteous. Rudolf Bultmann[15] and others claim that it only means a formal acquittal, a "declaring righteous" in court, but not an actual transformation of the believer. Martin Luther does sometimes accept the teaching of believer-transformation,[16] but he is better known for saying that righteousness is only "imputed" to believers, who remain basically sinful; he mocks "the popish schoolmen" for thinking "that righteousness is a certain quality poured into the soul."[17] But Paul *does* speak of being conformed to Christ and receiving righteousness from God in Romans 8:29; Philippians 1:11; 3:9; 2 Corinthians 5:21. Paul's religion is always transformative and experiential. The notion of a fictitious righteousness that leaves believers unchanged—that brings no new creation—is alien to Paul's thought. Rather, believers are transformed and renewed (Rom 12:2; 2 Cor 3:18; 4:16), receive "knowledge of the glory of God" (2 Cor 4:6) and "newness of life" (Rom 6:4).

Justification, acquittal, deification, christology, and God's righteousness are inseparable in Paul's theology. Justification is God's righteousness acting on us, both acquitting and transforming us. No one is justified

---

14. See Adolf Deissmann, *Paul: A Study in Social and Religious History* (2nd ed. New York: Harper & Brothers, 1957), 169–70.

15. Rudolf Bultmann, *Theology of the New Testament* (New York: Charles Scribner's Sons, 1951) 1:272–77.

16. See Jonathan Linman, "Martin Luther: 'Little Christs for the World'; Faith and Sacraments as Means to *Theosis*," in Michael Christensen and Jeffrey A. Wittung, eds., *Partakers of the Divine Nature: The History and Development of Deification in the Christian Traditions* (Madison, NJ: Fairleigh Dickinson University Press, 2006), 189–90.

17. *In Gal.* 2:19 and 5:17; *Martin Luther: Selections from His Writings*, ed. John Dillenberger (Garden City, NY: Doubleday, 1961), 131; 152–53.

or deified without Christ; no one is justified and then exempt from the deification process (which culminates in the afterlife: Phil 3:20-21). Some of the traditional interpretations of justification have been insufficiently attuned to Paul's concept of participation in God and Christ.

Paul returns to his earlier questions. Boasting in the Torah is ruled out because "a person is justified by faith apart from works prescribed by the law" (3:28). One can hardly say that God belongs to the Jews; he is God of the Gentiles as well (3:29), and he will justify everyone, circumcised or uncircumcised, on the basis of faith (3:30). Paul is not "overthrowing the law" but "upholding the law" on the basis of faith (3:31). Some have taken this last verse to mean that the Law is still in effect, at least the Law understood in the light of faith.[18] More likely Paul is trying to prevent any potential opposition from Jewish Christians in Rome. His critique of the Law is considerably milder than in Galatians, but the Law, which held us captive (7:6) and was unable to free us from "sin and death" (8:2), is still a problem. What he emphasizes is the prophetic function of the Law. The Law had foretold faith, Messiah, and church, so loyalty to *these* realities fulfills the Law's purpose.

Paul's teaching is one of fulfillment and replacement. The old glory is fading; the new and enduring glory "surpasses it" (2 Cor 3:10-11). The age of faith has superseded the age of the Law. The Abrahamic covenant is fulfilled, and the Mosaic covenant is replaced. The covenant idea is internationalized. Thus does the Gospel take up, fulfill, and supersede the Jewish tradition. Most scholars want to emphasize continuity and especially avoid the word "supersede," since it has in the past been associated with Christian arrogance and even anti-Semitism, but Paul is unavoidably supersessionist.[19] To minimize or deny the replacement theme is to minimize Paul's message in Galatians 2–3, 2 Corinthians 3, and Romans 3, 5, 7, and 8, especially. The Law was temporary, only "until the offspring would come" (Gal 3:19). Now "you are not under law but under grace"; "we are discharged from the law"; "Christ is the end of the law" (Rom 6:14; 7:6; 10:4; see below).

18. "Faith did not render the law invalid . . . (1) The law for Paul retained its function as a measure of righteousness. But (2) that measure could only be 'attained' through faith" (James D. G. Dunn, *The Theology of Paul the Apostle* [Grand Rapids: Eerdmans, 1998], 639, 641); "the law continued to have paraenetic force for the first Christians" (p. 658).

19. This is recognized by Dunn (the old "epoch is passé," *Theology*, 148). I would insist that this must mean that the Law's "measure" is only symbolic. The Law is not still in effect *judicially*.

The Faith of Abraham; Penal Substitution: Chapter 4

In Romans 4, as in Galatians 3, Paul uses Abraham as the example of faith, but he makes some crucial additional points. He begins with the issue of boasting, saying that Abraham *would* have the right to boast if his works had earned him righteousness, but it was his faith that "was reckoned to him as righteousness" (4:2-3; quoting Gen 15:6). Righteousness was not earned, like a wage, but was received, like a gift (4:4). Sins are "covered" (4:7).

The clever insight Paul articulates in Romans 4:10, which is absent from Galatians 3, is that righteousness was credited to Abraham (Genesis 15) before he was circumcised (Genesis 17). It was "the righteousness that he had by faith while he was still uncircumcised. The purpose was to make him the ancestor of all who believe without being circumcised and who thus have righteousness reckoned to them" (4:11). Uncircumcised Christian men can be made righteous by faith just as the uncircumcised Abraham was. It is faith that matters. Even the circumcised need to "follow the example of the faith that our ancestor Abraham had before he was circumcised" (4:12).

God spoke to faith, long before the Law came. "For the promise that he would inherit the world did not come to Abraham or to his descendants through the law"; rather, it was made "through the righteousness of faith" (4:13). If Law-adherence made one an heir, then "faith is null and the promise is void" (4:14). But "it depends on faith, in order that the promise may rest on grace," and it is given "to those who share the faith of Abraham" (4:16). In fact, he was "the father of many nations" (4:17; Gen 17:4), both literally and figuratively. Abraham "did not doubt God's promise" that he and his barren wife Sarah would have a child. He believed that God "gives life to the dead and calls into existence the things that do not exist" (4:17). He did not doubt that his old body ("he was about a hundred years old") and Sarah's "barren womb" (4:19) could do what was necessary. "Hoping against hope, he believed," "being fully convinced" (4:18, 21), and *therefore* "his faith was reckoned to him as righteousness" (4:22). But that was not for him alone, "but for our sake also," that we might be credited righteous (4:23-24), if we "believe in him who raised Jesus our Lord from the dead, who was handed over to death for our trespasses and was raised for our justification" (4:24-25). The Resurrection opened the door of salvation.

Verse 25 does not follow from the faith-argument of the rest of the chapter, but resumes the sin-and-death argument of Romans 3 (while adding resurrection). Pardon and salvation are linked to the death and resurrection of the Lord Jesus. That Jesus "was handed over to death for our transgressions" seems to be inescapably substitutionary, and in a penal sense. Although not stated repeatedly by Paul, penal substitutionary teaching does occur a few times, often in key summarizing statements. However, we cannot be sure that penal substitution is present in places where Paul says Christ died "for all of us" or "for our sake" (Rom 8:32; 1 Cor 15:3; 2 Cor 5:21). There are ways to die heroically "for others" that have nothing to do with penal substitution: on the battlefield, for instance, which is the setting of some of the noble death stories in Hellenic literature. But "for our trespasses" (Rom 4:25) does seem substitutionary, as does "becoming a curse for us" (Gal 3:13). This is "for" not only in the sense "for the benefit of," but also to take on something that would have been directed at others. Christ dies for sinners (5:8), *therefore* they are "saved . . . from the wrath" (5:9). Further, Romans 4:25 echoes Isaiah 53:5 ("he was wounded for our transgressions"), and the "handed over" verb (*paredothē*) is also found in Isaiah 53:12 LXX. The Gospel fulfills Scripture.

The Overflow of the Obedience of Christ: Chapter 5

Romans 5:6-9 is one of the few Pauline passages that *requires* a penal substitutionary interpretation to make sense. Many Christians assume the presence of penal substitution almost everywhere in the Bible, not just in Paul, but one has to search hard to find passages that *must* be interpreted in a penal substitutionary way. The *main* message of the whole of Romans 5, for instance, is not substitutionary, but participationist: it concerns the negative overflow of Adam's sin and the beneficial overflow of Christ's obedience.

Romans 5 begins with a judicial image ("justified by faith," 5:1), but there is also an implication of cultic activity, since having "peace with God" and "obtain[ing] access" to God's "grace" (5:2) are usually spoken of in a cultic setting. It is "through our Lord Jesus Christ" that this peace is had and this access obtained. There is actually a fairly complicated three-cornered relationship among God, Christ, and humans. God restores the relationship because Christ does something that achieves a judicial result *and* because believers practice faith-trust *and so* are connected with Christ. What believers experience is part of the story, starting with suffering and leading to a series of virtues: "suffering produces endurance, and endurance produces character, and character produces hope, and hope does not disappoint us, because God's love has been poured into our hearts" (5:3-5).

But, of course, it is not all about believers and what they experience. Christ's action made salvation possible: "For while we were still weak, at the right time Christ died for the ungodly" (5:6). The heroism of Christ is highlighted, though exactly *how* his death saved the ungodly is not clear at first. More important than the "how" is the "what." Furthermore, Paul wants to avoid the conclusion that a good and kindly Jesus propitiated a violent and unmerciful God. Rather, "God proves his love for us in that while we were still sinners Christ died for us" (5:8). The motives of God and of Christ are identical. As long as a sacrificial and substitutionary metaphor is used, however, it is necessary to continually deny the harshness of God, since the metaphor itself carries the implication that a kindly Son convinced a stern Father to do something. Justification through a sacrificial death implies that the wrath of God was soothed: "Much more surely then, now that we have been justified by his blood, will we be saved through him from the wrath of God" (5:9). Something had to be *done* to achieve this: "if while we were enemies, we were reconciled to God through the death of his Son, much more surely, having been reconciled, will we be saved by his life" (5:10). The *life* of Jesus has a saving, a life-giving, overflow.

We have difficulty understanding the participationist mentality common to the ancients, the idea that a nation has the characteristics of its ancestor, that an army takes on the attributes of its leader, that a king affects the character of the people. Paul is drawing on this way of thinking: "just as sin came into the world through one man, and death came through sin, and so death spread to all" (5:12); conversely, "much more surely have the grace of God and the free gift in the grace of the one man, Jesus Christ, abounded for the many" (5:15). Paul restates this concept several times in the verses from 12 to 21; perhaps this particular participationist concept was not easy to comprehend, even for people of his time.

Despite the basically simple outline, there is complexity here. For instance, the whole race suffers from Adam's sin ("one man's trespass led to condemnation for all," 5:18), yet Paul also says that "all have sinned" (5:12), though the sins of some "were not like the trespass of Adam" (5:14), but some other kind of sin, evidently. Yet Adam's sin brought death and condemnation to all (5:12, 14-18). There may be some free will involved in the fact that "all have sinned," and the rescue from sin does involve the choice to "receive." For "those who receive the abundance of grace and the free gift of righteousness exercise dominion in life through the one man, Jesus Christ" (5:17). As Adam shaped the human race in one way, Christ shapes it in another, empowering believers to "exercise dominion."

Adam "is a type of the one who was to come" (5:14), so Christ is a new Adam. All humans were disoriented by Adam's sin but can be reoriented, made righteous, by Christ's obedience. Further, the beneficial overflow from Christ exceeds the negative overflow from Adam. Paul makes this "how much more" point in 5:15, 17, 20; God shows an almost excessive love, leading to eternal life, so that "grace might also exercise dominion through justification leading to [*eis*] eternal life" (5:21). Does justification mean "made just" or "acquitted" here? It may make more sense to say that grace exercises dominion through a transformation leading to eternal life than to say that grace exercises dominion through an *acquittal* leading to eternal life, but the latter is not impossible. There is certainly a judicial setting here; transgression is mentioned repeatedly, and "judgment . . . brought condemnation, but the free gift following many trespasses brings justification" (5:16). But transformation seems equally unavoidable, since believers "exercise dominion in life" (5:17) and are "made righteous" (5:19). The "gift of justification" (5:17) seems to include both acquittal and real transformation. Both gifts are products of Christ's obedience: "one man's act of righteousness leads to justification and life for all" (5:18).

The *Pistis Christou* Debate

The *pistis Christou* debate was touched upon in discussing Galatians 2:16 and other passages. Now it may be examined in more depth, since Romans 5:17-19 is a key passage in the debate. Let us begin with Romans 3:22, 26, where *pistis Iēsou* and *pistis Iēsou Christou* occur. Luke Timothy Johnson sees the phrase as referring to Jesus' *own* faith, and he translates Romans 3:22 "through the faith of Jesus Christ for all who believe."[20] If so, however, the faith of Jesus certainly is "abruptly introduced" here.[21] It has not been mentioned in the preceding portion of Romans, which had to do with human sin. Further, the contrasts in Romans 3:27-30 do not have to do with Jesus' faith but with believers' faith issues: faith

20. Luke Timothy Johnson, *Reading Romans: A Literary and Theological Commentary* (New York: Crossroad, 1997), 59.
21. Dunn, *Theology*, 383.

instead of boasting, faith rather than works of the Law, faith instead of circumcision. Romans 4 is about *believers* needing to practice faith, as Abraham did. It seems strange that, if Paul intended to signify Jesus' faith, he did not make this more clear.[22]

If the subjective reading were correct, Paul would need to be repeatedly telling believers to imitate Christ's faith, but he only says this on one or two occasions (1 Thess 1:6; Phil 2:5).[23] Rather, he spends whole chapters speaking of *believers'* faith, of the "righteousness of faith" for "those who share the faith of Abraham" (Rom 4:13, 16), of "what was promised . . . to those who believe" (Gal 3:22), of our faith not being in vain (1 Cor 15:14-20). James D. G. Dunn argues that the "faith of Christ" position underestimates Paul's stress on the faithfulness of God: "What Paul is calling for throughout Romans is for faith in God's faithfulness, faith like that of Abraham."[24] Further, the "faith of Christ" advocates fail to distinguish between "faith of Christ" and "faithfulness of Christ."[25]

But there are interesting arguments on the other side as well. Richard B. Hays asks us to consider *dia pisteōs Iēsou Christou* (Rom 3:22) in light of the manifestation of the righteousness of God in 3:21. He finds it baffling to say that God's justice would be revealed through human believing. Rather, "God's eschatological justice can only have been shown forth by an act of God: Paul's claim is that the death of Jesus is just such an apocalyptic event."[26] So Paul is contrasting the faithful Jesus with the rebellious humans of the previous three chapters; God put "forward as a sacrifice the one perfectly faithful human being."[27]

It may be that the argument of the "faith of Christ" advocates depends on whether they can prove "the functional equivalence of faith and obedience"[28] while at the same time making *pistis Christou* a recognizable catchphrase for the faithfulness of Christ. Looking at "the obedience of

---

22. Mark A. Seifrid, *Justification by Faith: The Origin and Development of a Central Pauline Theme.* NovTSup 68 (Leiden: Brill, 1992), 220 n. 166.

23. More common is the notion that an *apostle* imitates Christ, while believers are to imitate the apostle (1 Cor 4:15-16; 11:1; Phil 3:14-17).

24. James D. G. Dunn, "Once More: ΠΙΣΤΙΣ ΧΡΙΣΤΟΥ," in Eugene H. Lovering, Jr., ed., *SBL Seminar Papers, 1991.* SBLSP 30 (Atlanta: Scholars Press, 1991), 742.

25. Ibid., 741.

26. Richard B. Hays, "ΠΙΣΤΙΣ and Pauline Christology: What Is at Stake?" in Lovering, ed., *SBL Seminar Papers, 1991,* 721.

27. Ibid., 720.

28. Luke Timothy Johnson, "Romans 3:21-26 and the Faith of Jesus," *CBQ* 44 (1982): 86.

faith" in Romans 1:5, Luke Timothy Johnson argues that faith and obedience are "mutually interpretative"; they do the same thing: faith leads
to righteousness in Galatians 3:6 and Romans 4:3; obedience leads to
righteousness in Romans 6:16.[29] In Romans 5:19 "the obedience of Jesus
is explicitly said to be the basis for the righteousness of others. . . . Jesus'
faith . . . is essentially obedience" and "it provides the basis for the faith
response of others."[30]

Indeed, Paul does contrast the effects on the human race of the "disobedience" of Adam and the "obedience" of Christ (5:19), and makes other
contrasts between Adam and Christ in 5:15-22, but he never contrasts
Christ's faith to any disbelief of Adam's, something that would be "crying
out" to be said,[31] if "the faith of Christ" were the focus of salvation. It seems
essential to the subjective genitive position that "faith of Christ" be the
recognized meaning of all occurrences of *pistis Christou*. The reader would
have to make some consistent linguistic conversions, turning all faith-
Christ constructions into references to the faith *of* Christ himself, and also
understanding "faith" whenever Paul speaks of "obedience." It may be
that Johnson and others are bringing out something that is *potential* within
Pauline thought, but that Paul himself did not develop.

There is another, possibly disappointingly mundane, interpretation
of these phrases. *Pistis Christou* could just mean "Christ-faith," being
shorthand for Christian faith (or "messianic faith," since Paul never uses
the word "Christian"). One could go back through and read "Christian
faith" or "our faith" into many of these passages and get plausible readings: God justifying through Christ-faith (Rom 3:26), people being justified through our Jesus-Christ-faith (Gal 2:16). This understanding unifies
the subjective and objective readings to some extent. Jesus-Christ-faith
would originally have been the faith he practiced, but is now the faith
practiced by his followers. This seems to be the revised position now
advocated by Sam Williams: believers' faith *is* in view, and *pistis Christou*
"is a double-sided expression, referring first to the faith of Christ himself
but including as well the answering faith of those who are in him,"[32]
who are *in Christ*.

This version of the subjective genitive position is more convincing
than versions that exclude believers' faith from the explanation. By the

29. Ibid., 85–86.
30. Ibid., 89.
31. Dunn, "Once More: ΠΙΣΤΙΣ ΧΡΙΣΤΟΥ," 743.
32. Sam K. Williams, *Galatians* (Nashville: Abingdon, 1997), 70.

same token, objective genitive readings are unconvincing when they overlook participation in Christ. Some preachers seem to understand faith as a mindless conformity to doctrine: "just believe this, and you're in." Faith, in Paul's teaching and in his experience, is not just the passive consent to a doctrine; it is an active fellowship with Christ through which "Christ is in you" (Rom 8:10; Gal 2:20) and we actually live "in Christ" (2 Cor 5:17), sharing his sufferings and his resurrection (Phil 3:10-11).

Nevertheless, Paul does speak of believing *in* Christ at least once: "we have come to believe in Christ Jesus [*eis Christon Iēsoun episteusamen*]" (Gal 2:16; *eis* can be "in" or "into"). There is saving power in believers' faith (Rom 10:9). Of course, that faith is a gift (Rom 12:3; 1 Cor 4:7; 12:9), and it is not passive consent but active participation in Christ, as we see in the next chapter of Romans.

Slaying the Body of Sin: Chapter 6

Romans 5 was participationist in showing that the sin of the racial ancestor infected the whole race, while the obedience of the Messiah undoes that damage and brings life to all. Now Romans 6 brings participationism down to the individual believer's experience.

Paul begins here by opposing any kind of lawless attitude: "Should we continue in sin in order that grace may abound? By no means!" (6:1). Believers have "died to sin" (6:2) and must think of their baptism as a form of participation in the Messiah's death: "Do you not know that all of us who have been baptized into Christ Jesus were baptized into his death?" (6:3). Paul says the Roman Christians are ignorant if they are not familiar with this teaching. "Therefore we have been buried with him by baptism into death" (6:4). The Pauline believer must exercise some imagination, must understand himself or herself as being co-buried (*sunetafēmen*) with Jesus. To what end? "So that, just as Christ was raised from the dead by the glory of the Father, so we too might walk in newness of life. For if we have been united with him in a death like his, we will certainly be united with him in a resurrection like his" (6:4-5). One must become a Christ-person through and through, seeing oneself as dying with Christ and experiencing (in "newness of life") a foretaste of the resurrection to come. One's fate is linked to the Messiah's.

But first something must die: the baptized person must experience the death of selfish bodily motivation: "We know that our old self was crucified with him so that the body of sin might be destroyed, and we might no longer be enslaved to sin" (6:6). Believers need to know that baptism represents the complete death of "the body of sin"—sensual and selfish motivation. Baptism is the death of the "old self" and the birth of a new one. The carnal world killed the innocent Messiah, but "death no longer has dominion over him"; now he "lives to God" (6:9-10) and his lively power spills over onto us: "so you also must consider yourselves dead to sin and alive to God in Christ Jesus" (6:11).

Consequently, Paul adjures them: "do not let sin exercise dominion in your mortal bodies, to make you obey their passions" (6:12)—our bodies' desires. "No longer present your members to sin . . . but . . . present your members to God as instruments of righteousness" (6:13). There is an interesting logic in his next sentence: "For sin will have no dominion over you, since you are not under law but under grace" (6:14). This means that sin *does* have dominion over those who are under the Law. This ties in with some of Paul's other comments on sin and the Law: "through the law comes the knowledge of sin" (3:20); "the law brings wrath; but where there is no law, neither is there violation" (4:15). The Law somehow increased the power of sin; sin was able to use "the commandment" to produce "in me all kinds of covetousness" (7:8). We will learn more when we read Romans 7.

Repeating the point he had made in Romans 6:1, Paul asks, "Should we sin because we are not under law but under grace? By no means!" (6:15). The real question is: whom do you serve? "You are slaves of the one whom you obey" (6:16). Fortunately, Paul's hearers "have become obedient from the heart to the form of teaching to which you were entrusted" (6:17). Correct teaching enables correct loyalty: "you, having been set free from sin, have become slaves of righteousness" (6:18). Occasionally Paul signals the reader or listener regarding his rhetorical method: "I am speaking in human terms because of your natural limitations" (6:19). He had used this language before when he asked if God were unjust (3:5) and when he compared God's covenants with a human will (Gal 3:15). Here he is not asking an absurd question, as in 3:5, or using a crude comparison, as in Galatians 3:15, but is boldly using slavery as a metaphor for all human behavior. These mortal bodies, in their various parts, will evidently be "slaves" of something, therefore "present your members as slaves to righteousness for sanctification" (v. 19).

Sanctification, in Greek, in Latin, and in English, means literally "making holy," often referring to the purification and prayer prior to entering a ritual setting. Figuratively it means moral self-correction and dedication to God, and Paul intends this. Formerly his auditors had sinned, but they are ashamed of the things they did, which lead to death (6:20-21).

Now, as slaves of God, they are sanctified to eternal life (6:22). "For the wages of sin is death, but the free gift of God is eternal life in Christ Jesus our Lord" (6:23). This seems to indicate that Paul did not believe in a hell of eternal punishment; rather, final death was the "reward" of sin; the sinful "perish" (2:12), and only the righteous enter into eternal life. Romans 6:23 is Paul's clearest statement of this principle, though there is cumulative support from Romans 2:7-8; 5:12, 21 (sin and death go together); 1 Corinthians 1:18; 2 Corinthians 2:15; 4:3 ("those who are perishing"); Galatians 6:8.

Dead to the Law: Chapter 7

Paul creates a metaphor that has caused agony to meticulous scholars but is easy to understand if one allows the main point to come through. He says that a woman is bound to her husband as long as he lives, but when he dies she is released from her legal obligation to him (7:1-4). In the same way, "my friends, you have died to the law through the body of Christ, so that you may belong to another, to him who has been raised from the dead " (7:4). If one is overly literal, the metaphor is confusing. Has the spouse died, as in the first part of the metaphor, or have *I* died, as in the second part? It does not matter. For a metaphor to be effective, all it needs is one point of comparison to the thing referred to. Here the common feature is the cessation of a legal bond, enabling one to get a new partner. That is *all* that is needed to make the metaphor work. If I say that I am as fat as a house, it does not mean I have something equivalent to windows, doors, a garage, and underground foundations; it only means I am *wide*. Wideness is the one and only necessary point of comparison. Paul just wants the reader/listener to imagine the Law as dead (or oneself as dead *to it*), and Christ as one's new partner. From this partnership come new offspring: "that we may bear fruit for God" (7:4).

Before following through on the implications of offspring, or "fruit," I would examine another aspect of verse 4, that is, the meaning of "you have died to the law through the body of Christ." It seems clear that our legal obligation to the Law ended with the death of Christ, but why the focus on the *body* of Christ? It is likely that this is another scapegoat image. The *body* of the scapegoat is tormented before it carries away sin, and the body of Christ seems to be carrying away both sin and the Law. Images of possession and banishment seem to be ever-present in Paul's mind. Our bodies are possessed by sin (7:8, 17-20, 23; 8:10), which needs to be killed or banished (6:6; 7:24-25; 8:13). The Christian is not really *in* the body any more: "While we were living in the flesh, our sinful passions, aroused by the law, were at work in our members to bear fruit for death" (7:5). Building on the opening metaphor, Paul says: "but now we are discharged from the law, dead to that which held us captive, so that we are slaves not under the old written code but in the new life of the Spirit" (7:6). Release and newness are contrasted with captivity and oldness.

It is necessary to look more closely now at "flesh," "sinful passions," and the earlier "body of sin . . . passions . . . your members . . . as instruments of wickedness" (6:6, 12, 13). The sexual implication of these phrases is as strong in Greek as it is in English. We need to notice that it was the law that "aroused" (NRSV) or "awakened" (NAB) those sinful passions (7:5). Sin, in fact, "seizing an opportunity in the commandment, produced in me all kinds of covetousness" (7:8). What commandment would do that? Is it not the one to "be fruitful and multiply" (Gen 1:22; 9:1)?[33] Bearing "fruit for death" (7:5) probably means bearing children into this domain of sin and death, "while Christians bear spiritual fruit."[34] Here Paul reflects the pessimism about sexuality that we see in Philo and other Jewish writers of the time, replicating the trend among Gentile philosophers,[35] for whom "sexual abstinence became foundational for single-minded commitment to the philosophic ideals, and sexual passion was described as the enemy of the holy."[36] Paul is convinced that the flesh harbors nothing but rebellion against God: no good dwells in his flesh; his flesh serves "the law of sin"; the fleshly way is the way of death (7:18, 25; 8:7, 13). Believers are those who "have crucified the flesh with its passions (*pathēmasin*) and desires (*epithymiais*)" (Gal 5:24). These words were widely recognized as referring to sexual desires.

The difficulty in perceiving this point is not just that it may cause us discomfort but that Paul is blending several points in a complicated way. He also wants to focus on the ironic helplessness of the Law and on how it heightens our awareness of sin: "if it had not been for the law, I would not have known sin. I would not have known what it is to covet if the law had not said, 'You shall not covet'" (7:7). The tenth commandment is here given in its shortest version, concentrating on coveting or desiring rather than on *what* is desired. Paul is engaging in "speech-in-character"

---

33. Boyarin, *Radical Jew*, 164.
34. Ibid., 177.
35. Calvin Roetzel, *Paul: The Man and the Myth* (Edinburgh: T&T Clark, 1999), 138–41.
36. Roetzel, *Paul: The Man*, 138.

here, creating a character to discuss a subject with literary flair, hoping to stimulate reflection in the listeners; this rhetorical device was common in diatribes, and much of Romans fits the diatribe style.[37] The character in Romans 7 is perplexed by the fact that the Law, especially the commandment against desire, induced a consciousness of sin in him. The Law, being powerless against sin, has the ironic effect of heightening the power of sin: "Apart from the law sin lies dead" (7:8). Next Paul gives us a clue as to who the fictional narrator is—"I was once alive apart from the law, but when the commandment came, sin revived" (7:9)—but scholars do not agree on what the clue indicates. Some see the character as Israel, some as Adam, and some as a hypothetical Gentile. If a Gentile, he formerly lived outside the Law, but when he became a God-fearer, "the commandment came" for him, and "sin became alive" for him. It would then be the sorrow of recognizing himself as a sinner that is meant by "the very commandment that promised life proved to be death to me" (7:10). Knowledge of the Torah only heightened his consciousness of sin. However, the same things could be said about "Israel" recognizing its failure to fully obey the Law. Verse 9 is not fatal to this position, since Israel *did* live outside the Law before Moses.[38] Whoever our character is, meditating on the command not to "covet," he found himself coveting; "sin, seizing an opportunity in the commandment, deceived me and through it killed me" (7:11).

Even though "the law is holy . . . It was sin, working death in me through what is good, in order that sin might be shown to be sin, and through the commandment might become sinful beyond measure" (7:12-13)—that is, that it might be exposed *as* sin. The Law was not at fault, but it proved to be helpless: "The law is spiritual, but I am of the flesh, sold into slavery under sin" (7:14). Paul is not concerned with the quantity of sins, but with sin as an evil power that dominates people's behavior. Here it dominates the narrator, leaving him helpless: "I do not do what I want, but I do the very thing I hate" (7:15). Again, "the law is

37. Thomas H. Tobin, *Paul's Rhetoric in Its Contexts: The Argument of Romans* (Peabody, MA: Hendrickson, 2004), 95–98, 226–27. Diatribe was a literary form that included "dialogues with imaginary interlocutors" (ibid., 91–93).

38. Some differing views are that the "I" character is Adam (Dunn, *Theology of Paul*, 473–76), a Gentile Christian (Tobin, *Paul's Rhetoric*, 229–30, 236–37), or Israel and Adam combined (Frank Thielman, "The Story of Israel and the Theology of Romans 5–8," in Eugene H. Lovering, Jr., ed., *SBL Seminar Papers, 1993*. SBLSP 32 [Atlanta: Scholars Press, 1991], 246–48).

good" (7:16), but "in fact it is no longer I that do it, but sin that dwells within me" (7:17, repeated in v. 20).

Paul is profoundly pessimistic about human inclinations: "nothing good dwells within me, that is, in my flesh" (7:18). With his mind he serves "the law of God," but with his "flesh I am a slave to the law of sin" (7:25). This echoes a theme in Greco-Roman authors: "He is not doing what he wants, and is doing what he does not want to do."[39] "I see what is better . . . but I follow the worse."[40] Paul's "I" delights in the law of God in his inner self (7:22), but "I see in my members another law at war with the law of my mind, making me captive to the law of sin that dwells in my members. Wretched man that I am! Who will rescue me from this body of death?" (7:23-24). The answer, of course, is "Jesus Christ our Lord" (7:25).

The Torah was unable to break the power of sin; in fact, sin used the Torah's prohibitions to heighten the appeal of sin. Only God's Son—who conquered the flesh and is the channel for God's life-giving power—enables humans to break free from sin and the flesh. But Paul is not done yet with the subjects of Son, Law, sin, and flesh. What he needs to nail down this discussion is an ingredient that mostly has been left out so far: the Spirit.

Spirit, Flesh, and Adoption: Chapter 8

A vivid image in Paul's mind is the dramatic way Christ rescues sinners from condemnation and becomes their new owner. "There is therefore now no condemnation for those who are in Christ Jesus. For the law of the Spirit of life in Christ Jesus has set you free you from the law of sin and of death" (8:1-2). The law of Christ is the way of Christ; it is a rhetorical expression signifying replacement of the Torah with a way that is truly life-giving. The "law of sin and of death" may not be Torah (Romans is not Galatians!), but the relentless power of sin that uses even Torah to enslave and stifle (7:5-10).

Paul sees God sidestepping Torah altogether, using the death of the Messiah to judge sin and so end its reign: "For God has done what the

39. Epictetus, *Diss.* 2.26.4; Stanley K. Stowers, *A Rereading of Romans: Justice, Jews, and Gentiles* (New Haven: Yale University Press, 1994), 262. Jewish authors like Philo and the author of 4 Maccabees also discuss the problem with desire, in ways similar to the Stoics (Tobin, *Paul's Rhetoric*, 229–32, 235).

40. Ovid, *Met.* 7.20; Stowers, *A Rereading*, 263.

law, weakened by the flesh, could not do: by sending his own Son in the likeness of sinful flesh, and to deal with sin, he condemned sin in the flesh" (8:3).

At least two things need to be clarified. The "likeness" does not mean any kind of unreal body; it just means he came in the *form* of flesh. The phrase "to deal with sin" is a translation of *peri hamartias*, but not the best translation, since *peri hamartias* was the technical term for the sin offering or purification offering. It occurs over seventy-five times in the LXX with this meaning, and this should be reflected in the translation of Romans 8:3: God, sending his own Son in the form of sinful flesh and *as a sin offering*, condemned sin in the flesh. Now we can see more clearly the metaphors Paul is mixing. He thoroughly blends the sacrificial and judicial metaphors: Christ dies as a solemn sacrificial offering *and* he allows his flesh to be the target of condemnation. There may be a third metaphor joining in here, the image of the scapegoat. Sacrificial animals were never seen as condemned, in the Jewish system, but the scapegoat was understood to bear condemnation and to be accursed. The notion of *condemned flesh* sounds more like the scapegoat than like a sacrifice. Paul explicitly mentions the sin offering, and he seems to be conflating it with scapegoat, even as he conjoins it with the judicial image.

This is more than a mixing of metaphors; the images mutually interpret each other. Scapegoat takes on a judicial meaning; condemnation takes on an aura of ritual holiness; sacrifice issues in judicial condemnation. All of these enable solemn meaning to be discerned in what was really an ugly act of violence. Paul treats the death of the innocent Messiah as the final sacrifice, the last scapegoat, the supreme condemnation of sin. This blending of meanings is now taken for granted, and most Christians are completely unaware of the extent to which they understand "sacrifice" as a kind of scapegoating and the extent to which they blend cultic and judicial concepts in their understanding of atonement. This is a product of the Pauline tradition. The martyrological interpretation began before Paul (1 Cor 15:3), but this blended atonement concept comes down to us in Paul's wording. Atonement is so associated with Paul in the mind of the church that even a work like Hebrews, probably not part of the Pauline tradition, was drawn in and treated as a work of Paul's.

Romans 8:4 gives the outcome of the sin-condemning act of 8:3: "so that the just requirement of the law might be fulfilled in us, who walk not according to the flesh but according to the Spirit." The "just requirement" (*dikaiōma*) can signify a regulation or decree (as in Deut 4:40; 6:1), an "act of justice" (Ari. *Eth.* 5.7.7 [1135a]; BAGD), or (more literally) a "righteous thing" or "just outcome." Paul means fulfilling the essence or intent of the Law, as he says later: "Love is the fulfillment of the law" (Rom 13:10). Ironically, we can now fulfill the Law's intention because God did something the Law was intended to do but was unable to do: *finally* condemn sin and show us how to live. Sin is condemned through the Son's substitutionary or representative death; life is revealed through the Spirit's instruction.

Believers live according to the Spirit, not the flesh. In Romans 7 we were told about the goodness-killing effect of the flesh; now we hear of the goodness-enabling power of the Spirit, a word that occurred only once in the previous chapter (7:6) but twenty-one times in this chapter. Paul offers a dualistic view of behavior: "To set the mind on the flesh is death, but to set the mind on the Spirit is life and peace. For this reason the mind that is set on the flesh is hostile to God; it does not submit to God's law" (8:6-7). The "law" or principle of God is the will and way of God. To follow this way, one needs the Spirit to overcome the flesh. "Those who are in the flesh cannot please God. But you are not in the flesh; you are in the Spirit" (8:8-9). This is essential, not optional: "Anyone who does not have the Spirit of Christ does not belong to him" (8:9). If the Spirit is essential, why has Paul hardly mentioned it until chapter 8? Apparently he first had to make a strong case about the enslaving power of sin, the saving death of Christ, and believer participation in Christ, and the narrative might have become too complicated if he had tried to bring in the Spirit earlier.

Paul is an ascetic, and he speaks as an ascetic when he says: "if Christ is in you, though the body is dead because of sin, the Spirit is life because of righteousness" (8:10). God dwells within a person *as* Christ within. Yet God also acts *as* the Spirit: God "will give life to your mortal bodies also through his Spirit that dwells in you" (8:11). We have the beginning of Trinitarian thought here. The Spirit dwells within (8:9, 11); Christ dwells within (8:10); both act for God (8:11, 14). But Paul is more interested in practical spirituality than in systematic theology.

We need to know that we owe nothing to the flesh (8:12): "for if you live according to the flesh, you will die; but if by the Spirit you put to death the deeds of the body, you will live" (8:13). This is not the occasional denial of some pleasures, a foregoing of candy during Lent. This is the constant mortification of the flesh, the way of a dedicated ascetic. There is no room for compromise. One either lives for the flesh or repudiates the flesh and lives for God, empowered by the Spirit.

Only those who follow the Spirit can be called children of God, according to Paul. There is no notion here of all human beings (or all Jews) being *naturally* the children of God. Rather, "all who are led by the Spirit of God are children of God. . . . you have received a spirit of adoption [through which] we cry, 'Abba, Father!'" (8:14-15). Here Paul uses the Aramaic that Jesus himself might have uttered when praying to "Dad," as in Galatians 4:6, which evidently was a prayer commonly uttered during worship in the Pauline churches. The point is that we are *adopted* into the status of children of God; it is a *granted* status, not a natural status. Adoption was an important Greco-Roman institution whereby someone who was not the natural heir was designated as the heir. Being the son (whether natural or adopted) of an important father carried great status. The Greek in 8:14 is *uioi,* meaning "sons," but in 8:16 Paul uses the neuter *tekna,* "children," showing that gender is not an issue.

"When we cry 'Abba! Father!' it is that very Spirit bearing witness with our spirit that we are children of God" (8:16). There are clearly two different spirits here, sensibly represented in English by capitalizing one and not capitalizing the other. Although Paul never mentions the story of Pentecost, which we have from Acts 2, the Spirit is clearly the Spirit of Christ, sent by God into our hearts (Gal 4:6; 2 Cor 1:22), *poured* by God into our hearts (Rom 5:5), received by us (Rom 8:15). The second spirit in 8:16, "our spirit," probably refers to the spirit within each individual, whether or not the individual has received the Spirit of Christ. Intriguingly, this spirit *agrees* with the message of Christ's Spirit, affirming that we are children of God. This seems to work against Paul's insistence that sonship is conferred and is not natural. The idea that the individual's spirit, not just Christ's Spirit, affirms one's sonship implies that sonship is *natural,* is spiritually inherent—a teaching inconsistent with Paul's own. Only in this verse does Paul allow this view of one of his sources (probably Jesus)[41] to show through. The metaphor of adoptive sonship, occurring in several places (Gal 4:5-7; Rom 8:15, 17, 23; 9:4), certainly represents Paul's own view.

Paul spells out the glorious significance of being adopted: "if children, then heirs, heirs of God and joint heirs with Christ—if, in fact, we suffer with him so that we may also be glorified with him" (8:17). This is the other aspect of participationism: Christians must suffer rejection by the world, as Christ did. Glorification is conditional upon willingness to

---

41. John 20:17; Matt 6:1, 4, 8, 32; 7:11; 10:20; 23:9; Luke 12:32; etc.

suffer. But be comforted, "the sufferings of this present time are not worth comparing with the glory about to be revealed to us" (8:18).

But it is not only believers who are changed by the life and death of the Messiah. In fact, "creation awaits with eager longing for the revealing of the children of God" (8:19). Paul is sensitive to the suffering and struggle in nature: "the creation itself will be set free from its bondage to decay and will obtain the freedom of the glory of the children of God" (8:21). This has been understood in various ways by Christians. Some believers have speculated that they need to achieve the power to remove death and decay (caused by sin in the first place) from the natural world. Some contemporary writers see a profound ecological sensitivity in Paul's remarks. At the very least, Paul says that there is a yearning within nature that coincides with our spiritual yearning: "We know that the whole creation has been groaning in labor pains until now . . . we ourselves . . . groan inwardly while we wait for adoption, the redemption of our bodies" (8:22-23). The compound verbs *synstenazō* (groaning-together-with) and *synōdinō* (suffering-with) are just two of the dozens of "with" compounds Paul uses to describe the deeply intertwined, *shared* life. "With" compounds describe shared suffering, dying, working, rejoicing, crucifixion, and resurrection (1 Cor 12:26; 2 Cor 7:3; 8:23; Phil 2:18; Rom 6:6; Col 2:12; etc.).[42]

The use of "redemption" in 8:23 is different from that in Romans 3:24, where it referred to the death of Jesus purchasing the freedom of the captives of sin. In 8:23 it speaks of a future "cashing-in" or fulfillment of the promised hope. The Spirit was a "first fruits" or "first installment" of this promise (8:23; 2 Cor 5:5); we will "redeem" this body after we die. "If there is a physical body, there is also a spiritual body" (1 Cor 15:44).

"For in hope we were saved" (Rom 8:24). Truly, we live on hope. Hope requires faith, for "hope that is seen is not hope. . . . But if we hope for what we do not see, we wait for it with patience" (8:24-25). Hope builds spiritual character; it is one of the treasures of faith, and it brings joy with it (12:12; 15:13). Nor does the believer have to do it alone. The Spirit aids us, "for we do not know how to pray as we ought, but that very Spirit intercedes with sighs too deep for words" (8:26). This is more than just help with prayer; it is real intercession with God. The Spirit "intercedes for the saints according to the will of God" (8:27). The Greek actually says "according to God" (*kata theon*), but it does suggest a unity of purpose between the Spirit and God.

---

42. And many more listed by Dunn, *Theology*, 402–3.

When intercession is mentioned again, it paints a picture of the divine courtroom: "Who will bring any charge against God's elect? It is God who justifies" (8:33). And the risen Christ also "intercedes for us" (8:34). If we are acquitted, why the need for intercession by both the Spirit and Christ? The reader will recall Paul's earlier teaching on the wrath of God (2:8; 3:5; 5:9), and will notice the repeated mention (and denial) of condemnation (8:1, 3, 33-34). Is Paul hinting that God could still decide to condemn, even after he has justified? Probably not. We should not assume that Paul is contradicting himself. Rather, he thinks in judicial categories and cannot avoid the image of Jesus or the Spirit interceding in the divine courtroom, even though he then has to deny the possibility of new charges being brought (8:33-34). There are other forms of intercession, not judicial, such as angelic advising, or even an angel making propitiatory offerings on one's behalf (Job 33:23; *T. Levi* 3:5), but with Paul intercession suggests a judicial setting.

What matters is that believers have an advocate in heaven: "all things work together for good for those who love God" (8:28). This is a truth that is never shaken by outward circumstances.

Verses 28b-29 speak of those "who are called according to his purpose. For those whom he foreknew he also predestined to be conformed to the image of his Son." Some theologians remove these verses from their context and take them to mean that only *some* are called to be saved, while others are predestined to be damned, a position that removes human choice from the equation. This is too literal-minded, and it fails to understand the practical motives behind Paul's rhetoric. Paul does not want anyone to take credit for his or her own salvation. The language of *being called* gives God the glory. Paul is not denying freedom of choice. He is constantly exhorting people to choose rightly, to "abstain from fornication" (1 Thess 4:3), to "be reconciled to God" (2 Cor 5:20). But he wants to emphasize that only God saves. Second, we should recall that God's foreknowledge is a major theme in the Hebrew Bible, where the point is not predestination but the almighty power of God. Paul stands in this biblical tradition when he stresses that God's plan is coming to fruition: God decided to create a community of those on whom God could confer divine qualities (conformation to the Son is the same as conformation to God, since the Son is the revelation of God). But everyone is called to this glorious destiny, and it is sad when some do not accept it; the rejection by many of his fellow Jews is a source of much sorrow for Paul (9:1-4). What is highlighted in these verses is not predestination, but *destiny*: Paul is not looking back, but looking ahead to the perfecting and glorifying of those who accept God's offer: "those whom he justified he also glorified" (8:30).

All of this was enabled by the death of the Son and the kindness of the Father: "He who did not withhold his own Son, but gave him up for all of us, will he not with him also give us everything else?" (8:32). The not-sparing of his own Son (*tou idiou huiou ouk epheisato*) is strongly suggestive of the Aqedah, Abraham's not-sparing of his Son Isaac (*ouk epheisō tou huiou*, Gen 22:12). The analogy works, even though one is an instance of a *human* showing readiness to give his son and the other of *God* actually giving his Son. Both stories involve the giving of a Son; we do not need to correlate each person in the two stories. The Aqedah was frequently cited by writers in the time of Paul as illustrative of Abraham's faithfulness, and even of Isaac's. The near-sacrifice of Isaac was sometimes treated *as* a sacrifice, so it is not surprising that it should appear in Paul as well. This is another example of typology: Christ fulfilling a *type* in the OT.

And so, what could "separate us from the love of Christ? Will hardship, or distress, or persecution . . . ?" (8:35). That "we are accounted as sheep to be slaughtered" (8:36; Ps 44:22) does not deter us. Rather, "in all these things we are more than conquerors through him who loved us" (8:37). Paul confidently takes his audience along with him, declaring, "neither death, nor life, nor angels, nor rulers, nor things present, nor things to come, nor powers . . . nor anything else in all creation will be able to separate us from the love of God in Christ Jesus our Lord" (8:38-39). Whether the "powers" are earthly authorities or heavenly powers not yet obedient to Christ, the message is the same.

Saving Israel: Chapters 9–11

Although Paul will now turn to the question of Israel, he uses terms (like "conscience")[43] and concepts (such as martyrology) that were important in Roman moral philosophy. He says, "I am speaking the truth in Christ . . . my conscience confirms it is by the Holy Spirit—I have great sorrow and unceasing anguish" (9:1-2) over the Jewish rejection of the Messiah. He goes so far as to say he would wish himself "accursed and cut off from Christ for the sake of my own people" (9:3) if it would mean their salvation. Of course this is excessive, but it dramatizes the

---

43. Seneca and Cicero, in particular, focused on conscience (Klaus Haacker, *The Theology of Paul's Letter to the Romans* [New York: Cambridge University Press, 2003], 130–31).

idea of being "willing to die for your country," something the Romans fully understood[44]—and yet Paul is speaking of his fellow Jews. All of this may be aimed at getting Jewish Christians and Gentile Christians to understand each other better.

The Gentiles need to be reminded that "They are Israelites, and to them belong the adoption, the glory, the covenants, the giving of the law, the worship, and the promises; to them belong the patriarchs, and from them, according to the flesh, comes the Messiah" (9:4-5). This sheds light on other passages in Paul. Even the Israelites were "adopted." The "covenants" intends the two main ones (with Abraham and with Moses); Paul shows no interest in the occasionally-mentioned covenant with David (Ps 89:4; Jer 33:21). The "worship" is the religious service at the tabernacle and later at the Temple. The promises are central to Paul's understanding of the covenant with Abraham and the function of Scripture itself. Paul shows the secondary significance of the flesh when he concedes that the Messiah is Jewish "according to the flesh."

Regarding genetics and spirituality, Paul will not mince words: "not all Israelites truly belong to Israel, and not all of Abraham's children are his true descendants" (9:6-7). Rather, "it is not the children of the flesh who are the children of God, but the children of the promise" (9:8). God works his plan through the promises he made to Sarah and (in the next generation) to Rebecca (9:9-12).

The logic of 9:13-16 is quite strained. Paul wants simultaneously to defend God's favoritism ("As it is written, 'I have loved Jacob, but I have hated Esau,'" 9:13) and God's justice (God is not unjust, 9:14) and generosity ("For he says to Moses, 'I will have mercy on whom I have mercy,'" 9:15), although favoritism returns in that last verse. Genesis and Exodus definitely speak of God favoring a certain family line and ethnic group, but Paul's whole argument requires that God be impartial and offer salvation to all. Romans 9–11 seems to be aimed at resolving this tension between God's impartiality and God's faithfulness.[45] Paul wants to prevent Christians from taking pride in being either Jewish or Gentile, or even Christian; rather, "it depends not on human will or exertion, but on God who shows mercy" (9:16). This allows room for the very ancient

---

44. Seneca, *Ep. Mor.* 76:27; LCL II:163; similar ideas in Livy, Cicero, Lucanus, and others (Haacker, *Theology of Paul's Letter*, 132–34).

45. E. Elizabeth Johnson, "Romans 9–11: The Faithfulness and Impartiality of God," in David M. Hay, et al., eds., *Pauline Theology.* Vol. III: *Romans* (Minneapolis: Fortress Press, 1995), especially 234–39.

idea of God hardening hearts: "he has mercy on whomever he chooses, and he hardens the heart of whomever he chooses" (9:18). If that is true, "Why then does he still find fault?" (9:19). Paul's response sounds like the last chapters of Job: "who indeed are you, a human being, to argue with God?" (9:20). Then he assumes an even harsher OT voice:

> What if God, desiring to show his wrath and to make known his power, has endured with much patience the objects of wrath that are made for destruction; and what if he has done so in order to make known the riches of his glory for the objects of mercy, which he has prepared beforehand for glory . . . (9:22-23)

This seems to make God entirely arbitrary. Those who are saved were "prepared" beforehand, were "called, not from the Jews only but also from the Gentiles" (9:24). But Paul *has* to deal with arbitrariness because he has to explain something that *already* seems shocking and arbitrary: the fact that more Gentiles than Jews are being saved (9:30). He finds this in the prophets:

> As indeed he says in Hosea, "Those who were not my people I will call 'my people,' and her who was not beloved I will call 'beloved.' And in the very place where it was said to them, 'You are not my people,' there they shall be called children of the living God." (9:25-26; Hos 2:25 [in NRSV 2:23] and Hos 2:1)

Paul makes this refer to the Gentiles, but Hosea was speaking of Israel! Hosea has God name Hosea's children "not beloved" and "not my people" (Hos 1:6-9) to symbolize God's rejection of disloyal Israel; God then renames them when he takes them back. Paul sees it as a prophecy of God taking in those who had *never been* his chosen people. As elsewhere in Paul, *the Gospel message itself controls the reading of the OT.* Further, Paul is trying to account for God's arbitrariness—God's arbitrary kindness and outreach toward undeserving Gentiles.

As for Israel, "only a remnant of them will be saved" (9:27, quoting Isa 10:22). But the whole earth will be subject to judgment (9:28), and had the Lord not showed mercy "we would have fared like Sodom" (9:29). Paul uses one Jewish text after another to explain why God has reached out to the Gentiles. It is strange that the ignorant Gentiles should have achieved righteousness while the righteousness-pursuing Jews have not (9:30-31), "because they did not strive for it on the basis of faith, but as if it were based on works" (9:32). This verse is used by Dunn to claim that Paul's problem was not the Law, but the Law pursued apart from faith.[46] Is this mistake, then, the "the stumbling stone" (9:32)? Or was the crucifixion the stumbling stone ("Christ crucified, a stumbling block to Jews," 1 Cor 1:23)? Or was Christ himself the stone? God was "laying in Zion a stone that will make people stumble," but whoever "believes in him will not be put to shame" (9:33, citing Isa 8:14). Evidently salvation by faith, Christ, and the crucifixion are so inseparable that all three can be called the stone of stumbling.

Paul returns to the question of Jewish righteousness: "they have a zeal for God, but it is not enlightened," for "being ignorant of the righteousness that comes from God, and seeking to establish their own, they have not submitted to God's righteousness" (10:2-3). A large wave of recent scholarship argues against the notion that Judaism was a religion of works-righteousness and against the idea that Paul said that it was, but Paul *does* sometimes paint with a broad brush, and here he attacks Jews who attempt to establish their own righteousness. Paul says things that *we* may find embarrassing. The point is, "Christ is the end of the law" (10:4). Scholars debate whether end (*telos*) means "finish" or "goal"; it can mean either one, just as "end" can in English. Christ was either the completion or the goal of the Law. The import is the same. Paul is drawing our gaze from Torah to that at which Torah was pointing—the Messiah. The Messiah is "the end of the law so that there may be righteousness for everyone who believes" (10:4). Moses had written about doing the things in the Law (10:5), but faith knows that "'the word is near you, on your lips and in your heart' (that is, the word of faith that we proclaim)" (10:8, using Deut 30:14 to make his point). The primary meaning of faith is trust, but the secondary meaning (believing a teaching) is important here: "because if you confess with your lips that Jesus is Lord and believe in your heart that God raised him from the dead, you will be saved" (10:9). Belief and confession both play a role in saving: "For one believes with the heart and so is justified, and one confesses with the mouth and so is saved" (10:10).

Although Paul had affirmed the dignity of the Jewish heritage, the larger point is God's impartiality in the present: "there is no distinction between Jew and Greek; the same Lord is Lord of all . . . 'Everyone who calls on the name of the Lord shall be saved'" (10:12-13)—and again he uses the OT to make his point (Joel 3:5 [NRSV 2:32]). Paul sees the OT affirming the truths of the Gospel. But for the Gospel to be heard,

---

46. Dunn, *Theology*, 639–40.

it must be proclaimed (10:14), and if it is to be proclaimed, some must be "sent" (10:15; apostles are "sent ones"). This, too, was prophesied: "'How beautiful are the feet of those who bring (the) good news" (10:15; quoting Isa 52:7). How, then, is it that Israel did not understand? Moses had foretold that God would make the Israelites jealous of "a foolish nation" (10:19), and Isaiah wrote, "I have been found by those did not seek me," while Israel itself was rebellious and disobedient (10:20-21; Isa 65:1-2).

But this will not last forever. God has not abandoned Israel, and Jewish identity is something of which to be proud: "I myself am an Israelite, a descendant of Abraham, a member of the tribe of Benjamin" (11:1). In Elijah's time God preserved a minority who had not "bowed the knee to Baal" (11:2-4; 1 Kgs 19:18). "So too at the present time there is a remnant, chosen by grace" (11:5). The "remnant" was a righteous minority that would weather the storm of God's punishment directed at the sinful majority. Paul uses "chosen" language to exalt God and suppress human pride: "But if it is by grace, it is no longer on the basis of works, otherwise grace would no longer be grace" (11:6). Jewish rejection was foretold in the OT (11:8-9), but "through their stumbling salvation has come to the Gentiles, so as to make Israel jealous. . . . their stumbling means riches for the world" (11:11-12). But Israel will be hardened only "until the full number of the Gentiles has come in. And so all Israel will be saved" (11:25-26). Paul's job, in saving Gentiles, was "in order to make my own people jealous, and thus save some of them" (11:14). Unbelieving Jews are like branches broken off an olive tree; the Gentiles are like a wild olive shoot grafted onto the tree (11:17). This gives them no right to boast; rather, they should be grateful to the root (11:18), which is Israel. Undoubtedly Paul is trying to curb a certain arrogance in the Gentile believers in Rome. "For if God did not spare the natural branches, perhaps he will not spare you" (11:21). Thus the danger of condemnation returns; "Note then the kindness and the severity of God . . . kindness toward you, provided you continue in his kindness" (11:22). Regarding the Jews, the Gentiles need to know that "God has the power to graft them in again. . . . so all Israel will be saved; as it is written, 'Out of Zion will come the Deliverer'" (11:23, 26). It was all foretold in the Bible: the hardening of Israel, the drawing in of a people that did not know God, and then the healing of Israel's disloyalty, "for the gifts and the calling of God are irrevocable" (11:29). The Jews will receive mercy, as the Gentiles have received mercy (11:31).

Transformation, Ethics, and Practicality: Chapters 12–13

These chapters are generally more practical than theoretical, except for the highly conceptual passage right at the beginning:

> I appeal to you therefore, brothers and sisters, by the mercies of God, to present your bodies as a living sacrifice, holy and acceptable to God, which is your spiritual worship. Do not be conformed to this world, but be transformed by the renewing of your minds, so that you may discern what is the will of God—what is good and acceptable and perfect. (12:1-2)

"Spiritual worship" and "living sacrifice" recall the "rational and bloodless oblation" offered by archangels in *T. Levi* 3:5-6, a Jewish document that incorporates some of the "spiritual" and rationalizing viewpoint of Hellenistic philosophy.

Not all of Paul's sacrificial metaphors concern the death of Christ; this one is about the believer's devotion and willingness to suffer. "Acceptable to God" is an OT technical term signifying the desired and expected result of sacrificial ritual. Then Paul makes the profoundly spiritual demand to be transformed, to be "metamorphosed," for that is the Greek verb. It takes courage and insight—qualities of soul—to be able to resist conforming to this world, to conform instead to the way of God, which is usually misunderstood and despised in this world. The means of such metamorphosis is *anakainōsis tou noos*, renewal of mind, which sharpens the ability to perceive the will of God—everything that is good, pleasing, and perfect. There have been many Christian philosophies that caution against thinking one can possibly know the will of God, but Paul's is not one of them. He boldly commands the Romans to be intellectually transformed and to discern the will of God. Paul's philosophy is not for the half-hearted or the intellectually timid. If you are not using your mind to discern the will of God, you are hardly "in Christ" at all. There is spiritual significance to the *mind's* attention (Rom 1:28; 6:11; 8:5-7; Phil 4:8).

Anakainōsis is a key Pauline teaching; believers are to be renewed daily (2 Cor 4:16; see the similar passage in Col 3:10). *Anakainōsis* and cognate words occur in some interesting OT passages: "your youth is renewed like the eagle's" in Ps 103:5; God renews the whole world in Ps 104:30. The final supplication in Lamentations is that God "renew our days as of old" (Lam 5:21). Paul speaks of "newness" of life or spirit (Rom 6:4; 7:6), a new covenant (1 Cor 11:25; 2 Cor 3:6), new creation (Gal 6:15; 2 Cor 5:17). One could say that the walk of faith is an *anakainoform* experience (having the *form* of *renewal*), both in this life and in the next as, step by step, "Christ is formed in you" (Gal 4:19).

The outcome is ethical. One does not think too highly of oneself, but thinks soberly or moderately (Rom 12:3). God gives "the measure of faith" (12:3) and provides the "mercies" (12:1) that enable one's dedication to be "holy and acceptable to God" (12:1). We recognize ourselves as parts of the body of Christ, each with "gifts that differ according to the grace given to us" (12:6), some teachers, some exhorters, but all manifesting love (12:7-10).[47] One can picture the interaction in a Pauline church: "love one another with mutual affection; outdo one another in showing honor. . . . persevere in prayer. Contribute to the needs of the saints" (12:10, 12-13). Some of the ethics of Jesus are certainly present here: "Do not repay anyone evil for evil . . . If it is possible, so far as depends on you, live peaceably with all. . . . overcome evil with good" (12:17-18, 21; cf. Matt 5:9, 39-44; Mark 9:50; John 16:33).

Next, Paul tells believers to "be subject to the governing authorities" (13:1), probably a sage piece of advice for a religious minority living in the imperial capital. But the intensity of Paul's advice may suggest that some specific threat is in mind: "whoever resists authority resists what God has appointed . . . for the authorities are God's servants" (13:2, 6). Is this the same Paul who rejects conformity to the world? He goes out of his way to recommend a non-threatening stance: "Do you wish to have no fear of the authority? Then do what is good, and you will receive its approval" (13:3). What happened to the inevitability of suffering with Christ (8:17-18)? It is likely that Paul is aware of a real and imminent danger to the Roman Christian community, and that his cautionary advice is somewhat overstated because he fears for their safety. The anti-Jewish actions of the emperor Claudius were in the recent past. This chapter causes difficulty, but is not fatal, to the argument that Paul is anti-imperial,[48] but it does compel a nuanced understanding. The survival and spiritual health of the church are not negotiable, but Paul will adjust his political stance as necessary to support these primary principles.

---

47. Possible connections with the moral reasoning in Aristotle's *Ethics* are explored by Luke Timothy Johnson, "Transformation of the Mind and Moral Discernment in Paul," in John T. Fitzgerald, et al., eds., *Early Christianity and Classical Culture: Comparative Studies in Honor of Abraham J. Malherbe*. NovTSup 110 (Leiden: Brill, 2003), 221–35.

48. In the OT, God also puts authorities in place as "the rod of my anger" (Isa 10:5), and as quickly removes them; "the present disposition of the authorities is . . . not permanent" (Neil Elliott, *Liberating Paul: The Justice of God and the Politics of the Apostle*. The Bible and Liberation [Maryknoll, NY: Orbis, 1994], 224). Scholars speculate about dangers posed by Roman and Jewish political attitudes (ibid., 218–22).

Believers should pay their taxes and show "respect to whom respect is due. Owe no one anything, except to love one another; for the one who loves another has fulfilled the law" (13:7-8). Love is the essential principle. Even the Ten Commandments are summed up in love: "'. . . You shall not steal; You shall not covet'; and any other commandment, are summed up in this word, 'Love your neighbor as yourself'" (13:9; cf. Matt 22:39; Lev 19:18). And again, "love is the fulfilling of the law" (13:10). When this is combined with Paul's remark in Galatians about love fulfilling "the whole law" (5:14), and his advice to the Corinthians about self-effacing love, we have to conclude that it was just as necessary in the new covenant to practice love as it was to follow the precepts of the Law in the old covenant. The urgency of this necessity is heightened by an awareness of the rapidly approaching end: "For salvation is nearer to us now than when we became believers; the night is far gone" (13:11-12), and believers must conduct themselves righteously, not participating in "reveling and drunkenness" (13:13). Was there really a danger of believers joining in orgies? Usually we assume that such advice has a causative basis. Paul wants them to go to the other end of the sensuality spectrum: "make no provision for the flesh, to gratify its desires" (13:14).

The Strong, the Weak, and the Prominent: Chapters 14–16

Chapter 14 advises the "strong" to show consideration for the "weak" who have scruples about diet. The weak could be Jewish Christians who are upset by the blatant consumption of non-kosher food by their fellows at table. However, the "weak" could equally well be former Pythagoreans who followed a vegetarian diet ("only vegetables," 14:2).[49] Paul's advice is similar to that in 1 Corinthians 10:28: abstain from eating things that will upset your fellows; do not "for the sake of food, destroy the work of God" (Rom 14:20). Food does not matter; trust and consideration do. Self-righteous judging of one's fellows' eating practices is wrong: "Who are you to pass judgment on servants of another? It is before their own lord that they stand or fall. . . . let us therefore no longer pass judgment on one another" (Rom 14:4, 13). Shades of the Sermon on the Mount (Matt 7:1)!

49. The "weak" may manifest "a composite of Jewish and pagan values current in first-century Rome" (Mark Reasoner, *The Strong and the Weak: Romans 14.1–15.13 in Context.* SNTSMS 103 [Cambridge: Cambridge University Press, 1999], 137).

Paul wants believers to respect each other's motives; those who eat, eat for the Lord; those who abstain, abstain for the Lord (14:6). "We do not live to ourselves, and we do not die to ourselves" (14:7). There is no place for picky self-righteous judgmentalism. "Nothing is unclean in itself" (14:14), so don't judge and hurt others "by what you eat" (14:15). Obviously "the kingdom of God is not food and drink but righteousness and peace and joy in the holy Spirit" (14:17), but it *is* necessary to consider others' feelings. This chapter is another example of how Paul's discussion of a specific ethical problem culminates in a statement of principle. If one is doubtful about eating something, "they do not act from faith; for whatever does not proceed from faith is sin" (14:23). Be thoughtful, be considerate, but do not be wishy-washy or doubtful about your actions.

Again, "we who are strong ought to put up with the failings of the weak" (15:1). Christ did not please himself, and we should not, either (15:2-3). Paul cites an OT verse and articulates a principle: "whatever was written in former days was written for our instruction, so that . . . we might have hope" (15:4). This is a thoroughly prophetic and typological approach to Scripture, one that sees it speaking directly to the present-day reader. What is the hopeful and helpful message?—"to live in harmony with one another, in accordance with Christ Jesus" (15:5); to glorify God, who is the Lord Jesus' Father (15:6); to welcome one another (15:7).

Changing tack, Paul says: "Christ became a servant of the circumcised . . . that he might confirm the promises given to the patriarchs, and in order that the Gentiles might glorify God for his mercy" (15:8-9), and he finds passages from all three parts of the Hebrew Bible to confirm the calling of the Gentiles, including one that is not in the Hebrew, but only in the LXX of Isaiah 42:4: "in him the Gentiles shall hope" (15:12).

Paul now speaks in the voice of the kindly pastor: "May the God of hope fill you with all joy and peace in believing, so that you may abound in hope by the power of the Holy Spirit" (15:13). He trusts that "you yourselves are full of goodness," but he knows that he had to speak boldly at some points (15:14-15). This is because he is "a minister . . . in the priestly service of the gospel of God, so that the offering of the Gentiles may be acceptable" (15:16). This recalls the sacrificial image of 12:2, which also concerned the sacrificial service believers offer. Paul is the "priest" overseeing the Gentiles' self-offering. He does "not venture to speak of anything except what Christ has accomplished through me to win obedience from the Gentiles" (15:18). In other words, he *does* dare to announce his success in reaching Gentiles, "by the power of signs and wonders, by the power of the Spirit of God" (15:19), and he yearns to preach where

Christ has not yet been proclaimed, in Spain (15:20, 24). Because of these plans, his visit to Rome has been delayed (15:22-23). Some scholars think this refers to Paul's attempt to organize a trip to Spain; others think it refers to a trip actually taken. First Paul goes to Jerusalem to deliver the collection for the poor believers ("saints") in that city (15:25-26). It is only right that the Gentiles should serve the poor Jews of Jerusalem by making contributions (15:27). Paul makes it hard for any Gentile believer to continue having contempt for Jewish believers.

Once Paul has delivered the collection, he will visit Rome on his way to Spain (15:28). He asks for their prayers "that I may be rescued from the unbelievers in Judea, and that my ministry to Jerusalem may be acceptable to the saints" (15:30-31). Clearly there are deep waters here, where Paul's honor is at stake as well as the welfare of the poor in Jerusalem. He has served the Gentiles, but he recognizes the need to serve Jewish believers in Jerusalem while remaining wary of the danger from unbelievers there. He was probably correct about the latter. Post-biblical tradition says the Jerusalem leaders persuaded the Romans to arrest him, that he was taken to Rome and eventually executed there.

Paul commends to the Roman church his coworker Phoebe, who is described as a "deacon" and "a benefactor of many and of myself as well" (16:1-2). This word for "benefactor" also means "patron."[50] She is a church leader, then. So are Prisca and her husband Aquila, Paul's "coworkers," who risked their lives for Paul (16:3-4). Paul is sending his greetings to a roll call of church leaders, male and female, some of whom are mentioned in other letters. By far the most interesting to us is the apostle Junia (16:7), clearly a female name, although it was changed to the male form "Junias" in the Latin translations. Paul says she is a relative, and was "in Christ" before him. This is the only female apostle named in the NT; further, she is "prominent among the apostles" (15:7).

Junia is not the only female leader. The fact that Paul can greet her as an apostle without skipping a beat, as though there is nothing unusual in a female apostle, is quite revealing. There were clearly other women leaders. Phoebe is a deacon, and possibly the host, of a church. Aquila and Prisca do host a church at their house, according to 1 Corinthians 16:19. They are credited as being important teachers in Acts 18:26.

Many of these church leaders were well-traveled, as Paul was. This is how he knew so many of them, even though he had not been to Rome.

---

50. Wendy Cotter, "Women's Authority Roles in Paul's Churches: Countercultural or Conventional?" in *Novum Testamentum* 36 (1994): 351.

As in 1 Corinthians 16:20 and 2 Corinthians 13:12, he urges people to "Greet one another with a holy kiss" and to "keep an eye on those who cause dissensions" (16:16-17). Some church leaders are with Paul, including Timothy, and he sends their greetings to the Romans (16:21). Tertius seems to be the secretary (16:22). Gaius is the host of a church (16:23), alerting us once again to the fact that many churches met in people's houses. Some of these people may have been wealthy, but some may have been what we would call middle-class: merchants and low-level government officials. "Erastus, the city treasurer" (16:23) is obviously a higher-level official, possibly the same person as in Acts 19:22.

In his sendoff Paul mentions "the proclamation of Jesus Christ, according to the revelation of the mystery that was kept secret for long ages but is now disclosed, and through the prophetic writings is made known to all the Gentiles, according to the command of the eternal God, to bring about the obedience of faith" (16:25-26). We have already encountered the OT prophecies of the Gospel, the revelation to the nations, and the linkage of obedience and faith (as in 1:5), but the concept of a past-eternal "mystery kept secret" probably has only one parallel, in 1 Corinthians 2:7: "God's wisdom, secret and hidden, which God decreed before the ages for our glory." It is not surprising, of course, that religious reflection would find all aspects of the Gospel story to have been planned beforehand. There is a certain fatalism that emerges sometimes in religious reflection, where everything is attributed to God. "The mystery that has been hidden throughout the ages" is mentioned in Colossians 1:26, but we must address the last two of the so-called undisputed letters before we move on to the very interesting case of Colossians, which has some conceptual connections to Romans.

Chapter 8

Philippians
and Philemon

PHILIPPIANS

Knowledge of God: Chapter 1

According to 1:1, Philippians is another letter either cowritten or cosponsored by Paul and Timothy, as seen in 2 Corinthians 1:1, 1 Thessalonians 1:1 (with Silvanus), and Colossians 1:1. With the exception of Colossians, most scholars treat these letters as written by Paul alone, with Timothy or Silvanus playing mainly a secretarial role[1] but probably responsible for some phrases and sentences.[2]

Paul writes Philippians while in prison (1:7, 13). Although one could contemplate the imprisonment at Ephesus in about 56 CE,[3] the final imprisonment at Rome around 60 CE is more likely,[4] both because "it has become known throughout the whole imperial guard and to everyone else that my imprisonment is for Christ" (1:13) and because he sends

---

1. Raymond F. Collins, "'I Command That This Letter Be Read': Writing as a Manner of Speaking," in Karl P. Donfried and Johannes Beutler, eds., *The Thessalonians Debate: Methodological Discord or Methodological Synthesis?* (Grand Rapids: Eerdmans, 2000), 329.

2. Jerome Murphy-O'Connor examines the possibility of "collaborators as coauthors" (*Paul the Letter-Writer: His World, His Options, His Skills* [Collegeville, MN: Liturgical Press, 1995], 16–34, 46–47, 104–7).

3. Hans-Josef Klauck, *Ancient Letters and the New Testament* (Waco, TX: Baylor University Press, 2006), 319.

4. Gordon D. Fee, *Paul's Letter to the Philippians*. NICNT (Grand Rapids: Eerdmans, 1995), 36.

greetings from some believers, "saints . . . of the emperor's household" (4:22), a tantalizing thought about which we would like to know more. In Philippians Paul delves into knowledge of God, christology, perfection, earthly and heavenly citizenship, and even hymnology. He seems to get more joy and satisfaction from his dealings with the congregation at Philippi than with some others (they "share in God's grace with me," 1:7), although some enemies of Paul are in view in chapter 3.

The first interesting teaching occurs in 1:6: "I am confident of this, that the one who began a good work among you will bring it to completion [*epiteleō*] by the day of Jesus Christ." The *teleō* verbs speak of perfection, maturity, or completion. Here, God and Christ will finish what they started: the perfecting of the believer. This, of course, implies the subject of the afterlife, as does the fact that Paul is in prison as he writes (1:7). But Paul's focus will be on the Philippians' own religious experience:

> . . . this is my prayer, that your love may overflow more and more with knowledge [*epignōsis*] and full insight [*aisthēsis*] to help you to determine [*dokimazō*] what is best, so that in the day of Christ you may be pure and blameless, having produced the harvest of righteousness that comes through Jesus Christ for the glory and praise of God. (1:9-11)

Paul had used *dokimazō* to speak of testing the words of prophets (1 Thess 5:21), of *being* tested by God (1 Thess 2:4; 1 Cor 3:13), and of examining ourselves (1 Cor 11:28; Gal 6:4). More interestingly, he used it in Romans 12:2, where one is transformed in order to *discern* the will of God. In Philippians 1 the sequence is somewhat different: knowledge is for the purpose of discerning, and discerning is in order to make believers blameless and righteous through Jesus. In other words, discernment leads to transformation, while in Romans 12 transformation leads to discernment. This is an interesting rhetorical switch, but hardly a contradiction, since the two have a reciprocal effect. In Philippians love leads to discernment, which leads to transformed blamelessness and righteousness (Phil 1:9-11). In Romans 12:2-12 the sequence is transformation to discernment to humility to gifts to love and joy. So transformation leads to discernment, which leads to more transformation.[5]

Philippians 1:9-10 is rich in both biblical and philosophical associations. Knowledge of God is a key OT concept, and *epignōsis* is the term used in some well-known passages in Hosea ("[no] knowledge of God

---

5. There is a similar reciprocal effect in Col 3:10-16.

in the land," 4:1; "I desire . . . knowledge of God rather than burnt offerings," 6:6) and Proverbs ("find the knowledge of God," 2:5). *Aisthēsis* occurs in Proverbs 1:7: "The fear of the LORD is the beginning of knowledge."[6]

Paul wants his readers to know that his arrest "has actually helped to spread the gospel" (1:12); apparently he is able to encourage fellow Christians under arrest (1:13-14). He trusts that "Christ will be exalted now as always in my body, whether by life or by death" (1:20). Paul is quite aware of the seriousness of his situation and is not just engaging in rhetoric when he says "to me, living is Christ, and dying is gain" (1:21). In fact, "my desire is to depart and be with Christ," but he knows that remaining is "more necessary for you" (1:24). He thinks that he can "know that I will remain" and serve his brothers and sisters (1:25), but we tend to think of this letter as one of his last acts of service.

Paul prays for unity among the Philippians, "striving side by side with one mind for the faith of the gospel" (1:27). They need to expect that they will have the "privilege" of suffering for Christ (1:29). Their struggle is the same as Paul's (1:30), and *he* is in chains. He decides to turn to a more comforting message next.

The Christ Hymn: Chapter 2

Believers are to manifest the encouragement, compassion, and mercy of Christ (2:1-2), while (again) being "of the same mind" and "being in full accord" (2:3). These repeated exhortations to unity, particularly unity of mind, strongly suggest the existence of disagreement and disunity in the congregation. They need to be humble and to care for others (2:3-4). They are to "let the same mind be in you that was in Christ Jesus" (2:5). It is not just mental unity and intellectual conformity to Christ that are being stressed; the outcome of having Christ-mind is self-forgetful love (2:3, 7-8, 14-17).

What follows has been, for well over a century, referred to by scholars as "the Christ hymn." Christ was in the form of God, even equal to God, but he did not grasp or cling to this status (2:6), "but emptied himself, taking the form of a slave, being born in human likeness" (2:7). Most scholars accept that this describes Christ's pre-existence and his decision

---

6. One wonders if any of the Philippian congregation had read the classics, where Sophocles used *epigignōskō* for "recognizing" a god (*Antig.* 960), and Plato used *aisthēseis* for "visible appearances of the gods" (*Phaedo* 111B; both from LSJ).

to be "emptied" and become a mere human, which is a slave-like status compared to his prior divine status. He became "obedient to the point of death—even death on a cross. Therefore God also highly exalted him and gave him the name that is above every name, so that at the name of Jesus every knee should bend" (2:8-10).[7] Notice that there is nothing of atonement or redemption payment here. Rather, what is emphasized is the obedience of Jesus throughout the humiliating experience, and his vindication at the hands of God, even to the point that everyone, in heaven and on earth (2:10) will have to acknowledge that "Jesus Christ is Lord" (2:11). Whether this was an early hymn or Paul's own composition, it certainly contains a very high christology. "Lord" is a divine status.

All of this attention to status, from the highest to the lowest and then to the highest again, speaks critically to the proud and grasping love of status within Roman patronage. Philippi was an important Roman colony, refounded as a colony by Augustus in 30 BCE,[8] shortly after the military victory that solidified his status as emperor. The city, which already held many Roman veterans, was now populated with still more veterans, and the city in many ways embodied Roman values and structures. A number of scholars study the ways this Roman background illuminates Paul's rhetoric. Joseph Hellermann points out that the Christ hymn deliberately confronts the Roman hierarchical value system. Christ, in this hymn, has power equal to God, yet he does not act like the Roman and Philippian elites, "known for grasping at honors."[9] He not only endures submission to human status, he allows himself to suffer a slave's death, yet God vindicates him and bestows on him the greatest honor. In fact, "it is precisely Jesus' willingness to relinquish his status in the interests of others that explains (*dio kai*, v. 9) his exaltation to the highest position."[10] Paul is turning the Philippian value system on its head and advocating a new value system, one that does not involve grasping at honors but consideration of what is good for others ("in humility regard others as better than yourselves," 2:3). Paul suggests that honors are

---

7. This mention of Jesus' actual experience (obedience and death) refutes Bultmann's view that "the Redeemer himself is a cosmic figure and not really an individual person" (Rudolf Bultmann, *Theology of the New Testament* [New York: Charles Scribner's Sons, 1951] 1:299), but it *is* true that knowing Christ in the Spirit is more important than knowing "Christ from a human point of view" (2 Cor 5:16).

8. Joseph Hellermann, *Reconstructing Honor in Roman Philippi:* Carmen Christi *as* Cursus Pudorum. SNTSMS 132 (Cambridge: Cambridge University Press, 2005), 160.

9. Ibid., 148.

10. Ibid., 149.

rubbish, and challenges the elites to use their power differently than the Roman value system has taught them.[11] Paul wants to see a different set of values operating in the Philippian congregation.

He uses himself as an example, in the sacrificial (or at least offertory) metaphor we find in this chapter: "I am being poured out as a libation over the sacrifice and the offering of your faith" (2:17). The sacrificial metaphor suggests itself to his mind to illustrate selfless service. This equation of sacrifice with service, which we now take for granted, was relatively new when Paul expressed it.

One verse that has troubled many interpreters is the instruction to "work out your own salvation with fear and trembling" (2:12). It does not signify *earning* salvation with effort, but rather working out the *consequences* of salvation with moral seriousness and spiritual wholeheartedness. God "is at work in you, enabling you both to will and to work for his good pleasure" (2:13)—God implants both the *desire* for good and the ability to *do* it—"so that you may be blameless and innocent" (2:15), which is a *transformed* condition. Again there is the theme of gaining discernment in order to allow oneself to be transformed, to be "children of God without blemish in the midst of a crooked and perverse generation" (2:15). If believers have not been transformed, how can they "shine like stars in the world" (2:15)?

Practical matters complete the chapter; Paul hopes to send his fellow apostle and representative, Timothy, to them (2:19); he had also sent Timothy to the Corinthians (1 Cor 4:17) and Thessalonians (1 Thess 3:2). Timothy was a man of character and was well-liked (2:20-23). Epaphroditus, who apparently went back and forth between Philippi and Paul (2:25-26, 28; 4:18), became ill and nearly died "for the work of Christ" (2:27, 30). Imitation of models is a key theme in Philippians, and Timothy and Epaphroditus are being offered as models.[12] Later, Paul will present himself as a model for imitation (3:13-17).

Resisting Judaizers, Appreciating Gifts: Chapters 3–4

Philippians 3 returns to the theme that dominated Galatians, the danger posed by the circumcision party. But who is the true circumcision?

---

11. Ibid., 162, 165–66.

12. Benjamin Fiore, S.J., "Paul, Exemplification, and Imitation," in J. Paul Sampley, ed., *Paul in the Greco-Roman World: A Handbook* (Harrisburg, PA: Trinity Press International, 2003), 240–41.

"Beware of the dogs, beware of the evil workers, beware of those who mutilate the flesh! For it is we who are the circumcision, who worship in the Spirit of God and boast in Christ Jesus and have no confidence in the flesh" (3:2-3). Again Spirit is contrasted with flesh, and figurative circumcision with literal circumcision.

Paul has as much basis for fleshly boasting as anyone, if he so chose. He was "circumcised on the eighth day," is thoroughly Hebrew, "of the tribe of Benjamin," a zealous Pharisee "a persecutor of the church," and he was actually "blameless," as regards the Law (3:5-6). But all these gains are "loss because of Christ" (3:7). They are rubbish compared to "the surpassing value of knowing Christ Jesus my Lord" (3:8). What matters is not "righteousness of my own that comes from the law, but one that comes through faith in Christ" (3:9). (This could be one of those passages where *dia pisteōs Christou* is shorthand for "Christian faith.")

This part of the chapter shows that Paul does have an issue with the Law; he is not just saying that the Law had been approached in the wrong way. He *contrasts* law-works and Spirit-faith, as he did in Galatians and (to a lesser degree) in Romans (4:16; 6:14; 7:6). The result of this faith is believer transformation, "having . . . righteousness from God based on faith" (3:9). This is literally a from-God righteousness (*ek theou dikaiosynēn*). Faith means "to know Christ and the power of his resurrection and the sharing of his sufferings by becoming like him in his death" (3:10). The believer is actually re-formed into a fellow-sufferer,[13] but also takes on a certain resurrection power even while still in the flesh. The attempt to deny that there is any trace of "mystical participation" in Paul, and that he is "telling essentially the same story that we find in the Gospels and Acts,"[14] is unconvincing. We can certainly argue against an excessively mystical understanding of Paul's message, but to eliminate it entirely is to "quench the Spirit" (1 Thess 5:19).

Paul strives for perfection. He knows he has not reached it, but "Christ Jesus has made me his own" (3:12). He strains forward, pursuing "the prize of the heavenly call of God in Christ Jesus" (3:14). Perfection is the prize (3:15), and the Philippians should "join in imitating" Paul (3:17) in progress along this way. They should do what they have learned from and seen in Paul (4:9). They should not imitate the "enemies of the cross of Christ," whose "God is the belly" and who are earthly-minded

13. See the comments on Col 1:24 in chapter 9 on Colossians.
14. David A. Brondos, *Paul on the Cross: Reconstructing the Apostle's Story of Redemption* (Minneapolis: Fortress Press, 2006), 172, 100; cf. 189.

(3:18-19). This is probably the circumcision party, whose motives are fleshly (Gal 6:12), who are "confident in the flesh" (Phil 3:4).

Paul wants to direct their eyes to the higher goal: "our citizenship is in heaven, and it is from there that we are expecting a Savior, the Lord Jesus Christ" (3:20). This takes the concept of political loyalty and redirects it to the heavenly level, which has its own set of values. Aligning oneself with the heavenly system means adopting these values and also learning what awaits us on the next level: "He will transform the body of our humiliation that it may be conformed to the body of his glory, by the power that also enables him to make all things subject to himself" (3:21). There is a change from humiliation to glory. Jesus is the transformer, and his glorified (resurrection) body will apparently be the model for believers' resurrection bodies. Jesus is in charge of this whole resurrection process. In fact, he is assuming control of all things. In 1 Corinthians 15:28 God *subjects* all things to the Son. Here the Son himself does it. Father and Son work together.

Paul tells the Philippians to "stand firm" (4:1). In Galatians that advice was linked to not giving in to the circumcision party ("stand firm . . . and do not submit again to a yoke of slavery," Gal 5:1). Here Paul is speaking to a congregation towards whom he feels more affection. Evidently there is a conflict between two women in the congregation (which implies that they have some leadership role[15]), and he calmly urges them to "be of the same mind in the Lord" (4:2). He greets some coworkers and encourages the believers to "rejoice in the Lord always" (4:4). Prayer should be trusting: "Do not worry about anything . . . let your requests be made known to God" (4:6). This culminates in some majestic affirmations:

> And the peace of God, which surpasses all understanding, will guard your hearts and your minds in Christ Jesus. Finally, beloved, whatever is true, whatever is honorable, whatever is just, whatever is pure, whatever is pleasing, whatever is commendable, if there is any excellence and if there is anything worthy of praise, think about these things. (4:7-8)

Mental attention to truthful and gracious things is part of the walk of faith. We are reminded of the beginning of the letter, where love and knowledge lead to a discernment of everything that is of value (1:9-10). The Philippians should stay the course, do as Paul does (4:9). He has

---

15. On female leadership, see Wendy Cotter, "Women's Authority Roles in Paul's Churches: Countercultural or Conventional?" in *Novum Testamentum* 36 (1994): 350–72.

learned to be satisfied, whether "well-fed" or "going hungry" (4:12). The Philippians have shared with Paul; in fact, they were the only ones who offered him financial support early in his missionary travels (4:14-15). What he received from them (through Epaphroditus) was "a fragrant offering, a sacrifice acceptable and pleasing to God" (4:18). The act of giving is pictured as "sacrifice," a metaphorical meaning we now take for granted. This is Paul's last theological point in what may be the last multi-page communication we have from him.

PHILEMON

Although probably written earlier than Philippians, Philemon tends to receive separate consideration since it is the briefest of Paul's surviving letters and the only one not addressed to a church.

Philemon is one of the most important one-page letters ever written. It is also one of the most underappreciated letters in the NT. Many Christians and scholars do not notice the subtlety of Paul's advice to Philemon, the letter's recipient. There is a forcefulness that lurks under the polite tone, an ethical power that lies behind the gentle advice.

Philemon is a Christian slaveowner whose slave (vv. 15-16),[16] Onesimus, has run away, converted to Christianity, and become a coworker with Paul. Some property may have been damaged, given Paul's remark about damages owed (vv. 18-19). Onesimus is in some trouble, then, and he still legally belongs to Philemon. Paul, who is not a political revolutionary, is sending Onesimus back to Philemon with this letter. The advice in the letter, however, is more revolutionary than any strictly political position could possibly be.

The Subtlety of Paul's Advice

Paul starts with the same friendly greetings as in his other letters (vv. 1-2), he remembers the Philemon household in his prayers, and he hears reports of their love and faith (vv. 4-5). The first subtle dig, the first hint that Paul wants a certain behavior from Philemon, is in the purpose clause at the end of that sentence; his prayer is "that the sharing of your faith may become effective when you perceive all the good that we may

---

16. I find completely unconvincing Allen Dwight Callahan's argument that Onesimus was not a slave (*Embassy of Onesimus: The Letter of Paul to Philemon* [Valley Forge, PA: Trinity Press International, 1997], 5–10, 44–49).

do for Christ" (v. 6). Is your faith good enough to be recognized? Paul prays so! There is something Philemon needs to do, or his faith is worthless, manifesting none of the good that leads to (and comes from) Christ.

Paul does not allow the dig to hurt yet, as he goes on to say "I have indeed received much joy and encouragement from your love" (v. 7). But he *could* order Philemon around if he wanted to: "I am bold enough in Christ to command you to do your duty" (v. 8), but instead he will only *urge:* "I would rather appeal to you on the basis of love—and I, Paul, do this as an old man, and now also as a prisoner of Christ Jesus" (v. 9).

Philemon could choose to ignore the advice of a senior statesman who is suffering for the faith! Or he could choose to listen when Paul says, "I am appealing to you for my child, Onesimus, whose father I have become during my imprisonment" (v. 10); the reference is to spiritual fatherhood. Paul loves the kindly Onesimus, who takes good care of him in prison. The Roman administration allowed outsiders to lend assistance and spend time with high-status prisoners. The fact that Paul receives such attention may lend support to Acts' assertion that Paul was a Roman citizen (16:37; 22:25-28). Paul does not say whether he suffers from any injuries or illness, but this may be one reason why he needs a helper.

However, Paul finds it necessary to say, "I am sending him, that is, my own heart, back to you" (v. 12). He would like to have kept Onesimus, "so that he might be of service to me in your place during my imprisonment for the gospel" (v. 13), but he will not do so just on the basis of his own needs. What he is building up to is that he wants Philemon to voluntarily free Onesimus from slavery: "I preferred to do nothing without your consent, in order that your good deed might be voluntary and not something forced" (v. 14).

Paul seems to plead with Philemon for Onesimus' freedom. In fact, however, he is applying as much pressure as he can, in a cautious and calculated way, toward that end. Maybe Onesimus ran away precisely so that this would happen, so that his soul would be saved forever, which is what he means by "so that you might have him back forever, no longer as a slave but more than a slave, a beloved brother" (vv. 15-16). He is appealing to Philemon's Christian values; Philemon must value a fellow believer as a brother. Paul uses his position to ask Philemon to "welcome him as you would welcome me," and if he "owes you anything, charge that to my account" (vv. 17-18). Paul is clearly acting as Onesimus' patron and protector. Anything Philemon does to Onesimus, he is doing to Paul.

All this carries weight because Paul is Philemon's spiritual father as well, having led him to the Gospel. For that reason he owes Paul "even your own self" (v. 19). Philemon is indebted to Paul, and he can undo that debt by accepting Onesimus as a brother.[17] This kind of debt-paying is what Paul has in mind when he says "yes, brother, let me have this benefit from you in the Lord!" (v. 20). It is a spiritual debt, and Paul is looking for spiritual profit. Even so, it follows the patronage pattern; Paul is calling in his debt, forcing his high-status client Philemon to show mercy to his low-status client Onesimus. But he applies this force with a velvet glove (so much so that many commentators miss it completely)— "Refresh my heart in Christ" (v. 20)—do what your patron asks; make your patron happy!

"Confident of your obedience, I am writing to you, knowing that you will do even more than I say" (v. 21). This bluff confidence in Philemon's willingness to cooperate is also a strategic move, applying affection and pressure at the same time. But there is an iron fist inside the velvet glove, as Paul hints when he threatens a visit: "One thing more—prepare a guest room for me" (v. 22). This is like a warning shot. You had better do what your patron asks, or he will visit you! (Paul assumes that he will be released from prison.)

Paul finishes by sending greetings from a fellow prisoner and from some friends who are possibly also visiting him in his imprisonment, two of whose names jump out at us: "Mark . . . and Luke, my fellow workers" (v. 24). Acts seems to provide valid historical background of Paul's association with two of the likely authors of our NT Gospels: John Mark (Acts 12:12, 25; 15:37-39) and Luke ("we" traveled with Paul [Acts 20:7, 13; 21:4; 27:1, 3]).

Philemon raises a different set of ethical questions than Paul's other letters, putting him face to face with the slavery issue, quite different from the issues of religious inclusion and interpersonal consideration he faced in the other letters, but it gives us an opportunity for rethinking the ethical significance of the whole Pauline message. We begin with the slavery issue and move on to the broader question of brotherhood.

---

17. Norman R. Petersen, *Rediscovering Paul: Philemon and the Sociology of Paul's Narrative World* (Philadelphia: Fortress Press, 1985), 168.

The Issue of Slavery

What is Paul's attitude toward slavery? He does not directly question Philemon's right to own slaves, but indirectly the principle of Christian brotherhood and sisterhood does challenge the Roman class system, especially the unfree condition of slaves. If one truly treats all fellow believers as brothers and sisters, one could not treat them as people without rights, without freedom. Philemon, Paul suggests, needs to think of Onesimus differently: Onesimus is to be "no longer as a slave but more than a slave, a beloved brother" (v. 16). Socially this makes Onesimus a new person.

It is still true that Paul's is not a political program. He would change slavery, one owner at a time, but this does set in motion a series of shifts that results in political change (however long it might take). The spiritual insight (all believers are brothers and sisters) leads to a moral insight (all should be *treated* as brothers or sisters; see 1 Thess 4:6, 8) which eventually compels a political principle (no one should have slave status). Of course, there are several hurdles to be jumped in reaching the final conclusion. One is that all people, not just fellow believers, should be treated this way. It is one thing to practice brotherhood and sisterhood within one's immediate religious community; it is quite another to extend that principle, that behavior, outward to all people, even to the point of changing social customs, rights, structures of power, and lines of authority.

The extension of spiritual principles beyond one's immediate circle is to some degree coordinate with the extension of the concept of community. When once one considers all people to be deserving of the consideration one practices within one's religious community, then the principles start having political effect, but that takes time. By the time many or most people in the empire had become Christians, Christianity itself was no longer the same. It had taken on a hierarchical authority structure, it had systematically avoided conflict with society over issues of power and freedom, and the radicalism of Jesus and Paul were long gone. In fact, with the advent of Christian emperors, Christianity took on imperial values. It began to serve the interests of social stability. Social classes and hierarchies were considered to be God-ordained, and there was no opportunity for the gospels or Philemon to have any world-changing implications. Compassion was certainly encouraged, and practiced, but basic social structure was not changed. Political change had to await a rediscovery of the ethics of the Gospel (along with certain changes in the facts of material culture) during the Protestant Reformation, followed by further developments in moral and political philosophy in subsequent centuries.

Paul wants people to think about things that are deeper than political structures; he wants us to reflect on the nature of discipleship and on life itself. We are all slaves, either of righteousness or of sin (Rom 6:16-19). The freed person becomes a "slave of Christ" and *therefore* is not to be enslaved to anyone (1 Cor 7:22-23). *This* slavery brings freedom. As a "slave of Christ," Paul does not seek "to please people" (Gal 1:10). Jesus himself came in "the form of a slave, being born in human likeness" (Phil 2:7). The concept of "slave" is a focus of religious reflection for him. Nevertheless, literal slavery is negative; the new covenant is not a covenant of slavery (Gal 4:7, 25, 30-31; 5:1; Rom 8:15). If slaves are presented with an opportunity to be freed, they should take it (1 Cor 7:21).

Jennifer Glancy offers quite a different view on slavery and Paul's stance: Paul speaks of a suspension of social categories like slave and free, male and female, but people's "places in society . . . are defined by these very categories."[18] Paul's opposition to adultery and other forms of *porneia* is complicated by the fact that slaves were commonly used as sexual objects by their owners.[19] Glancy is inclined to think that "Paul implicitly suggests that slaves who oblige their masters sexually are engaged in *porneia*."[20] She does not seem to recognize that, if this is true, Paul's position would be tantamount to advising these slaves to resist such usage and would therefore constitute a very strong resistance to one aspect of slavery, even though he is somewhat indirect about it (simply condemning *porneia*). Whether or not Glancy is right on this particular point, her book is a crucial source of information about the demeaning and harsh condition of slavery, although we also learn from ancient sources that well-positioned slaves in managerial positions had considerable social power. Glancy resists the scholarly trend of assimilating slavery to the patronage system as though slaves were free to seek out other patrons, which they were not.[21]

18. Jennifer A. Glancy, *Slavery in Early Christianity* (Oxford: Oxford University Press, 2002), 38.

19. Ibid., 21–23 (on slaves, not Paul), and 35–38, 61–70.

20. Ibid., 64.

21. Ibid., 115, 124–27.

The Issue of Making Moral Judgments about Ancient Texts

Is it appropriate for us to make judgments about the morality contained in ancient writings? Inasmuch as humans in all times and places have had moral instincts and principles, we inevitably will assess the moral message in ancient writings, but we must exercise caution and we must educate ourselves. We need to learn about ancient cultures and value systems so that we know what to expect, and so that we recognize the originality of such sayings as "There is no longer Jew or Greek, there is no longer slave or free, there is no longer male and female" (Gal 3:28). If we do not notice that such a statement is applying a standard of values completely at odds with the political system we will fail to appreciate how daring it was.

Further, it is neither fair nor sensible to expect ancient people to utter modern viewpoints. Our ideologies have taken centuries to evolve; some of our slogans and ideas have only developed within the last generation or two. Any approach to historical matters or to ancient literature requires some understanding of how culture shapes thinking. Even the discourse of opposition to prevailing values is shaped by the culture being criticized. This is why it is entirely appropriate when scholars notice similarities between Paul's rhetoric and that found in the Cynic epistles. It does not mean that Paul was a Gentile philosopher; it just means that he is adapting the style and some of the reasoning of this recognized form of social critique. It also likely means that some Gentiles, hearing Paul's message, would be reminded of Cynic critique. This does not contradict the fact that, to a *greater* degree, they would be confronted with Jewish concepts of a prophecy-inspiring God and a Messiah sent by God. Even with such a Jewish background, however, the reader would have to grapple with the fact that Paul is speaking of a new way to interpret the Jewish scriptures and a new, more cosmic way of understanding "Messiah." Both Paul's continuity with the surrounding culture(s) and his discontinuity with them are important.

Even today Paul's message is not for the mentally lazy or conventionally-minded. Regardless of one's background, the hearer of Paul's Gospel must question his or her assumptions and rethink long-cherished dogmas. Paul asks us to reconsider the way God has been working with the human race and to recognize that God has always been working on saving the whole human race, despite having made a covenant with Moses that created a distinct covenant people. There still is a distinct covenant people, in Paul's view, but now it is entered by everyone who humbly believes in God and in Jesus the Messiah (Rom 10:1-10).

Covenant Ethics

The biblical covenant has always moved in an ethicizing direction. Covenant principles always included a commitment to justice (Isa 5:7; 58:6; Jer 22:16), to "kindness and mercy to . . . the widow, the orphan, the alien . . . the poor" (Zech 7:9-10). Along with the prophets' concept of ethical deepening of the covenant went the expansion of its social scope. If ethics matter more than ritual practice (Hos 6:4-10), the next logical step is to say that God will honor these values whenever they are manifested by Gentiles (Rom 2:14-16).

Reflection on Gospel principles can lead one to question whether God ever made a covenant with an ethnic group as such, despite the traditional understanding. Later tradition would speak of "the God of Abraham, Isaac, and Jacob," showing how thoroughly the covenant was assimilated to the tribal or clan concept, but the Abrahamic covenant itself was not so clannish. Abraham's principal allies were some Amorites (Gen 14:13), including Mamre, in whose locale Abraham built an altar and in whose territory the Lord appeared to Abraham (Gen 13:18; 18:1). Similarly, Moses' religious ally and judicial advisor Jethro was a Midianite (Exod 18:1, 11-22), and he had Kenite allies (Judg 1:16; 4:11, 17). God has never been God of the Jews only (Rom 3:29). Of course, Paul has to swim upstream to make this argument, but so had the prophets: "Blessed be Egypt my people, and Assyria the work of my hands, and Israel my heritage," (Isa 19:25; cf. Amos 9:7). Paul's universalizing teaching was not wholly unprecedented. Prophets had foretold, "Many nations shall join themselves to the LORD on that day" (Zech 2:11 [NAB 2:15]). "I am coming to gather all nations and tongues," even taking some of them to be priests (Isa 66:18, 21). Clearly "the Holy One of Israel" was also "God of the whole earth" (Isa 54:5). Luke has Jesus pointing out this theme in the OT, "that repentance and forgiveness of sins is to be proclaimed in his name to all nations" (Luke 24:47). Mark has Jesus preaching in the Gentile regions of Sidon and the Decapolis (7:31; cf. Matt 15:21). Luke has Jesus pointing out that Elijah and Elisha healed only Gentiles (4:25-27). Matthew has Jesus saying "make disciples of all nations" (28:19). Gentiles come to Jesus (Mark 3:8; 7:26; Luke 7:2-9; John 12:20).

Paul's universalism could be called ethical, but even more, it can be called christological: Jesus became human and humbled himself even to death, so "that at the name of Jesus every knee should bend, in heaven and on earth and under the earth, and every tongue should confess that Jesus Christ is Lord, to the glory of God the Father" (Phil 2:10-11). "Our citizenship is in heaven" (Phil 3:20). Just as Jesus brings all things into subjection to himself (3:21), the ethics of the Gospel aspire to universality. There will come a day when everyone enslaved to status, money, and sensuality will be no longer "a slave but . . . a beloved brother" (Phlm 16). These are Paul's parting messages to those who will read his letters.

Chapter 9

Colossians
and Ephesians

COLOSSIANS

Questions of Authorship and Literary Relationships: Chapter 1

Colossians offers three or four choices for the interpreter as regards authorship: (1) it was written by Paul, as the church has traditionally accepted; (2) it is deutero-Pauline, as many scholars of the last hundred years have held; (3) it is deutero-Pauline, but is *very* close to Paul, both conceptually and in terms of time of composition; (4) Timothy was truly a coauthor, as the prescript says ("and Timothy our brother," 1:1), or even the principal author, of Colossians.[1] The issue is different for Ephesians, which incorporates most of Colossians but with some crucial changes.

There are some expressions in Colossians that do not occur in the seven "undisputed letters" of Paul, but there are many things that reflect not only Pauline teaching but the unique attitude of Paul. A number of passages remind us of Philippians passages on discernment, knowing God, and sharing Christ's sufferings. The first example is this: "we have not ceased praying for you and asking that you may be filled with the knowledge

---

1. It may contain "the theology of Paul as . . . interpreted by Timothy. . . . with Paul's approval . . . 4:18" (James D. G. Dunn, *The Epistles to the Colossians and to Philemon: A Commentary on the Greek Text*. NIGTC [Grand Rapids: Eerdmans, 1996], 38; cf. 47).

(*epignōsis*) of God's will in all spiritual wisdom and understanding[2] . . . so that you may live lives . . . fully pleasing to him, as you bear fruit in every good work and as you grow in the knowledge of God" (Col 1:9-10). The same focus on *epignōsis*, righteousness, and pleasing God occurs near the beginning of Philippians (1:9-11). This, of course, neither proves nor disproves Pauline authorship, since a close disciple of Paul may be inclined to make the same points. But it is a piece of circumstantial evidence.

Colossians has the strong christology we saw in the longer letters. God rescued believers "from the power of darkness and transferred us into the kingdom of his beloved Son" (1:13). This can be described as redemption, *apolytrōsis*, the same word we saw in Romans 3:24. But Colossians adds a phrase that does not occur in Paul: "in whom we have redemption, the forgiveness of sins" (1:14). Although Paul is very much interested in rescue from sin and restoration of right relations, he never elsewhere speaks of "forgiveness of sins" except once when he is quoting Psalm 32:1 (at Rom 4:7). However, this is not sufficient by itself to rule out Pauline authorship. We would need more evidence to do that.

The christology continues: "He is the image of the invisible God, the firstborn of all creation; for in him all things in heaven and on earth were created, things visible and invisible, whether thrones or dominions or rulers or powers—all things have been created through him and for him" (1:15-16). Jesus as the image of God is found in 2 Corinthians 4:4 and Philippians 2:6. Jesus as cocreator, or as the one *through* whom God created, is found in 1 Corinthians 8:6. The *Testament of Levi* had spoken of "thrones and authorities" being present with God, while the archangels offered "bloodless oblation" (*T. Levi* 3:6, 8). Thrones and authorities are some kind of middle-management figures in heaven. But Christ is over them: he "is the head of the body, the church; he is the beginning, the firstborn from the dead, so that he might come to have first place in everything" (Col 1:18). That he is the first resurrected is also the point of the "firstborn" saying in 1 Corinthians 15:20, but Colossians 1:16 concerns his origin, not the resurrection.

What about the following statement? Does it go beyond what is found in the other letters? "For in him all the fullness of God was pleased to dwell" (1:19). The Greek actually does not contain "of God" in this verse, but the author is talking about "the invisible God" in 1:15, and speaks of the "fullness of deity" in 2:9. The statement is not much different from

---

2. Echoing "the spirit of wisdom and of understanding" in the messianic passage, Isa 11:2.

"he was in the form of God" (Phil 2:6), "is the image of God" (2 Cor 4:4), and is subjecting all things to himself (1 Cor 15:28; Phil 3:21).

Familiar soteriology follows.

> God was pleased through him . . . to reconcile to himself all things, whether on earth or in heaven, by making peace through the blood of his cross. And you who were once estranged and hostile in mind, doing evil deeds, he has now reconciled in his fleshly body through death, so as to present you holy and blameless and irreproachable before him. (Col 1:20-22)

"Blood" and "cross," being "estranged" and then "reconciled" in his "fleshly body through death" all sound very Pauline, even if the precise phrase "blood of his cross" is unique.

The one passage that it is very difficult to imagine anyone but Paul saying is this: "in my flesh I am completing what is lacking in Christ's afflictions for the sake of his body, that is, the church" (1:24). The later church will not endorse any statement that makes such a close connection between apostle and savior, that even connects one's own afflictions with those of Christ. Ephesians contains nothing like it, despite restating most of what is in Colossians. Paul envisions a burden of pain that Christ and God are bearing on behalf of the human race and which is not finished yet. Eventually the full measure of suffering will be completed, and then the *parousia* and the rectification of all things will take place. It is the apostle's duty (and the believer's, too, to a lesser degree) to join in the suffering of Christ, to join in the work of God. It is a participationist saying, along the lines of what we saw in Romans 6. If one despises the word "mysticism," then one must find some other word to describe the active involvement in Christ's suffering that Paul is describing. He interprets his suffering as *part of Christ's suffering*, just as he did in 2 Corinthians ("always carrying in the body the death of Jesus," 4:10) and Philippians ("the sharing of his sufferings by becoming like him in his death," 3:10). The Colossians statement may seem more shocking, but it is saying the same thing as these other passages.

Evidently people had a hard time understanding Paul's participationist teaching, and they still do. One interpreter says that Paul's affliction, Seneca's tales of heroic suffering, and the deaths of the Maccabean martyrs are "examples of obedience" meant to inspire the community to remain loyal to its values.[3] Certainly, but Paul does much more than this. When he links his suffering to the Savior's he is telling a story of God

3. Jerry L. Sumney, "'I Fill Up What Is Lacking in the Afflictions of Christ': Paul's Vicarious Suffering in Colossians," *CBQ* 68 (2006): 672–73.

and of the believer's active participation in God's work of salvific suffering. Indeed, people resisted this deeply personal involvement in God's suffering work! It was much safer to speak of the saving deed that was done *for* us. But Paul makes believers, or at least apostles, participants in the saving activity of God that is ongoing. He holds back from calling apostles co-saviors, but only just barely! Apostles participate in God's saving activity, which means they must participate in God's suffering. This is what is left out of the simplistic and popular views of atonement in which only Christ has to bear this suffering. What if each one of us had to bear it?

The early church had a hard time understanding or accepting Paul's deeply participationist view of suffering, especially when it seemed to complicate the notion of Christ's work. The church was willing to accept Paul's metaphors as long as they could be simplified and turned into slogans. The saving blood of Christ is a simple enough metaphor that the church was able to use. It is a major image in Ephesians, with no hint of the apostle helping to fill up the measure of suffering. Colossians still shows the deep participationism and fluidity of metaphor one sees in Paul's own writings.

There follow some phrases that are not found in Paul but do recall known Pauline passages: "the mystery that has been hidden throughout the ages . . . how great among the Gentiles are the riches of the glory of this mystery" (1:26-27). The "mystery" in Romans 11:25 is the hardening of Israel "until the full number of the Gentiles has come in," and the "mystery that was kept secret for long ages" (Rom 16:25) also concerns "all the Gentiles" (16:26). What is the saving content of the mystery? It is "Christ in you, the hope of glory" (Col 1:27). And what is Paul's assignment?—"teaching everyone in all wisdom, so that we may present everyone mature in Christ" (1:28). Being presented to God or "preserved blameless" for the Lord's coming is also found in 1 Thessalonians 5:23; Romans 15:16; 1 Corinthians 1:8.

Knowledge of God and Transformation: 2:1–3:17

Love has a cognitive purpose in Colossians 2. The author prays that believers may be "united in love, so that they may have all the riches of assured understanding and have the knowledge (*epignōsin*) of God's mystery, that is, Christ himself, in whom are hidden all the treasures of wisdom and knowledge" (2:2-3). Love *enables* knowledge, just as love made knowledge and insight overflow in Philippians 1:9. This is a protection against being deceived. The believer is to be "rooted" in Christ, and "established in the faith, just as you were taught" (2:7). The latter phrase suggests systematic doctrinal teaching.

We have to handle some of the passages in the second half of chapter 2 non-consecutively. One of the subjects is the "philosophy and empty deceit" (2:8) that consumed the thinking of many of the Colossians. It involved food regulations, observances of "festivals, or new moons, or sabbaths" (2:16), "self-abasement" (2:18, 23) and other restrictive regulations (2:20-22). It encouraged visions, participation in angelic worship or veneration of angels, and "wisdom" (2:18, 23). The identity of this philosophy continues to be debated among scholars. Suggestions have included a Pythagorean philosophy (which had dietary restrictions and a focus on wisdom), an ascetic Gnostic sect, an astrological mystery cult, a Jewish sect that imagined (like the Qumran community of the Dead Sea Scrolls) participating in the heavenly liturgy ("worship of angels," 2:18), and a blend of local folk beliefs with local Judaism.[4] The philosophy probably had a Christian veneer. When the author condemns the "visions" he says they are based on "a human way of thinking, and not holding fast to the head," who is Christ (2:18-19). Why would one *expect* the visions to hold to Christ unless they claimed to be Christian?

Whatever the identity of the group, the author's point is that these observances are futile and do not really bring self-control (2:22-23). As in Galatians, serving such a religion is serving "elemental spirits [*stoicheia*]" (2:8; cf. Gal 4:3). Who needs them? Rather, "in him the whole fullness of deity dwells bodily, and you have come to fullness in him, who is the head of every ruler and authority" (2:9-10). This lends support to the likelihood that Paul saw these powers as personal beings[5] over whom Christ asserts control. There was a public conquest of these invisible powers, evidently, since when Christ removed the condemnation that was against us he also "disarmed the rulers and authorities and made a public example of them, triumphing over them in it" (2:15). This was a military victory parade.

---

4. Arguments are summarized and critiqued in Clinton E. Arnold, *The Colossian Syncretism: The Interface between Christianity and Folk Belief at Colossae* (WUNT 2/77; Tübingen: Mohr Siebeck, 1995), who argues for a blend of mystery religion, "Phrygian folk belief, local folk Judaism, and Christianity" (243). Folk Judaism outside Palestine often includes "Solomonic magical tradition" (226; cf. 101).

5. Arnold, *Colossian Syncretism*, 182–84.

In keeping with his strongly spiritualizing approach our author says that "you were circumcised with a spiritual circumcision, by putting off the body of the flesh in the circumcision of Christ" (2:11). By "strongly spiritualizing" I mean the author asserts that there is a spiritual practice that is *more true* than the literal ritual practice. The next line has a more familiar ring: "when you were buried with him in baptism, you were also raised with him through faith in the power of God" (2:12) This echoes Romans 6:3-4 closely. Yet the next two verses have some very un-Pauline thoughts:

> And when you were dead in trespasses and the uncircumcision of your flesh, God made you alive together with him, when he forgave us all our trespasses, erasing the record that stood against us with its legal demands. He set this aside, nailing it to the cross. (Col 2:13-14)

Is this Pauline? Paul does not think literal circumcision matters at all (Rom 3:30; 4:9). Perhaps he is addressing the Godfearers among the Colossians, those men who *were* uncircumcised but became proselytes to Judaism before they became Christians. Regarding the next clause, it has already been mentioned that forgiveness of sins is not an expression Paul uses, but we should not be too dogmatic about this. It may just be that he usually found a metaphor (redemption, justification) that would communicate the concept effectively. The next clause is a little strange, since it assumes that the Law has legal claims over his audience, but there are two plausible explanations: (1) he is speaking to Godfearers who do think they will be judged by the Torah, as well they might be (Rom 2:12), or (2) he is not referring to the Torah here, but to the Colossians' own (Gentile) concepts of the power of legal decrees,[6] or even to the indictment nailed to the cross of crucifixion victims.[7] Thus we cannot be certain that Paul did not write these verses, though we can say that they look suspect. Since that is probably the most we can say, these problems are really outweighed by the many Pauline concepts in chapters 1–2: being transferred into the kingdom of the Son, being presented holy to God, apostolic participation in the suffering of Christ, the mystery of Gentile inclusion, the reciprocal effect of love and knowledge, divinity dwelling in the Son, and the enslaving *stoicheia* being led away in a military victory parade. There is a good chance that most of chapters 1–2 was written or cowritten by Paul.

---

6. As he did to his Galatian audience.
7. Dunn, *Epistles to the Colossians and Philemon*, 166. On the Jewish elements in 2:11-16, see pp. 33–34.

Chapters 3–4 seem to depart further from Pauline expression. Paul's notion of future resurrection hope is changed into a present resurrection experience, and spiritual-mindedness seems to amount to otherworldliness: "So if you have been raised with Christ, seek the things that are above . . . Set your minds on things that are above, not on things that are on earth" (3:1-2). There is still a *parousia* hope, but with an unusual addition: "When Christ who is your life is revealed, then you also will be revealed with him in glory" (3:4). This sounds as if believers will be gloriously displayed, which differs from Paul's account. According to 1 Thessalonians 4:13-17 we will be caught up in the air, but not in glory, and 1 Corinthians 15:51-53 says that we will be changed and raised incorruptible, but not displayed with Christ.

However, as soon as the reader is ready to conclude that the author is not Paul, some material that is very Pauline in expression as well as in concept follows: "Put to death, therefore, whatever in you is earthly: fornication, impurity, passion, evil desire" (3:5; cf. Rom 8:13). "On account of these the wrath of God is coming" (3:6; cf. Rom 1:18). Putting away the old behaviors (anger, obscenity, dishonesty) in 3:7-9 reminds one of the putting off of the "old self" in Romans 6:6 and the "works of the flesh" in Galatians 5:19-21. We hear a strong echo of Galatians 3:28 in Colossians 3:11: "In that renewal there is no longer Greek and Jew, circumcised and uncircumcised, barbarian, Scythian, slave and free; but Christ is all and in all." There is no mention of male and female, however. Maybe that teaching was the hardest to implement, meeting with the strongest opposition. We can only guess.

One of the great "renewal" sayings follows: "you have stripped off the old self with its practices and have clothed yourselves with the new self, which is being renewed (*anakainoumenon*) in knowledge (*epignōsin*) according to the image of its creator" (3:9-10). This recalls the renewal and new creation sayings in 2 Corinthians 3:18; 4:16; 5:17; and elsewhere. Knowledge is linked with transformation or renewal, as we saw in Philippians 1:9-10 and Romans 12:1-2. Just as renewal was followed by an exhortation to love in Romans 12, so renewal here is followed by advocacy of "compassion, kindness, humility, meekness . . . forgiv[ing] one another . . . love, which binds everything together in perfect harmony" (3:12-14). This leads to perfection of relationships. When "Christ is all and in all," social barriers are eliminated, and compassion creates unity (3:11-14), makes Christians "one body" (3:15). Then believers can "let the peace of Christ rule in your hearts" (3:15); they teach and admonish one another and rejoice together (3:16).

In all these letters the life of faith has both a "cruciform"[8] and an "anakainoform" (renewing, transforming) dimension. I coin the latter term because of the importance of *anakainōsis* in Romans 12:2; 2 Corinthians 4:16; Colossians 3:10; and other *kain*-words in Romans 6:4; 7:6; 2 Corinthians 3:6, and elsewhere. The life of faith, for Paul, involves both suffering with Christ and transformation into Christ-likeness.

The Household Code: 3:18–4:18

The modern reader may find what follows to be less palatable. Wives are exhorted to be subordinate to husbands, and husbands to love wives and avoid bitterness (Col 3:18-19). Children are to be obedient, but fathers are not to provoke children or make them discouraged (3:20-21). Slaves are to be obedient from the heart, and "not only while being watched" (3:22). Masters are to be fair, remembering that they "too have a Master in heaven" (4:1).

These "household codes" occur in most of the deutero-Pauline letters. The household codes have a recognizable literary form in which one group after another is instructed to be self-effacing and to act as expected in their recognized social roles. Here in Colossians the emphasis is on humility, consideration for others, and avoidance of any disturbance of the outward order of society. This is quite different from Paul's confronting the "wise" and the powerful. The household codes may come from a time when Christian communities were under attack and decided to assume a cautious social profile in order to reduce the hostility that was being directed against them. This may be the import of the advice: "Conduct yourselves wisely toward outsiders . . . Let your speech always be gracious, seasoned with salt" (4:5-6). This last remark probably refers to salt's ability to prevent corruption, thus: let your speech not become rotten.[9]

Colossians 4 continues with autobiographical information (if authentic). "Paul" is in prison for proclaiming the mystery of Christ (4:3). The author claims to be sending the letter along with Tychicus . . . and Onesimus (4:7, 9)! His fellow prisoner is Aristarchus (4:10), also mentioned in Philemon 24. In fact, all five people mentioned in Philemon 23-24

---

8. Michael J. Gorman, *Cruciformity: Paul's Narrative Spirituality of the Cross* (Grand Rapids: Eerdmans, 2001).

9. J. B. Lightfoot, *Saint Paul's Epistles to the Colossians and to Philemon* (London: Macmillan, 1904), 230.

(Aristarchus, Mark, Epaphras, Luke, and Demas) are also here in Colossians 4:10, 12, 14. The author asks the recipients to send greetings to the church in Laodicea (a region) and "to Nympha and the church in her house" (4:15). Laodicea is mentioned twice more in 4:16, including a letter "from Laodicea." Paul's own handwriting is said to appear in the last line: "I, Paul, write this greeting with my own hand. Remember my chains. Grace be with you" (4:18).

On balance, Colossians looks like a letter cowritten by Paul and Timothy. Paul seems to be the main author of most of what occurs up through 3:17, although Timothy may give us some concepts, such as believers appearing in glory (3:4), and "the record that stood against us" in 2:14. It may be Timothy's voice that is dominant from 3:18 onward. The co-authorship theory would mean that, although Paul did not write the household code, he did allow it to be included.

Of course, this is just one possibility. Other scholarly views need to be considered. Eduard Lohse says, "the receding of eschatology" and resurrection hope, and their replacement with the notion of being already resurrected with Christ (3:1) are "considerable differences" from the Pauline letters,[10] yet he finds significant similarities to the Pauline letters in the idea that church members (not just leaders) should admonish one another (3:16), and in the absence of anything like the "fixed order of offices of bishops, elders, and deacons" in the Pastorals or even like the list of five official roles in Ephesians 4:11.[11] At the time of the composition of Colossians, fixed administrative offices have not yet emerged in the church, but they are emerging in Ephesians and are fully evident in the Pastorals.

EPHESIANS

The "consensus view" is "that Eph was composed after the apostle's death by a Jewish Christian follower of Paul's on the basis of Col and a collection of Pauline letters."[12] There are many variations within this consensus, of course. According to George van Kooten, the author of

10. Eduard Lohse, "Pauline Theology in the Letter to the Colossians," *NTS* 15 (1968–69): 217.

11. Ibid., 216.

12. Pheme Perkins, "God, Cosmos and Church Universal: The Theology of Ephesians," in *SBL Seminar Papers, 2000.* SBLSP 39 (Atlanta: Scholars Press, 2000), 753.

Ephesians wanted his creation to be seen as the letter to the Laodiceans.[13] Inasmuch as the letter was canonized by the Christian tradition, his aspiration was a success, although the Laodicean detail was forgotten. Ephesians is largely an expansion and "reworking" of Colossians. One could even say "the author of *Eph* in fact offers a sort of commentary on *Col* in order to modify its cosmology" and clarify certain obscure concepts.[14] Christians have studied and cherished the longer and clearer epistle (Ephesians), and interpreted Colossians with the ideas of Ephesians in mind.

The Fullness in the Church: Chapter 1 and Elsewhere

Ephesians departs from Colossians in significant ways. In Colossians 1:18 Christ is head *of the church* (genitive case), but in Ephesians 1:22 he is "head over all things *for* the church" (dative case; emphasis added). Everything is now *for the church.* In Colossians 1:19 "all the fullness" dwells in Christ, but in Ephesians 1:23 the church itself is "the fullness of him who fills all in all." The church takes Christ's place in some ways: "The cosmic Christ of Col in whom the fullness of divinity dwells . . . shifts to Christ's body, the church."[15] In Colossians, christology is about Christ and God, with the church as a byproduct. In Ephesians, ecclesiology takes over christology; believers are even raised up with Christ and are seated "with him in the heavenly places" (2:6). Are there church services in heaven? God, in fact, now speaks "through the church . . . to the rulers and authorities in the heavenly places" (3:10). Even more remarkable is that Christ gave himself "for" the church (5:25), and is married to her (5:23-29). Salvation is pictured in collective terms; Christ saves *the church.*

Ephesians has many of the recognizable Pauline themes, but with a heightening of ecclesiasticism and predestination: believers were chosen "before the foundation of the world to be holy and blameless before him in love. He destined us for adoption . . ." (1:4-5). "In him we have redemption through his blood, the forgiveness of our trespasses" (1:7). The lengthier Pauline statements about redemption and justification by

---

13. George H. van Kooten, *Cosmic Christology in Paul and the Pauline School: Colossians and Ephesians in the Context of Graeco-Roman Cosmology, with a New Synopsis of the Greek Texts.* WUNT 2/171 (Tübingen: Mohr Siebeck, 2003), 197–201. Of course, Col 4:16 mentions a letter *from* Laodicea.

14. Ibid., 203–4.

15. Perkins, "God, Cosmos and Church," 755.

Christ's blood (Rom 3:24-26; 5:8-10) have been simplified, and augmented with the (Timothean?) mention of forgiveness. Also reminiscent of Colossians is "he has made known to us the mystery of his will" (1:9; cf. Col 1:26-27). Our author reflects the idea of Christ subjecting all things to himself (1 Cor 15:27-28; Phil 3:21), but he stresses the church's role in this effort: God's favor was "set forth in Christ, as a plan for the fullness of time, to gather up all things in him, things in heaven and things on earth" (1:9-10). Christians help to make the glory of Christ known: "having been destined according to . . . his counsel and will, so that we . . . might live for the praise of his glory" (1:11-12).

Using a manner of expression found in Romans 8:23, the author speaks of redemption as future: the "Holy Spirit . . . the pledge of our inheritance toward redemption as God's own people" (1:13-14). In the meantime, believers need to receive "a spirit of wisdom and revelation" (1:17) so they may know God.

The Gentiles Drawn Near: 2:1–3:9

Formerly, "You were dead through . . . trespasses and sins . . . following the ruler of the power of the air" (2:1-2), a phrase unique to Ephesians but probably meaning the same as "the god of this world" (2 Cor 4:4). People are lost in sin until rescued by Christ: "we were by nature children of wrath . . . But God, who is rich in mercy . . . made us alive together with Christ . . . raised us up with him and seated us with him in the heavenly places in Christ Jesus" (2:3-6), which goes beyond anything we see in Paul. But what follows is standard Pauline soteriology: "For by grace you have been saved through faith, and this is not your own doing; it is the gift of God—not the result of works, so that no one may boast" (2:8-9; cf. Rom 11:6; 1 Cor 1:29).

The inclusion of the Gentiles is pictured in vivid and compelling imagery. The Gentiles formerly had "no hope and [were] without God," but those "who once were far off have been brought near by the blood of Christ" (2:12-13). Christ "has broken down the dividing wall, that is, the hostility between us," creating one people in place of two, "making peace" and "putting to death that hostility" (vv. 14-16). Now Jews and Gentiles "have access in one Spirit to the Father" and Gentiles are "members of the household of God" (2:18-19). It sounds like 1 Corinthians 12:13, but it lacks Paul's own reasoning from Scripture and use of the figure of Abraham. One phrase that suggests deutero-Pauline authorship is what follows: "built upon the foundation of the apostles and prophets"

(2:20). This notion of the apostles as a foundation on which to build speaks of an apostolic *tradition*, which means some time has passed. The concept of "church" has grown: the church is a "structure" that "grows into a holy temple in the Lord" (2:21); "you also are built together spiritually into a dwelling place for God" (2:22). A similar idea is present in 2 Corinthians 6:16, but without the hierarchic image of "foundation" and "structure."

The claimed Pauline authorship is brought out in 3:1: "I, Paul, am a prisoner for Christ Jesus," and in subsequent verses. The "mystery was made known to me by revelation, as I wrote above in a few words" (3:3, recalling Galatians 1:12, but why would the Ephesians know what was written to Galatia unless there is now a letter *collection*?). This mystery "has now been revealed," namely that "the Gentiles have become fellow heirs, members of the same body, and sharers in the promise in Christ Jesus" (3:5-6). The "grace" of his calling and the "riches of Christ" (3:7-8) recall Romans 1:5; 11:33; Galatians 1:15-16, even though the passage is based on Colossians 1:27. While still based on Colossians, Ephesians 2:1–3:8 draws heavily on Romans, 1 Corinthians, and Galatians.

Making Known the Mystery: 3:10–4:32

The "mystery of Christ" (3:4)—the inclusion of the Gentiles (3:6)—is also "through the church . . . made known to the rulers and authorities in the heavenly places" (3:10). This is a mixture of themes from Galatians and Colossians. Gentile inclusion is a church issue, but it is revealed in the heavens; again Ephesians raises the church to the heavenly level.

The author discerns reflections of the heavenly in the earthly: "I bow my knees before the Father, from whom every family in heaven and on earth takes its name" (3:14-15). God's father-pattern is reproduced in the world. The point of this passage is encouragement. The believer is to be "strengthened in your inner being with power through his Spirit" (3:16). "Rooted and grounded in love," the believer joins the companies of the angels, able "to comprehend with all the saints . . . to know the love of Christ . . . so that you may be filled with all the fullness [*plērōma*] of God" (3:17-19). Believers now get to receive the fullness of God that, in Colossians 1:19; 2:9, was in Christ! This is not individualistic, however, but manifests God's power (3:20), expressed as "glory in the church" (3:21). In Ephesians everything is centered on the church.

Some of the early readers of Ephesians, however, found other theological centers. The *plērōma* concept became very important in Christian

Gnosticism, being used to describe a corporate Godhead. In the system of Valentinus (second century), the *plērōma* consisted of either thirty or thirty-two individual "aeons," or persons within the Godhead, two of whom were Jesus and Sophia. Gnosticism is characterized by the generation of many different cosmological theories, some of which used Ephesians as a jumping-off point.

But the orthodox have loved this letter as well. It is a masterpiece of expansive, universalizing Christian thought, with almost no controversy to distract from its positive message. It is the supreme theological production of the deutero-Pauline tradition. An example is the masterful discussion of love (4:2, 15-16, 32) and spiritual maturity (4:13-15) leading to spiritual unity (4:3-6, 13, 16-25). Believers are "knit together" in Christ (4:16), "grow up . . . into Christ" (4:15), and are clothed "with the new self" (4:24).

The Household Codes: Chapters 5–6

The "paraenetic," or advice, section begins in chapter 5. The first piece of advice is to "be imitators of God" (5:1), something Paul himself only touches upon, and lightly, once (1 Thess 1:6). Closer to the Pauline view is the advice to live selflessly, as did Christ, who "loved us and gave himself up for us, a fragrant offering and sacrifice to God" (Eph 5:2). This lush sacrificial image, with technical language ("fragrant offering and sacrifice") taken from the Pentateuch, is used with more subtlety, and with reference to believers, by Paul himself ("we are the aroma of Christ to God," 2 Cor 2:15). The vice list that follows, condemning "fornication and impurity . . . greed . . . obscene, silly, or vulgar talk" (5:3-5), is modeled on the one in Colossians 3:5-8. The dependence on Colossians is obvious: "because of these things the wrath of God comes" (5:6); "On account of these the wrath of God is coming" (Col 3:6). Believers must show they are not with "those who are disobedient"; they are to live "as children of light," producing "all that is good and right and true" (5:6-9). This means nonparticipation in all "works of darkness," which will be exposed by the light (5:11, 13). A church hymn is used to finalize this point: "Sleeper, awake! Rise from the dead, and Christ will shine on you" (5:14). The advice continues: believers are to be careful, not foolish; to seek the will of God, to avoid debauchery (evidently an actual option), to sing spiritual songs to one another (5:15-19).

The structured household code, as such, begins with the advice to "be subject to one another" (5:21), but in particular, "Wives, be subject to your husbands as to the Lord. For the husband is the head of the wife just as Christ is the head of the church" (5:22-23). This goes beyond what Paul said in 1 Corinthians 11:3 ("the husband is the head of his wife, and God is the head of Christ"). Paul had not used the strong word *hypotassō,* "submit" (not counting the probable interpolation at 1 Cor 14:34). But Colossians had used it: "Wives, be subject to your husbands" (Col 3:18). Lest the point be missed, Ephesians repeats it in 5:24. There is advice to husbands as well, but not to *submit:* "Husbands, love your wives, just as Christ loved the church and gave himself up for her" (5:25). They "should love their wives as they do their own bodies" (5:28). They should love them and care for them "just as Christ does for the church" (5:29). The man has the Christ-role in this relationship. Paul may have the same attitude, but his remarks in 1 Corinthians 11 are stressing church orderliness rather than submission in the home. It may not have been possible to expect the women of Corinth to be submissive! But the orthodox wing of the deutero-Pauline church of a generation later was considerably more conservative, and did expect women to fit into traditional roles.

Children are not exempt from the controlling advice. Fathers are not to provoke their children, but children need to obey and respect their parents (6:1-4, as in Col 3:20-21). As before, unequal social relationships are to be ameliorated by mutual consideration, but the basic inequality is not challenged. So also, "slaves, obey your earthly masters . . . not only while being watched" (6:5-6, in almost identical wording to Col 3:22). One serves humans as though serving the Lord, and trusts in due compensation in the afterlife (6:7-8). Masters are not to be bullies, since "you have the same Master in heaven" (6:9, as Col 4:1). It is God who gives strength (6:10).

Martial imagery is used for this. The believer puts on armor (6:11, 13), "for our struggle is not against enemies of blood and flesh, but against the rulers, against the authorities, against the cosmic powers of this present darkness, against the spiritual forces of evil in the heavenly places" (6:12). From the "rulers and authorities" of Colossians 2:15, Ephesians gives an expanded list of four kinds of powers, as was also done at 1:21, but with two differences. The list in 1:21 ("rule and authority and power and dominion") shares three elements with the list in Colossians 1:16, where Jesus is their creator—a major difference from Ephesians. Where Colossians had shown Christ asserting his authority over these principalities and powers, Ephesians 6:12 shows them as still dangerous and powerfully evil. Ephesians 1:20-21 says Christ was placed over all rule and authority and power and dominion, but says nothing about bringing them into line, as Colossians does (he conquers them, 2:15; he is their "head," 2:10). The revelation of Gentile-inclusion to the "rulers and authorities" in Ephesians 3:10 does not necessarily mean that these authorities are brought into line. It may just mean that they are being shown the rules: they will not be allowed to prevent Gentile inclusion.

The believer in Ephesians is at war with the heavenly principalities and must have truth as a belt, "the breastplate of righteousness," "whatever will make you ready" as shoes, "the shield of faith," and the helmet of salvation in order to resist the "flaming arrows of the evil one" (6:14-17). The church must be vigilant and prayerful (6:18), knowing that peace, love, and faith come from God and Christ (6:23). The author, and presumably the audience, perceive the church to be under a form of spiritual attack. Believers need strengthening.

Tychicus brings the letter, "to encourage your hearts" (6:21-22, exactly as in Col 4:7-8).

Chapter 10

The
Pastoral Epistles

The majority of scholars group 1 Timothy, 2 Timothy, and Titus together and attribute them to an author or authors in the Pauline tradition, a generation or two after Paul's time. The roles of overseers, deacons, and elders are emerging as distinct church offices in these letters in ways that are not in evidence in Paul's letters. While Paul had emphasized consideration and understanding between groups in the church, the author of the Pastorals is alarmed by the danger of independent conversation or speculation by, especially, "the older women" or "old wives" (Titus 2:3; 1 Tim 4:7; cf. 2 Tim 3:6) but also younger women (1 Tim 5:11-14; Titus 2:4-5), older men (1 Tim 5:1; Titus 2:2), younger men (1 Tim 5:1; Titus 2:6), "those of the circumcision," i.e., Jewish Christians (Titus 1:10), and some kind of dangerous "teachers" (2 Tim 4:3; 1 Tim 1:7; 4:1). In a line that could not possibly be more un-Pauline, one of the letters says "[women] will be saved through childbearing (*teknogonia*)" (1 Tim 2:15).

The Pastorals come from a circle of the inheritors of Paul, but they are not the only ones who tried to lay claim to the Pauline tradition. First Timothy gives us some hints as to the nature of the rival groups, as we will see.

FIRST TIMOTHY

Authority Issues: Chapters 1–2

This epistle claims to be written by "Paul, an apostle of Christ Jesus" (similar to 1 Cor 1:1) "to Timothy, my loyal child in the faith" (1:1-2). The author gets right to his concern, telling "Timothy" to "remain in Ephesus so that you may instruct certain people not to teach any different doctrine, and not to occupy themselves with myths and endless genealogies" (1:3-4). The Pastor (as scholars sometimes refer to the unknown author) coins a new word, the verb *heterodidaskalō* ("false-doctrine-teaching"). The problem with this false teaching is not only its content but its motives. The "divine training" stands in contrast, because "the aim of such instruction is love that comes from a pure heart, a good conscience, and sincere faith" (1:4-5). It is difficult to learn much about the opposing teaching from most of the comments made about it; it is "meaningless talk" (1:6) consisting of "controversy and . . . disputes about words" (6:4), even "profane chatter" (6:20). Thus we are grateful to get a hint of its actual content, as we do when we hear that these persons are "desiring to be teachers of the law" (1:7), which tells us it is probably a form of Jewish Christianity. The Pastor approves of the Law "if one uses it legitimately" (1:8), since it was not made for the righteous but "for the lawless and disobedient . . . for the unholy and profane, for those who kill their father or mother . . . sodomites, slave traders, liars . . . and whatever else is contrary to the sound teaching" (1:9-10). Here "teaching" evidently refers to ethical teaching, which is being disobeyed by liars and mother-killers.

"Sound teaching," which, in the nominative case would be *hygiainousa didaskalia*, and "sound words" are expressions frequently repeated in the Pastorals. The phrase is used to refer to moral teachings or rules, as here; to the Christian teaching as a whole, as in 2 Timothy 1:13; 4:3; Titus 1:9; or to teachings about keeping to one's social station, as in 1 Timothy 6:1-3, where "sound words" and "the teaching" include the demand that slaves not slack off just because they have Christian masters, and in Titus 2:1-5, where "sound doctrine" means self-control, temperance, and chastity. Unsound teaching is socially disturbing; it is upsetting "whole families" (Titus 1:11), leading to "disputes . . . envy, dissension" (1 Tim 6:4), and causing women to become unchaste or get out of their husbands' control (Titus 2:5).

The discussion of proper, controlled, and inoffensive behavior can also lead to a depiction of God and salvation. A believer should "lead a quiet and peaceable life," should offer prayers "for kings and all who are in high positions" (1 Tim 2:2). This pleases "God our savior, who desires everyone to be saved" (2:3-4).

> For there is one God;
>   there is also one mediator between God and humankind,
> Christ Jesus, himself human,
>   who gave himself a ransom for all. (1 Tim 2:5-6)

This has the sound of a doctrinal formula. Although "ransom" is a metaphor, it appears that it is being taken quite literally. The creative and mixed metaphors of Paul have been stripped down to one metaphor at a time and hardened into doctrinal formulas. Although the image is very Pauline, new terms have emerged. "Mediator" (*mesitēs*) occurs in Paul's letters only in reference to Moses (Gal 3:19-20), but it is used for Jesus in Hebrews 8:6; 9:15; 12:24. "Ransom" (*antilytron*) reminds us of the (*agorazō*) passages in 1 Corinthians 6:20; Galatians 3:13 and of the *lytron* passage in Mark 10:45.[1] The language of salvation is becoming standardized; the Savior has a technical title (Mediator), as in another post-Pauline letter (Hebrews), and the saving act may have a technical name (ransom, which occurs in a verbal form in Titus 2:14 and in a related noun form in Heb 9:12).

Further, "Paul" has been turned into a stern overseer. He orders women to adorn themselves "modestly and decently in suitable clothing, not with their hair braided, or with gold, pearls, or expensive clothes" (1 Tim 2:9), which tells us that some of the troublesome, independent-minded women are wealthy.[2] Rather,

> Let a woman learn in silence with full submission. I permit no woman to teach or to have authority over a man; she is to keep silent. For Adam was formed first, then Eve; and Adam was not deceived, but the woman was deceived and became a transgressor. (1 Tim 2:11-14)

End of discussion! Primal history has determined that women come second. This leaves no room for any women apostles or coworkers in *this* Paul's world, unlike in Romans 16. Rather, young women need to get married, for "she will be saved through childbearing" (2:15) and, again, with "modesty" (NRSV) or "self-control" (NAB). In chapter 5 there will be provision for saintly and chaste widows, but there is no mention of women prophets or preachers.

Church Offices: Chapter 3

It may come as a shock to some readers that "a bishop must be above reproach, married only once, temperate, sensible, respectable" (3:2). The

---

1. Occurring in the context of a saying about the Son of Man coming to serve others. The parallel passage in Luke 22:27 also focuses on service but does not contain the ransom term.

2. Margaret Y. MacDonald, *The Pauline Churches: A Socio-historical Study of Institutionalization in the Pauline and Deutero-Pauline Writings* (Cambridge: Cambridge University Press, 1988), 199.

choice of the word "bishop" is misleading, since that evokes the concept of a later time in church history. "Overseer" (NIV, NASB) would be a better translation of the word *episkopos* for this early period. It refers to the leader of an individual congregation. This and other passages in the Pastoral Epistles do indeed witness to the very earliest stages in the emergence of Christian clergy (and the word *episkopos* does eventually come to mean "bishop"), but we are not yet at the stage of a priesthood, much less a celibate priesthood. The Pastorals do not share Paul's high regard for celibacy.

Self-restraint and decorum are of utmost importance. The overseer must not be a drunkard, aggressive, or a lover of money, but must be gentle (3:3). "He must manage his own household well, keeping his children submissive and respectful in every way" (3:4). *Everyone* must be under control; this is the main social message of the Pastoral Epistles. The author is hyper-conscious of how Christians look to outsiders: "He must be well thought of by outsiders" (3:7), probably a strategy that emerged as a response to increasing hostility from outsiders. The rules for deacons (the Greek signifies someone who serves or assists) are the same as for overseers: dignified, not drinkers, not greedy, having clear consciences, married only once, managing their children well (3:8-9, 12). Additionally, they are subjected to some sort of test before they can serve (3:10). Women should also be dignified and temperate (3:11); there is no indication of the role these women are playing, but one may guess that they are teaching other women.

Imitating what occurs in some Pauline letters, the author has "Paul" say, "I hope to come to you soon, but . . . if I am delayed, you may know how one ought to behave in the household of God, which is the church" (3:14-15). This last image is not found in Paul, but is a good characterization of the view of the church as represented by Ephesians, the Pastoral Epistles, Hebrews, and 1 Peter (Eph 2:22; 2 Tim 2:20; Heb 3:4-6; 1 Pet 2:5), each of which has a lengthy household code. If overseers and deacons are to tightly manage their households, and if the church is a household, then "the ecclesiastical hierarchy becomes closely associated with the domestic hierarchy, with the ideology for the household . . . becoming an ideology for the church."[3] The new message of Christianity is here being wedded to the old message of the strict patriarchal household, which means the Christian message is being changed, domesticated.

3. David G. Horrell, *The Social Ethos of the Corinthian Correspondence: Interests and Ideology from 1 Corinthians to 1 Clement* (Edinburgh: T&T Clark, 1996), 287.

The third church office is mentioned in the next chapter, when Timothy is exhorted: "Do not neglect the gift that is in you, which was given to you through prophecy with the laying on of hands by the council of elders" (4:14). The *presbyteroi* are the elders. There seems to be a body of male elders in the congregation who ordain both the deacons and the overseer. These appear to be three distinct church offices.

This is the place to mention the one verse in the undisputed letters of Paul that mentions "bishops and deacons" (NRSV) or "overseers and deacons" (NIV), namely Philippians 1:1, but the reference is probably not to actual church "offices" there. Philippi would have only one overseer if it followed the Pastorals model, but the word is in the plural in Philippians, where it probably just means "leaders." Deacon may indeed have been a recognized church role in Paul's own time (Rom 16:1), though it usually means just "servant" (Rom 15:8; Gal 2:17). There is no hint of the hierarchical organization we see in the Pastorals.

Defaming the Enemies: Chapter 4

In this chapter "Paul" attacks false believers in his own day and in the future (the real author's present). These people are led astray by "deceitful spirits and teachings of demons, through the hypocrisy of liars" (4:1-2). There will be no ecumenical roundtable here. The group being attacked has an emphasis on asceticism ("they forbid marriage," 4:3) and has some kind of theology that can be attacked as "profane myths" (4:7). This has led some scholars to think that the enemies are a Gnostic Christian group, and this is possible, but not certain. Others think the opponents are a Jewish Christian group, because of the mention of law in 1:9-11 and because of food restrictions: they "demand abstinence from foods, which God created to be received with thanksgiving" (4:3). In order to achieve sufficient differentiation from the other group, Timothy must "put these instructions before the brothers and sisters . . . these are the things you must insist on and teach" (4:6, 11). That slogan of conformity, "sound teaching," occurs again: one must be "nourished on the words of the faith and of the sound teaching that you have followed" (4:6). Sound teaching defines and differentiates one's own group from the wrong group.

A biblical phrase, "the living God," is important for the Pastor. He had used it in 3:15 ("church of the living God"), and now he uses it again: "we have our hope set on the living God, who is the Savior of all people"

(4:10).[4] Timothy, for and with the congregation, is to "give attention to the public reading of scripture, to exhorting, to teaching. . . . devote yourself to them" (4:13, 15). Attending to the teaching will result in one's own salvation and in that of "your hearers" (4:16).

Fighting for Pauline Authority

After Paul's lifetime there was evidently a heated dispute within and between Pauline churches, with different groups and authors, including the Pastor, claiming to be the legitimate heirs of the Pauline tradition. The different heirs of Paul become clearer when we look at a wide body of literature emanating from these circles. We can make some guesses about the Pastor's foes based on what is in 1 Timothy, but we get a bigger picture when we look at other works that survive from the ancient world. The best place to start is with the *Acts of Paul,* which assembles several ancient works, including the second-century writing called *The Acts of Thecla,* which speak of a very radical Paul who draws women away from marriage into asceticism. Thecla is a betrothed woman who hears Paul preaching "blessed are those who keep the flesh chaste" (*Acts Thec.* 5). She decides to leave her fiancé and devote herself to the saintly life. The angry fiancé gets her arrested and the equally angry city governor orders her burnt at the stake, but God sends a thunderstorm to douse the fire. A later attempt to have her killed in the arena in Antioch, against the protests of the women in the city, is thwarted when the lioness becomes docile and friendly.[5] Females, even an animal, are mostly sympathetic to Thecla's stance (the sole exception being Thecla's own mother), while the men are deeply threatened. Stories of Thecla's renunciation of marriage and of her repeated rescues from martyrdom through God's miraculous intervention were already circulating orally throughout Asia Minor, Syria, and Egypt before a certain deacon put them down in writing.[6] This is probably the wing of the Pauline movement the Pastor is attacking when he speaks of "forbidding marriage," and against which he offers salvation through childbearing (1 Tim 4:3; 2:15). The Thecla wing, if we may call it

---

4. See Deut 5:26; Josh 3:10; 1 Sam 17:26; 2 Kgs 19:16; Jer 10:10 (all of which involve divine violence or the threat of it); Jer 23:36; Dan 6:27; Hos 2:1 (NRSV 1:10).

5. Bart D. Ehrman, *Lost Christianities: The Battles for Scripture and the Faiths We Never Knew* (Oxford: Oxford University Press, 2003), 29, 33–35.

6. Ibid., 29, 36.

that, honored women ascetics, not just Thecla, as heroes and leaders of the faith, and evidently allowed women to teach and baptize,[7] in sharp contrast to the advice of 1 Timothy 2:11-12; Titus 2:5 that women be quiet and submit to their husbands (cf. also Col 3:18; Eph 5:22).

In 2 Timothy 3:6 there is a warning against teachers who make captives of "little women" (the literal translation of *gynaikaria*), which "is precisely what Paul does with Thecla" in *The Acts of Thecla*.[8] It may be that the Pastorals "were written to contradict the image of Paul in popular legends . . . told by women to justify their celibate ministries."[9]

Frances Young offers the very plausible suggestion that there were three distinct groups competing for the Pauline tradition: a strongly ascetic apocalyptic group at odds with surrounding society (such as we see in *The Acts of Thecla*), a more cautious and non-ascetic group that retained eschatological hope but tried to avoid arousing the anxieties of surrounding society (which we see in the Pastoral Epistles), and Gnosticizing groups that believed they had already experienced resurrection, and that had contempt for surrounding society (such as we see in Gnostic texts, though most of them are from slightly later, the second through fifth centuries).[10]

The Pastoral Epistles attempt to take a more world-conforming path, rejecting any "teachings, either of a too spiritual and other-worldly kind (gnostic) or of too radical and social disruptive kind (as in the Apocryphal Acts)."[11] Apocalyptic, while not completely absent from the Pastorals, is greatly reduced, and there is an attempt not to look provocative to surrounding society. Both the intellectualizing Gnostics and the marriage-avoiding ascetics were contemptuous of the world, and were perceived as provocative.

The socially cautious stance of the Pastorals becomes more understandable the more one considers the confrontational stance of the other two groups and the political situation at the end of the first century. The Gnostics were anti-traditional and were perceived as arrogant. They thought they possessed hidden wisdom that the masses were too igno-

---

7. Ibid., 35, 37.

8. Dennis Ronald MacDonald, *The Legend and the Apostle: The Battle for Paul in Story and Canon* (Philadelphia: Westminster, 1983), 57.

9. Ibid., 76–77.

10. Frances Young, *The Theology of the Pastoral Epistles* (Cambridge: Cambridge University Press, 1994), 14–23.

11. Ibid., 40.

rant to understand. Thus the Gnostics tended to produce small isolated groups. For different reasons, the Thecla-wing ascetics were perceived as upsetting to the way of the world, breaking up families and creating dissension. Further, they expressed "anti-Roman hostility."[12] This was considerably more dangerous than the attitudes of a few Gnostic intellectuals, and the Thecla wing was persecuted. The Pastor seeks to avoid both provocation and isolation, a policy that seems to look sensible, however tiresome his authoritarian and conformist ethic. The Pastor's position is the one that won out, socially. It may be that the Thecla wing reached its most powerful manifestation in the movement known as Montanists from the visionary Montanus, who was known to have annulled some marriages.[13] Montanus' co-leaders were female prophets who believed they were channeling the Holy Spirit. The movement was very important for a few centuries but seems to have been overtaken by churches that were better organized and less confrontational—the approach adopted in the Pastorals.

The ancient world was very conservative as regards people claiming to have religious authority. One way to get an audience for one's religious writings was to attribute them to a known authority; thus there were several late documents claiming to be written by Plato. In the Jewish tradition the equivalent was to pass one's writing off as the *Apocalypse of Abraham* or the *Testament of Moses* or as a revelation of Enoch. However, if one wanted to claim Pauline authority one would need to write a Pauline letter. Third Corinthians was one such forged letter; later there was a so-called letter to the Laodiceans. The most successful of such pseudepigraphical letters, however, if our theory is correct, were the Pastoral Epistles.

The Pastorals were not universally recognized, however, in the period before a list of books to be respected and read in the churches (what we call the NT), was collected (mid-fourth century). The influential Gnostic-leaning preacher, Marcion, did not use them, and they were probably not included in the earliest known collection of Pauline letters, the Chester Beatty papyrus, $\mathfrak{P}$46.[14] But the very important church father Irenaeus (ca. 180 CE) did use them, and the subsequent church has considered them to be authored by Paul. In fact, the Pastorals have dominated the way the church has thought of Paul. Most Christians imagine the firm

12. MacDonald, *Legend and the Apostle*, 66.
13. Ibid., 58.
14. Young, *Theology of the Pastoral Epistles*, 142.

and proper Paul of the Pastorals, not the tongues-praying Paul of 1 Corinthians 14:18, the visionary Paul of 2 Corinthians 12:2, the ascetic Paul
of Romans 8:6-13, or the status-criticizing Paul of 1 Corinthians 1:27-31
and 4:7-14. An institutional church could not accept a complex and many-
sided Paul. It domesticated Paul and made him a saintly disciplinarian
who approved of the very authority structure that had evolved. Are we
ready, even yet, for a many-sided Paul?

Orderly Roles and Ethical Conduct: Chapters 5–6

This chapter begins with advice that leaders be considerate and respectful when correcting people in the congregation. "[Speak to] younger men
as brothers, to older women as mothers" (5:1-2). But there is a bite to some
of these remarks: "Honor widows who are really widows" (5:3). The
widows evidently received financial support from the church (5:16), and
some who were not "really" widows had managed to get into the group.
If they have offspring, those children should "learn their religious duty
to their own family" (5:4); they are worse than unbelievers if they do not
support their own (5:8). But the widow who is all alone should devote
herself to prayer and be irreproachable (5:5, 7). Again there is an awareness of what others might say. Younger women are trouble because of
"their sensual desires" (5:11). They become "idle . . . but also gossips
and busybodies, saying what they should not say" (5:13). Let them "marry,
bear children, and manage their households, so as to give the adversary
no occasion to revile us" (5:14). A widow must be over sixty, only married
once, and most importantly, have a good reputation (5:9-10).

Presbyters deserve honor, especially those who preach and teach
(5:17-18). There is public reprimand for those who do wrong, but no
accusation against a presbyter is to be accepted without two or three
witnesses (5:19-20). The Pastor charges the leaders "in the presence of
God and of Christ Jesus and of the elect angels" (a most un-Pauline
expression) to show no favoritism (5:21). In another anti-ascetic move,
the Pastor advises Timothy to "take a little wine for the sake of your
stomach" (5:23).

Chapter 6 is a household code that bears some resemblance to those
of Colossians and Ephesians but is even more conservative; it never
advises any restraint for slave owners (such as the fairness and no-bul-
lying rules in Col 4:1; Eph 6:9). All the advice is for slaves, who must
respect their masters for the sake of the reputation of "the teaching," and
must not take advantage of Christian masters (6:1-2). Anyone who

teaches differently "does not agree with the sound words of our Lord Jesus Christ" (6:3). Evidently sound teaching concerns social order and hierarchy, not just doctrinal teaching. Fundamentalists who want absolute literalness should be asked whether this includes the instructions to slaves.

The Pastor says any dissent from this order is conceited, argumentative, envious, and selfish (6:4-5). Contented piety is gain; we came into the world with nothing, and we will leave with nothing (6:6-7). If you have food and clothing, be content (6:8). "For the love of money is a root of all kinds of evil" (6:10 NRSV)[15]—now popularly remembered and repeated in a form based on the KJV, "money is the root of all evil," but even the KJV correctly had "the love of money," not just "money." This demonstrates how oral tradition often changes and replaces what was originally said.

Self-effacing values like patience and gentleness are appropriate for "Timothy" and all the Timothies who might read this epistle (6:11). What follows seems to describe a public confession associated with ordination. Timothy is to remember that "you made the good confession in the presence of many witnesses" (6:12, recalling the laying-on-of-hands passage in 4:14). The Pastor associates this with some confession of Jesus, "who in his testimony before Pontius Pilate made the good confession" (6:13). We can only guess what confession Jesus is thought to have given before Pontius Pilate. It could indicate Jesus' direct (Mark 14:62) or roundabout (Matt 26:63-64) acknowledgment of his messiahship before Pilate, and that the deacon, in being ordained, makes a public confession of Jesus as Messiah. Courage is being commanded ("fight the good fight of the faith," 6:12), as well as doctrinal conservatism ("guard what has been entrusted to you. . . . some have missed the mark as regards the faith," 6:20, 21), and social conservatism ("keep the commandment without spot or blame . . . avoid . . . profane chatter," 6:14, 20). "Blame" is a socially shameful experience, and "chatter" is an insulting characterization, much to be guarded against, according to the Pastor. The Pastor also wants Timothy to avoid "what is falsely called knowledge [*gnōsis*]," which is a deviation from the faith (6:20-21). This probably is a reference to Gnostics, or proto-Gnostics (before any complex Gnostic philosophies have developed).

The gap between rich and poor is not questioned in any way, but the rich need to take care of the poor (6:17-19). This has been called "the

---

15. A more accurate translation than NAB's "*the* root."

ethos of love-patriarchalism."[16] When we emphasize the authoritarian nature of control in the Pastor's church we do not imply an absence of care for others; we merely describe the structure and the tight control over discourse.

SECOND TIMOTHY

Guarding the Sound Words: Chapters 1–2

There is a strong personal touch in 2 Timothy, and an attention to Pauline details: "me his prisoner . . . I suffer . . . my chain" (1:8, 12, 16). The author says, "Recalling your tears, I long to see you"; he recalls the "sincere faith" of Timothy's mother and grandmother (1:4-5). But in this letter Timothy's ordination took place "through the laying on of my hands" (1:6), not the presbyters' hands (*contra* 1 Tim 4:14; 6:12).

Exhortation to courage is an important part of this letter. "I remind you to rekindle the gift of God . . . for God did not give us a spirit of cowardice, but rather a spirit of power and of love and of self-discipline. Do not be ashamed, then, of the testimony about our Lord" (1:6-8). Believers were called "with a holy calling . . . before the ages began" (1:9). The "Savior Christ Jesus . . . abolished death and brought life and immortality to light through the gospel" (1:10). Notice that it is through the *Gospel,* not through the death, as it would have been for Paul. This shows a heightened concept of the Gospel as saving doctrine. We also can see that 2 Timothy uses "Savior" for Jesus, while 1 Timothy used "Savior" for God (1:1; 2:3, 10; 4:10). (In Titus the term is applied to both God and Jesus.)[17] This suggests different authorship for the three letters, despite the significant similarity of viewpoint and the repetition of "sound teaching" and similar terms. One such occurs in 2 Timothy 1:13: "Hold to the standard of sound teaching that you have heard from me." The advice is to *conserve:* "Guard the good treasure" (1:14).

Timothy should be ready to bear hardship "like a good soldier of Christ Jesus" (2:3). Christian iconography has often depicted Timothy as a soldier, although the author soon switches to an athletic metaphor

16. I agree with Horrell that the term is useful for the deutero-Pauline period but is completely inappropriate as a description of Paul's own ethic (*Social Ethos,* 154–55, 282–83). The "patriarchal trajectory of Pauline Christianity" may be due to the "male householders" and others who inherited control of the Pauline churches after Paul's death (290–91).

17. See Young, *Theology of the Pastoral Epistles,* 53.

("competing according to the rules," 2:5), and then to a farming metaphor (getting a share of the crop, 2:6). The author mentions Christ, raised from the dead, but it is specifically "my gospel, for which I suffer hardship" (2:8-9). A conceptual shift has taken place: Paul would suffer for Christ; this author suffers for the Gospel.

There is a passage that sounds like Romans 6 ("The saying is sure: If we have died with him, we will also live with him," 2:11), but the author is aware of it as an established *saying*, indicating a passage of time since it was first said. "We will also reign with him," or be denied if we have denied him (2:12), echoes the gospels (Matt 19:28; 10:33; Mark 8:38).

The silencing of religious disputes is as important in this letter as in 1 Timothy: "avoid wrangling over words. . . . have nothing to do with stupid and senseless controversies" (2:14, 23). It is better to be "a worker who has no need to be ashamed," avoiding "profane chatter" (2:15-16). Keep your nose to the grindstone and stop the chatter! Be a useful vessel, whether of silver or of clay (2:20). Some of the enemies are those who are "claiming that the resurrection has already taken place" (2:18). Do not quarrel with them, but gently correct them, and they may come "to know the truth, and . . . escape from the snare of the devil" (2:24-26).

Fighting for the Tradition: Chapters 3–4

Chapter 3 focuses on dangers "in the last days" (the author's present). The skill of the pseudepigrapher is shown in his ability to simulate Paul's contemporary situation while really attacking the author's own ideological enemies.[18] The polemical rhetoric is even stronger than that in 1 Timothy 4. "People will be lovers of themselves . . . arrogant, abusive, disobedient to their parents . . . profligates . . . treacherous, reckless . . . holding to the outward form of godliness but denying its power" (3:2-5). They "make their way into households and captivate women" who are "always being instructed and can never arrive at a knowledge of the truth" (3:6-7). Evidently these women need the protection of the patriarch-Pastor. Eternal vigilance is needed. Enemies, "people of corrupt mind," are acting upon members of the congregation (3:8).

This is a fight for the Pauline tradition. "You have observed my teaching," but there are reckless and improper interpretations of that teaching; therefore, "continue in what you have learned and firmly believed" (3:10, 14). In another famous but often misquoted passage, the author says,

18. Richard Bauckham, "Pseudo-Apostolic Letters," *JBL* 107 (1988): 493.

"All scripture is inspired by God and is useful for teaching, for reproof, for correction, and for training in righteousness" (3:16). The word for "inspired" means literally "God-breathed." At that time "Scripture" would mean the Septuagint, but here it might also include a collection of Pauline letters that these churches are using and that, for these *particular* churches, is functioning as Scripture (long before there is an agreed-upon "New Testament").

The "Timothy" addressed in this letter (standing for preachers and overseers) is exhorted to "proclaim the message," to "convince, rebuke, and encourage" (4:2). The "Paul" of this letter foresees that "the time will come when people will not put up with sound doctrine but having itching ears, they will accumulate for themselves teachers to suit their own desires and will turn away from listening to the truth and wander away to myths" (4:3-4). There must be some appeal to the foes' teaching. It is—or it "will" be—drawing people away from the Pastor's sound teaching. The enemy teachers are popular enough to be "accumulated," and their teaching is appealing enough to satisfy "itching ears." Timothy should keep preaching the Pauline Gospel. Using a phrase from Philippians 2:17, the author is "already being poured out as a libation" (4:6), and the image of death is used very effectively here, picturing a Paul preparing to be martyred: "I have fought the good fight, I have finished the race, I have kept the faith. From now on there is reserved for me the crown of righteousness" (4:7-8). The author names those who have been loyal or disloyal; Demas deserted him; Luke is loyal; he asks for Mark to be sent to him (4:10-11). One wonders whether this group possessed Mark's gospel. In another indication of reverence for the Pauline letters, even their physical form, the author has Paul ask that "the books, and above all the parchments" be brought to him (4:13). Another enemy is Alexander (4:14; cf. 1 Tim 1:20), and one can only wonder whether this was a figure important to one of the competing wings of the Pauline tradition: "beware of him" (4:15).

Verse 16 speaks of Paul's being deserted at his "first defense," which may be meant to refer to Acts 22. More names well known to us ("Prisca and Aquila . . . Erastus," 4:19-20) and others unknown to us ("Eubulus, Pudens, Linus, Claudia," 4:21) are dropped as the letter draws to a close.

If possible, 2 Timothy is even more focused on social and factional issues in the church than 1 Timothy is, and makes more of an effort to present a believable portrait of a Paul who, while preparing himself to die, is moved to prophesy of haughty and persuasive teachers in the future. It spends no time defining the roles of church leaders, as 1 Timothy does. Perhaps those roles have become clearer, and it is more pressing to fight the rival preachers, who are causing too much discussion and speculation, especially among the women.

TITUS

Sound Doctrine to Silence Idle Talk: Chapter 1

The Pastoral Paul writes to "Titus, my loyal child in the faith we share" (1:4) in this letter, for the purpose of "the knowledge of the truth that is in accordance with godliness" (1:1). This Titus has been sent to "appoint elders in every town," ones who are "blameless, married only once, whose children are believers" (1:5-6). These criteria for presbyters are the same as the criteria for overseers in 1 Timothy 3:2-6, which leads some scholars to think that the office of overseer/bishop is still evolving, and that the overseer at this point is "simply the president of a college of elders."[19] The presbyter being appointed in Titus 1:5, then, is a chief presbyter or overseer. This makes sense, since there would be no need for an outsider to appoint presbyters (a congregation would know who its own elders were), but may need some nudging to choose an overseer. The argument is probably clinched by the fact that the author switches over to referring to the individual as "bishop" in 1:7; he is "not . . . addicted to wine or violent or greedy for gain," and so on. Crucially, he is "able both to preach with sound doctrine and to refute those who contradict it" (1:9).

Thus "sound doctrine" is characteristic of a proper hierarch. Sound doctrine attempts to correct "rebellious people, idle talkers and deceivers, especially those of the circumcision," who "are upsetting whole families" (1:10-11). This is the only place in the Pastorals that zeroes in on Jewish Christians, but the problem is not the same as Paul's a generation earlier; this has nothing to do with circumcision or works of the Law. Rather, the likely reference of "Jewish myths" (1:14) is gnosticizing speculation, similar to the "myths" and "speculations" of 1 Timothy 1:4 and "the contradictions of what is falsely called knowledge [*gnōsis*]" of 1 Timothy 6:20.[20] Jewish Gnosticism lies behind the earliest Christian Gnosticism or proto-Gnosticism.

Titus is supposed to be a bishop of Crete, so the ones who are being misled by the Jewish Christians are Cretans. In one of the strangest and

---

19. Young, *Theology of the Pastoral Epistles*, 98. She sees the first evidence of a powerful "monoepiscopate" in the letters of Ignatius, for which we have a section below.

20. William W. Meissner, *The Cultic Origins of Christianity: The Dynamics of Religious Development* (Collegeville, MN: Liturgical Press, 2000), 171.

most embarrassing sayings of the NT we are told that one of their own "said, 'Cretans are always liars, vicious brutes, lazy gluttons.' That testimony is true" (1:12-13). It turns out that this axiom was so common that the word "to Cretanize" was coined, meaning to lie.[21] What is shocking is that a biblical author should repeat such a vulgarity, labeling a whole nation lazy and gluttonous. However, the statement seems to be ironic. The quotation comes from "their very own prophet" (1:12)—but if a Cretan is saying that all Cretans are liars, he would have to be *lying*! This is called the liar's paradox, something the Stoics used in their discussions of reasoning and logic.[22]

The author of Titus, then, may be using this quotation in support of his attack on those who abuse speech and create controversies.[23] He prefers straight talk: "rebuke them sharply, so that they may become sound in the faith" (1:13). Who is *not* being admonished in the Pastoral Epistles? In this case it is in order to get them to ignore "Jewish myths or . . . commandments," including those concerning defilement (1:14-15). Were these Jewish teachers also using Stoic logical paradoxes? This is not likely. Probably the author is attacking two groups at once, both of whom engage in unsound speech, from his point of view.

Avoid Controversy and Argument: Chapters 2–3

The reader can hardly fail to get the point, but the point will be repeated anyway: "teach what is consistent with sound doctrine" (2:1), which in this case means quietness and contentedness with one's assigned role. The older men should be temperate and sound in faith (2:2). The older women must not be slanderers or drinkers (2:3); they should teach the younger women to "love their husbands, to love their children, to be self-controlled . . . being submissive to their husbands" (2:4-5). Why?—"so that the word of God may not be discredited" (2:5). As in 1 Timothy there is a sharp concern that Christians not be viewed negatively by outsiders. Arguments with nonbelievers should end so that the opponent is "put to shame, having nothing evil to say of us" (2:8).

The stress on marrying off the younger women and getting them under control strongly implies that the rival teaching was releasing women from

21. Reflected in Plutarch, Lucian, and others (Patrick Gray, "The Liar Paradox and the Letter to Titus," *CBQ* 69 [2007]: 302).
22. Ibid., 304–7.
23. Ibid., 310–11.

marriage and from "control." People like the author were embarrassed by the result, and the talk it stimulated. Slaves, too, must know their place: "to be submissive to their masters and to give satisfaction in every respect; they are not to talk back" (2:9). This confronts us with the fact that there are commandments in the Bible we can no longer follow, since they are linked to outmoded social systems and outdated household codes. Perhaps we can preserve the underlying instinct for ethical and considerate behavior, to show "complete and perfect fidelity" (2:10) toward others, "and in the present age to live lives that are self-controlled, upright, and godly" (2:12). This is the policy the author commends in the time of waiting for the *parousia:* "while we wait for the blessed hope and the manifestation of the glory of our great God and Savior, Jesus Christ" (2:13).

Atonement is present, too: "who gave himself for us that he might redeem us from all iniquity and purify for himself a people as his own" (2:14). This notion of sanctifying a people may be reworking the OT idea of the election and sanctification of Israel (Exod 19:5; Deut 26:18; Ezek 36:24-25; Mal 3:17).[24] In any case, the import is to tell believers "to be subject to rulers and authorities, to be obedient," to "speak evil of no one, to be gentle" and no longer the "slaves to various passions and pleasures" (3:1-3). They are to remember the mercy of God, and their baptism, "the water of rebirth and renewal by the Holy Spirit" (3:4-5). This was "so that, having been justified by his grace, we might become heirs according to the hope of eternal life" (3:7)—an actual bit of Pauline theology! Not as Pauline, although good advice, is the instruction "to devote themselves to good works" (3:8, 14). But, again, part of what this means is avoiding certain discussions: "Avoid stupid controversies . . . and quarrels about the law" (3:9). Walk away from such people if they continue arguing (3:10-11). The ever-present Tychicus (Col 4:7; Eph 6:21; 2 Tim 4:12) will be sent to the recipients (3:12).

The send-off says, "Greet those who love us in the faith" (3:15), which might indicate that there are some in the congregation who do not love the Pastoral Paul. In fact, one wonders if some of the Thecla group or of the proto-Gnostic group were present in the churches at which these letters were aimed. If so, probably not for long.

---

24. According to Stanislas Lyonnet ("The Pauline Conception of Redemption," in John R. Sheets, ed., *The Theology of Atonement: Readings in Soteriology* [Englewood Cliffs, NJ: Prentice-Hall, 1967] 174–76), but he sees this theme in numerous NT passages, so his thesis seems overstated.

Chapter 11

Hebrews and Other Letters

The Epistle to the Hebrews is anonymous; the name of Paul is never mentioned. Its vocabulary and style are more "literary" and polished than Paul's, yet its thought is far more repetitive, lacking Paul's scope of thinking. However, because of the views of the influential church fathers Pantaenus and Clement of Alexandria, the Egyptian church came to consider it to be Pauline. Gradually, other segments of the church began treating it as a Pauline letter, largely because of its sacrificial imagery. What they seem not to have noticed is that Hebrews lacks Paul's range of different metaphors. Hebrews returns to the same sacrificial image over and over, and uses a metaphor that does not occur elsewhere in the NT: Jesus as high priest. Further, Paul never indicates that Jesus' cultic death cleanses the consciences of believers, while this is a principal point in Hebrews.

Since there is no scholarly support for Pauline authorship of Hebrews, it will not be treated chapter by chapter here, but its sacrificial theme will be examined, since any study of Paul is also a study of sacrificial imagery, and Hebrews offers us another Christian use of sacrificial imagery.

Sacrificial Salvation in Hebrews

The soteriology of Hebrews is thoroughly sacrificial, to a much greater degree than in Paul. The logic of sacrifice governs the interpretation of Christ's person, his death, and its results. Christ came "to remove away sin by the sacrifice of himself" (9:26); he "offered himself without blemish

182

to God" (9:14); his death accomplished "purification for sins" (1:3) and brought about the consecration of believers (10:10, 14). Even believers' internal reformation is a result of this sacrifice: "the blood of Christ . . . will . . . purify our conscience" (9:14; cf. 10:22).

The author asserts the limited and futile nature of the Jewish sacrificial cult, yet affirms the sacrificial principle itself: "not even the first covenant was inaugurated without blood" (9:18). Sacrificial cleansing takes place on the earthly and heavenly levels (9:22-24). Sacrificial blood sanctifies and cleanses (9:13-14, 22); the payment aspect of sacrifice is not mentioned. For the higher cleansing there is the Melchizedek order of priesthood, higher than the Levitical order (7:1-15). Christ is the priest who "enters the inner shrine behind the curtain . . . having become a high priest forever according to the order of Melchizedek" (6:19-20). Christ is the "high priest . . . undefiled, separated from sinners," yet he also "offered himself" as sacrificial victim (7:26-27). Paul never calls Christ a priest, though he does apply the priestly metaphor to himself and other believers at Romans 12:1; 15:16; Philippians 2:17; 4:18.

Hebrews makes allegorical use of many details of the sacrificial cult—the veil, the inner sanctuary, the ark of the covenant, the blood: "since we have confidence to enter the sanctuary by the blood of Jesus, by the new and living way that he opened for us through the curtain (that is, through his flesh)" (10:19-20). The literal sacrificial cult was a symbol, but also something of a barrier; it "indicates that the way into the sanctuary has not yet been disclosed," and that literal sacrifices do not cleanse the conscience (9:8-9). Yet what replaces it, Christ's death, is also a "sacrifice," an "offering" (9:26; 10:12, 14). "He entered once for all into the Holy Place . . . with his own blood" (9:12)—the heavenly sanctuary, in this case. This is considerably more detailed and extended than anything Paul does. Paul never goes into such allegorical detail.

Hebrews actually describes the ark of the covenant (9:4), culminating with "the cherubim of glory overshadowing the mercy seat" (9:5). When Paul mentions the *hilastērion* in Romans 3:25 he conflates that metaphor with two others: redemption and justification. For Paul the sacrificial metaphor is always part of a mixture of metaphors. Hebrews dwells on a single metaphor, the sacrificial one.

And yet Hebrews is one of only two NT books to directly criticize the Jewish sacrificial cult.[1] The law on sacrifices was "only a shadow"; it

---

1. Matthew is the other; in that gospel the anti-sacrificial remark of Hos 6:6 is quoted by Jesus on two occasions when arguing with his opponents' excessive attachment to ritual:

can never "make perfect those who approach" (Heb 10:1). The reasoning here is that the sacrifices are not effective because they have to be performed over and over again (9:25; 10:1-3, 11). This seems to imply a *limited* effectiveness for the sacrificial cult, but then the author bluntly denies that effectiveness when he says: "it is impossible for the blood of bulls and goats to take away sins" (10:4). In fact, Jesus himself is said to have cited an antisacrificial psalm: "when Christ came into the world, he said, 'Sacrifices and offerings you have not desired . . . in burnt offerings and sin offerings you have taken no pleasure'" (10:5-8; citing Ps 40:6-8). Christ's sacrifice made the sacrificial cult obsolete: "He abolishes the first in order to establish the second" (10:9).

The way to unify these apparently contradictory statements is to recognize that, for Hebrews, the Law has been superseded. The new covenant "has made the first one obsolete" (8:13). Christ is the new high priest, and "When there is a change in the priesthood, there is necessarily a change in the law as well" (7:12). "There is . . . the abrogation of an earlier commandment because it was weak and ineffectual" (7:18). The offering for sin is no longer necessary (10:18).

Thus sacrifice is both defended and rejected. It is a sacrificial carcass that seals us in the new covenant: "we have been sanctified through the offering of the body of Jesus Christ once for all" (10:10). The new covenant transcends the old, but it is interpreted in terms of the old. This is largely due to the fundamentally Platonic viewpoint of Hebrews, whereby the earthly temple and sacrifice are copies of the heavenly and ideal temple and sacrifice. The earthly copy, though inferior, was necessary: "It was necessary for the *sketches* of the heavenly things to be purified with these rites, but the heavenly things *themselves* need better sacrifices than these" (9:23; italics supplied). This speaks of continuity as well as transcendence. A better sacrifice is still a sacrifice.

Part of what Hebrews wants to communicate with its priestly and sacrificial metaphor is the ethics of Christ's participation in the human condition. In fact, Hebrews has more to say about the Incarnation, as such, than any other book in the NT except the Gospel of John. Some of it involves Christ *earning* his status as savior: God made "the pioneer of their salvation perfect through sufferings" (2:10). "He learned obedience

---

Matt 9:13; 12:7. In the latter instance he links the Pharisees' willingness to commit violence to their ritualism and their failure to understand the Hosea quotation. Of course, there are anti-ritual (not anti-sacrificial) implications to some spiritualizing sayings such as "circumcision is a matter of the heart" (Rom 2:29).

through what he suffered" (5:8). This perfection through suffering sounds quite Stoic, but the incarnational idea itself is not derived from Stoicism or from any other antecedent, which may be why the author has to weld it to other metaphors and ideas. Ethically, the point is Christ's (and God's) solidarity with suffering humans. Christ qualifies as a priest because he knows what we have to suffer: "For we do not have a high priest who is unable to sympathize with our weaknesses, but we have one who in every respect has been tested as we are" (4:15). It was a step down for Jesus to become incarnated, but he had to do this in order to truly sympathize with human beings:

> Therefore he had to become like his brothers and sisters in every respect, so that he might be a merciful and faithful high priest in the service of God, to make a sacrifice of atonement for the sins of the people. Because he himself was tested by what he suffered, he is able to help those who are being tested. (Heb 2:17-18)

The incarnational concept is welded to the sacrificial one. In fact, the common image of sacrifice functions as the vehicle for the (uncommon) idea of the compassionate Incarnation of the Son of God.

Paul had also spoken of the compassion of Christ—and of God—in Christ's dying for the ungodly (Rom 5:6-8), and of grace overflowing (Rom 5:20), but there is nothing about sympathetic Incarnation as a fulfillment or demonstration of Christ's qualifications. Thus the irony is that the letter that is more crude and repetitive (Hebrews) is also the one that has more to say about the Son's Incarnation being a deep participation in human life and its many tests.

Besides the fact that Hebrews is still considered Pauline by some Christians, the reason to spend time on it here is because its extensive sacrificial metaphor and its incarnational theology offer an interesting contrast and complement to Paul's much-less-developed sacrificial theology and generally more down-to-earth concept of love. Most of Paul's remarks about love are focused on practical problems between people in the church.

We have seen that Hebrews differs from Paul in important ways. Hebrews has the human conscience being transformed through the cultic action of Christ (9:14; 10:14, 22)—something not found in Paul. But did the author of Hebrews get the sacrificial idea from Pauline circles, despite changing it? This cannot be demonstrated literarily, but it has to be allowed as a possibility. We do know that it was not long before the images in Hebrews were being used by the successors of Paul, who blended its images with Paul's. Thus the Hebrews stream flows into the Pauline stream, and its aftereffects are seen within the Pauline tradition.

Even though sacrifice is an ancient and violent image, the church has been unable to discard it because sacrifice has functioned as the vehicle for ideas of permanent importance—the compassion of God and Christ embodied in the Incarnation, which was the thorough participation of Divinity in human life. Another metaphor may some day do the work that the sacrificial metaphor has been doing. The image of God as loving parent, selflessly and patiently working for the children's growth, conveys the message of self-giving and care, but without any hint of a ritual killing or of sacrificial payment. In fact, Jesus is our source for the "new" metaphor, through his insistent referral to God as a Father, and one who knows what his children need and gives it to them. Unfortunately, the ethical and spiritual implications of Jesus' metaphor were undermined by the reassertion of the authoritarian family concept (seen in the deutero-Pauline household codes), and then put into a dormant condition by Christianity becoming the religion of the empire.

Pauline Elements in First Peter

It was not long before blended Pauline and Hebrews ideas could be observed . . . within *another* stream of Christian literature: the Petrine stream. First Peter purports to be a letter by the apostle Peter to the "exiles" scattered throughout five named districts of Asia Minor (1:1). Some scholars believe that the core of First Peter was authored by the apostle Peter, but that the letter was expanded and rewritten by someone (or several people) with high levels of Greek proficiency (something Peter is not likely to have had). At least one of the hands that helped shape 1 Peter was probably a Pauline hand. A few passages will show the similarities.

In 1:14 the author commands "Like obedient children, do not be conformed to the desires that you formerly had," using the same verb (*syschēmatizomai*) as in the "do not be conformed" passage of Romans 12:2. His atonement language blends elements from the deutero-Paulines and Hebrews. "You were ransomed . . . with the precious blood of Christ, like that of a lamb without defect or blemish" (1:18-19). First Peter's "ransomed" is the same verb as "redeem us from all iniquity" in Titus 2:14, and 1 Peter shares "unblemished" terms with Ephesians 5:27 and Hebrews 9:14. The editor of 1 Peter seems to be consciously fitting this letter within a body of recognized apostolic letters.

The atonement theology summarizes what we have seen elsewhere: "He himself bore [*anapherō*] our sins in his body on the cross, so that, free from sins, we might live for righteousness" (2:24). Christ also bore [*anapherō*] the sins of many in Hebrews 9:28. We were freed from sin and live for righteousness in Romans 6:6, 18, 22. What is unusual is that the author uses Isaiah 53 to describe Jesus' suffering: "by his wounds you have been healed" (2:24, citing Isa 53:5), something that becomes common later but only occurs a few times in the NT, some of them Pauline (Luke 22:37; Acts 8:32-35; Rom 4:25; possibly 5:19; possibly Heb 9:28; and more instances if one sees a reference to the "lamb" of Isa 53:7 in Rev 5:6, 12; John 1:29, etc.).

First Peter uses phrases common to Hebrews and to Romans: "Christ also suffered for sins once for all, the righteous for the unrighteous" (3:18). The angels and powers are subject to him (3:22; cf. Phil 2:10; Col 2:10). The household code ("Slaves, accept the authority of your masters . . . Wives, in the same way, accept the authority of your husbands . . . paying honor to the woman as the weaker sex," 2:18; 3:1, 7) resembles that in the deutero-Paulines, and the desire to look good to the Gentiles (2:12; 3:2, 16) matches the concern in the Pastorals.

Still, we can speak of a "Petrine" tradition with its own distinctives: believers as "exiles" and "aliens" in this world (1:1, 17; 2:11), using the Leviticus command "be holy" (1:16; Lev 11:44) and the Exodus image of a royal priesthood (2:5, 9; Exod 19:6), the image of a house of living stones (2:4-5), a description of the non-retaliation of Jesus (2:23), and the risen Jesus preaching "to the spirits in prison" (3:19-20). But a good quantity of deutero-Pauline thought was poured into the text at some point early in its transmission.

Pauline Elements in First John

It is not difficult to discern distinctly Pauline elements in First Peter, since it uses some specifically Pauline terminology. This cannot be said regarding First John, even though there are some clearly sacrificial metaphors in it. The mere presence of a sacrificial metaphor does not make a passage "Pauline." The metaphor in Hebrews, for instance, cannot with certainty be called Pauline, although it may have been influenced by Paul's theology. First John may also show *some* Pauline influence without actually being "Pauline" in the sense of coming from a follower of Paul or using distinctly Pauline terminology. First John uses *hilasmos* (sacrificial victim) for Christ (2:2; 4:10); it does not use Paul's *peri hamartias* (sin offering, Rom 8:3) or *hilastērion* (place of atonement, Rom 3:25, NRSV margin).

The Pauline Tradition outside the New Testament

The early compositions of the deutero-Pauline tradition are contained in the NT itself. We come now to further Pauline developments outside the NT.

First Clement

The first figure to consider is Clement of Rome, the overseer of the Roman congregation. His epistle, *1 Clement,* was written to the Corinthian congregation at the very end of the first century, during a time of persecution. Clement picks up on many Pauline themes and social issues, but Clement is no Paul. In contrast to Paul's constant uplifting of the "lowly" and criticism of those who think they "are something" (cf. 1 Cor 1:28), Clement supports the social status quo, and "the socially weak are urged to be submissive and obedient."[2] Nothing like Paul's advice to "the strong" to humble themselves for the sake of "the weak" ever occurs in *1 Clement.* Clement's is a program of "sober and selfless Christian piety . . . deferring to those over you."[3] "Humility and obedient submissiveness"[4] are the supreme values.

Clement is a great advocate of Paul, however, and uses him as a warrant for his own arguments; *1 Clement* 47.3-7 echoes 1 Corinthians 1:10-13, *1 Clement* 37.5 is based on 1 Corinthians 12:21, and there are many more examples. His favorites sources are 1 Corinthians, Hebrews, and the Pastoral Epistles,[5] but allusions and quotations from Philippians, Romans, and the Synoptic Gospels can be detected. He frequently moralizes on the OT. He uses Hebrews to distance himself from the Jewish tradition, while affirming that the OT had testified to Christ. He also quotes from an unknown "verse of Scripture" (23.3-4; 17.6). We are unaware of some of the

2. David G. Horrell, *The Social Ethos of the Corinthian Correspondence: Interests and Ideology from 1 Corinthians to 1 Clement* (Edinburgh: T&T Clark, 1996), 287.

3. *1 Clement* 1–2; Frances Young, *The Theology of the Pastoral Epistles* (Cambridge: Cambridge University Press, 1994), 44.

4. *1 Clem* 19.1.

5. Clayton Jefford argues that Hebrews and the Pastorals borrow from Clement (Clayton N. Jefford, *The Apostolic Fathers and the New Testament* [Peabody, MA: Hendrickson, 2006], 129), but this is a minority view.

works he considered Scripture. Of course, there is no "New Testament," as such, at this early date. He does not seem to know the Johannine writings. Especially does he want his Corinthian audience to "pick up the letter of the blessed apostle Paul" (47.1), by which he means 1 Corinthians. Paul wrote "under the Spirit's guidance" (47.3). Clement calls Paul a "pillar" (*1 Clem* 5.2), quite oblivious to the irony of calling Paul by a term that Paul sarcastically applied to the Jerusalem apostles (Gal 2:9). Even when he is not citing 1 Corinthians, he will often quote the same OT passages Paul does; for instance, 34.8 quotes "what no eye has seen, nor ear heard" from Isaiah 64:4, also cited at 1 Corinthians 2:9.[6] His exhortation to "fix our eyes on the blood of Christ" (7.4) probably borrows from Paul, though differing significantly from Paul's own wording (compare also "Christ whose blood was given for us," 21.6). The symbol is taken very literally. The blood of Christ has become the actual source of salvation; it is "precious . . . since it was poured out for our salvation" (7.4).

Like the author(s) of the Pastoral Epistles, this author stands for a clear hierarchy in the church and accepts the hierarchy in society: "Let us respect those who rule over us. . . . Let us rear the young in the fear of God. Let us direct our women to what is good" (21.6). Worldly "imperial power" is God-given (61.1). He advocates "lack of self-assertion, and submission . . . the order of this world was to be respected."[7] In his moralism Clement is like many other teachers of the time, both Jewish and Stoic, repeatedly using a favorite Stoic term, "harmony" (*homonoia*, 20.3, 11; 30.3; 49.5; 50.5; 60.4; and many more). He will use Gentile myths: to illustrate the future resurrection he uses the story of the phoenix, even down to the details of where it nests and what kind of incense it is said to put into its nest (25.1-6).

Most prominent is his emphasis on church order: "Not everybody is a general, colonel, captain" (37.3). The correct stance is to be "obeying orders rather than issuing them" (2.1). It is not surprising that Clement of Rome should be taken as a primary example of "early Catholicism," a term that was coined to signify the increased focus on church order, clergy, sacraments, moral rules, even a concept of apostolic succession (the latter is seen in 42.1-5). This term is generally not used now because of the Protestant bias of many of its users. However, we do need to notice the stages of increasing clerical organization and control in this period. Clement compares Christian clergy to the Jewish priesthood (43.3-6).

6. Jefford, *Apostolic Fathers and the NT*, 132.
7. Young, *Theology of the Pastoral Epistles*, 44.

Ordained presbyter-bishops[8] have rightly "offered the sacrifices" (44.4), probably meaning the Eucharist. Our next clerical figure, Ignatius of Antioch, has much to say about this subject.

Ignatius of Antioch

In the matter of strengthening the power of the *episkopos* and sharpening all the lines of authority within the church, there is a logical progression from the Pastorals to Clement of Rome to Ignatius of Antioch, writing around 111 CE. In the letters of Ignatius the *episkopos* emerges as an authority figure, a supervisor of approved rituals, a teacher and preacher, and a model of martyrdom. We can certainly translate *episkopos* as "bishop" in the case of Ignatius. "Without the bishop's supervision, no baptisms or love feasts are permitted" (*Ign. Smyrn.* 8.2). The Eucharist was still, evidently, part of a larger meal, an *agapē* feast. In fact, anyone who "does anything without bishop, presbytery, and deacons does not have a clear conscience" (*Ign. Trall.* 7.2). The bishop presides "in God's place," the deacons represent Christ, and the presbyters are an "apostolic council" (*Ign. Magn.* 6.1).

This is an extraordinary claim. Does he really mean it when he says: "regard the bishop as the Lord himself" (*Ign. Eph.* 6.1)? Are believers really to "obey the bishop as if he were Jesus Christ" (*Ign. Trall.* 2.1)? Yes!—he is to be respected "as you respect the authority of God" (*Ign. Magn.* 3.1). In fact, there is a threefold correlation to the divine level: "the deacons . . . represent Jesus Christ, just as the bishop has the role of the Father, and the presbyters are like God's council and an apostolic band" (*Ign. Trall.* 3.1). This seems to be a very literal-minded Platonism. Ignatius sees the revelatory pattern (Father to Son to apostles) *actually* reproduced in the congregation in the revelatory pattern of bishop to deacons to elders. To us it may be shocking to hear Ignatius comparing himself (or his job title) to God, and his deacons to Christ. But this is how Middle-Platonic thinking worked; divine patterns were reproduced on earth. In fact, Ignatius gives his life for the divine structure of the church: "I give my life as a sacrifice (poor as it is) for those who are obedient to the bishop, the presbyters, and the deacons" (*Ign. Poly.* 6.1). It is the Spirit who tells him this: "it was the Spirit that kept on preaching . . . 'Do nothing apart from the bishop'" (*Ign. Phld.* 7.2).

---

8. Clement uses *presbyteros* and *episkopos* interchangeably, strengthening the view, mentioned in our section on Titus 1, that the *episkopos* was chosen from among the ranks of the *presbyteroi*.

It is not surprising, then, that this bishop maintains a fairly conservative social philosophy. He advises Christian slave owners not to "treat slaves and slave girls contemptuously," but he adds that slaves should not expect the church to purchase their freedom (*Ign. Poly.* 4.3).

Ignatius sees himself as another Paul, not only in his role as a martyr but as an inspired writer of letters to the churches, using them to instruct, command, correct, and create a permanent legacy. Further, he imitates Christ: "Let me imitate the Passion of my God" (*Ign. Rom.* 6.3). His martyrological enthusiasm, atonement concept, and eucharistic mysticism all bleed into one: "It is with a passion for death that I am writing to you. . . . What I want is God's bread, which is the flesh of Christ . . . and for drink I want his blood: an immortal love feast indeed!" (*Ign. Rom.* 7.2-3). Ignatius prays to "become God's sacrifice" (*Ign. Rom.* 4.2). He speaks of being "initiated into the mysteries with Paul, a real saint and martyr" (*Ign. Eph.* 12.2). Like Paul (1 Cor 4:13), he is a *peripsēma* (*Ign. Eph.* 8.1; "rubbish" or "scapegoat" would be better than Richardson's "sacrifice"). There are many allusions, echoes, and (probable) brief quotations from the "Pauline" literature, especially from 1 Corinthians, Ephesians, 1 Timothy, and Hebrews.

There is a crude literalism (or one could say a vivid "realism") in Ignatius' use of symbols. He says "by faith (that's the Lord's flesh) and by love (that's Jesus Christ's blood) make yourselves new creatures" (*Ign. Trall.* 8.1). The Eucharist is the "flesh of our Lord" (*Ign. Phld.* 4.1). It "is the medicine of immortality, and the antidote which wards off death" (*Ign. Eph.* 20.2). More than just *symbolizing* immortality, the sacrament *conveys* it. The sacrament *itself* has life-giving power. It has dangerous power as well. All creatures, even "angels, and principalities" who disbelieve "in Christ's blood, they too are doomed" (*Ign. Smyrn.* 6.1). This is the church militant, sacramentally militant! The blood functions like a person; "it was God's blood that stirred you up" (*Ign. Eph.* 1.1).

Obviously, all of this vivid martyrology and sacramentalism goes far beyond anything we see in Clement, or in Paul. It probably goes beyond what we would call normal and healthy; but we must recall that Ignatius was anticipating being tormented and killed in the arena in Rome, and it was important that he remain an ardent witness for Christ. Some of his excessive rhetoric can be explained as self-training in preparation for martyrdom, and some of it is the product of taking symbols hyper-literally.

At Antioch, Ignatius stands in a long martyrological tradition. The Antiochene Jewish community commemorated the Maccabean martyrdoms annually. Antioch had been Paul's headquarters for some time (Acts 15:35), and Paul's theology may draw on this stream as well.

We see Ignatius's ethic of devotion when he exhorts the Ephesians to "'keep on praying'[9] for others too, for there is a chance of their being converted. . . . Return their bad temper with gentleness. . . . By our patience let us show we are their brothers, intent on imitating the Lord, seeing which of us can be the more wronged, robbed, and despised" (*Ign. Eph.* 10.1-3).

Clement and Ignatius are really the heirs of the hierarchical ecclesiology and conservative social stance of the Pastoral Epistles more than they are successors of Paul the theologian. Ignatius is closer to Paul in most ways, though with a fiercely literal-minded interpretation of the sacraments and of martyrdom that differs from Paul's. Clement wants to live at peace in this world, while Ignatius is eager to move on: "I do not want to live any more on a human plane" (*Ign. Rom.* 8.1).

Different as they are in style and psychology, Clement and Ignatius together exemplify the authority of bishops in the early church. A well-organized, hierarchical clergy emerges within the Pauline tradition, but nothing approaching a papacy yet. It is true that the bishop of Rome (Clement) presumes to give advice to the Corinthian congregation, but it is the content of his message rather than the Roman see (bishop's office) that gives him that authority. The Antiochene bishop is even more eager to give advice to many churches. In my view the first bishop who can really be called a pope is Leo the Great, in the fifth century. Through a combination of surrounding circumstances and of his intellect and courage Leo gained an unprecedented prestige, and he was able to argue that the Roman see had the mission of protecting doctrine for the wider church. He articulated the Chalcedonian doctrine that Jesus Christ was both fully human and fully divine, which is the backbone of Christian doctrine, whether Catholic, Orthodox, or Protestant.

What of the rise of celibacy, or encratism, in Christianity?[10] One may or may not want to call Paul an encratite, depending on how one defines the term, since he tolerated marriage, saying it was better for most men and women to be married, and that the two should not withhold sex from each other (1 Cor 7:2, 5). But even married people seem to be obliged (at least in their imaginations) to "crucif[y] their flesh with its passions and desires" (Gal 5:24), and to "put to death the deeds of the body" (Rom 8:13). Surrounded by all our creature comforts, we often fail to appreciate

---

9. A quotation of 1 Thess 5:17.

10. Encratism is the term preferred by academics, signifying not just celibacy but a thoroughgoing ascetic lifestyle and an accompanying anti-sexual ideology.

how seriously ascetic this teaching is. Encratism was a growing influence in Paul's time, a trend mainly observed among Gentile Stoics and Gnostics, but also appearing within Judaism. The prevailing view was that "repression of passions and desires distinguished the philosopher from the common lot," and "sexual chastity was a prerequisite for the divine encounter."[11] Paul is not single-handedly responsible for bringing encratism into Christianity, but he is a key figure in this trend. Church fathers such as Origen and Tertullian placed a high value on celibacy, and as this became more common, celibacy became the norm for bishops.

Marcion and His Opponents

The next important figure is Marcion of Sinope, considered by many orthodox believers to be the original heretic, or at least the most dangerous of the early heretics. Yet Marcion is our earliest known advocate of a canonical list that included a gospel and Paul's letters, in 144 CE.[12] The process of canon-formation is slow. It took over a thousand years for the process of composition, collection, revision, and agreement on a final list of books for the Hebrew Bible, but all the books had already been revered for centuries by then. Although all the NT books were written between 50 and 110 CE, the development of their reputations and of the concept of a definitive list of books took considerable time. The development of a canon is the work of many generations of believers, not of a group of monks in a smoke-filled—or incense-filled—room. In the first century and a half of the movement there were probably churches that knew of only one or two gospels, others that knew of some gospels that are now lost or that we call non-canonical (like *Thomas*).[13] Other works like *1 Clement* and the *Epistle of Barnabas* came close to being included in the NT. The earliest known list that *exactly* matches our list of twenty-seven NT books dates from the mid-fourth century, three hundred years after Paul wrote his letters!

There were several steps in the gradual formation of the canon. Marcion made one very important move when he criticized the distortions of the Jesus message that he perceived in most of the available texts. He

---

11. Calvin Roetzel, *Paul: The Man and the Myth* (Edinburgh: T&T Clark, 1999), 138–39.

12. J. N. D. Kelly, *Early Christian Doctrines* (rev. ed. New York: Harper & Row, 1978), 57.

13. Most of the Gnostic Gospels come from the third and fourth centuries CE. *Thomas* is the only (proto)-Gnostic Gospel with any plausible claim of having first-century roots, although this is hotly debated among scholars.

believed that Jesus presented the truth about God, but that most of the apostles had misunderstood and distorted Jesus' message. Marcion believed Jesus had proclaimed a radical break with the religion of the OT, and that his revelation of the loving Father exposed the falsehood in OT concepts of God. Because Jesus' apostles had a hard time understanding this radically new teaching, Marcion said, they reintroduced much old and familiar Jewish theology, idealizing and harmonizing it with the teachings of Jesus, thus distorting the latter.[14] The church had really failed to preserve the originality of Jesus' revelation of the kindly Father God, in contrast to the OT's despotic Creator God.[15] Paul, however, came closest to preserving the Gospel of Jesus in its pure form, so Marcion produced a list of Pauline letters for his churches to use. The Pastoral Epistles were not on this list (nor was Hebrews). Marcion also produced an edited version of the Gospel of Luke, which, to his way of thinking, was the least distorted of the written gospels. With a gospel and epistles, Marcion's list is the predecessor of our NT.

The opponents of Marcion responded by discussing which works they thought should be recognized. Forty years after Marcion, Irenaeus, bishop of Lyons, affirms the four gospels, the Pauline letters (including the Pastorals), and Acts. Not recognized as authoritative by Irenaeus are Hebrews, Revelation, the Epistles of John, James, Peter, and Jude.[16] Clement of Alexandria does accept Hebrews, 1 Peter, 1 John, 2 John, and Jude, but also *Barnabas*.[17] The NT work that probably came closest to not making it into the canon was Revelation, but it had an important third-century defender in Tertullian.

Marcion was certainly a Christian (Jesus is divine and is truly the Savior), but there is some debate over whether he should be called a Christian Gnostic. I think he should be, since he articulates the defining belief (in my view) of Christian Gnosticism: that the OT was the product of a lesser god or "demiurge," not of the highest God. Marcion distinguishes himself from other Gnostics by refusing to label the demiurge as evil,[18] but he does not affirm what all the orthodox affirm: that the God of the OT is also the Father of Jesus. Marcion asserts a radical dis-

14. Hans von Campenhausen, *The Formation of the Christian Bible* (Philadelphia: Fortress Press, 1972), 150.

15. Ibid., 151.

16. Ibid., 203.

17. Ibid., 212–13.

18. Kelly, *Early Christian Doctrines*, 57.

continuity between the OT and Jesus, something the majority of the church could not accept. The four gospels that won acceptance all had Jesus quoting the prophets and fulfilling Scripture (e.g., Matt 26:54; Mark 12:10; Luke 24:44; John 5:46). This spoke of continuity more than discontinuity, despite Jesus' improvement on, and deepening of, biblical commandments ("You have heard that it was said . . . But I say to you," Matt 5:21-22, 27-28, 31-34, 43-45).

After Marcion, Christian Gnostics like Valentinus claimed to be true followers of Paul, and the Gnostic *Gospel of Philip* (103–5, 109, 127) paraphrases and interprets several Pauline letters. All of this led some orthodox believers to refer to Paul as "the apostle of the heretics," and this is probably why some orthodox thinkers, such as Justin Martyr, simply do not mention or quote from Paul.[19] But most orthodox teachers used Paul, including those heroes of the faith, the martyrs Polycarp and Ignatius of Antioch.

Irenaeus and Other Interpreters

Irenaeus wrote his greatest work, *Against Heresies,* in the 180s CE. A thorough discussion of Irenaeus would need to address his key role in affirming the four gospels we now have in the canon and in articulating a doctrine of the Incarnation that describes Jesus rescuing sinful humanity by living through ("recapitulating") every stage of life, thus blessing and rescuing each stage of life that had been corrupted by sin. The Incarnation is essential for his doctrine of salvation, because in the Incarnation, divinity came *into* humanity, and "how shall man pass into God unless God has first passed into man?"[20] Because he became human, Christ can actually remake our disordered human nature and rejoin us to God.[21] Relying on the image of the life-giving Christ in 1 Corinthians 15:22, 45, Irenaeus argues that Christ restores to us the "likeness of God" that was lost in Adam.[22]

---

19. von Campenhausen, *Formation,* 177.

20. *Against Heresies* (*Adversus haereses,* hereafter *Haer.*) 4.33.4, quoted from Jeffrey Finch, "Irenaeus on the Christological Basis of Human Divinization," in Stephen Finlan and Vladimir Kharlamov, eds., *Theōsis: Deification in Christian Tradition.* PTMS 52. (Eugene, OR: Pickwick Publishers [Wipf & Stock], 2006), 86–103, at 99.

21. *Haer.* 3.16.6; 4.6.2; 4.20.4; Finch, "Irenaeus," 100.

22. *Haer.* 3.18.1; 5.1.3. Maurice F. Wiles, *The Divine Apostle: The Interpretation of St. Paul's Epistles in the Early Church* (Cambridge: Cambridge University Press, 1967), 74.

Paul's writings were an important source of teaching for use against
Gnostic and Marcionite positions, and later against Arian views. Irenaeus
uses Galatians 4:4 and Romans 1:3-4 against a Gnostic Docetism that
denied Christ had a human body.[23] ("Docetism," the idea that Christ
only *seemed* to suffer and die, is named from the Greek verb *dokeō*,
"seem.") The theologians seek to ward off wrong interpretations: Tertullian argues that "likeness of sinful flesh" in Romans 8:3 does not mean
that the flesh was illusory.[24] And in the remark, "those who are in the
flesh cannot please God" (Rom 8:8), it is not the flesh itself that "is cen-
sured but its actions"; likewise, Irenaeus says the flesh is not evil, but it
needs the Spirit "infused into it."[25] Of course these are exegetically valid
interpretations, but we can see that the motivation is less exegetical than
theological, that is, concerned with contemporary theological debates.

Nevertheless, there is material in Paul that influences the content of
the debate. Pauline christology contributes greatly to patristic development of the doctrine of the full divinity and full humanity of Christ. On
the divinity of Christ and his being with God in the beginning, some
passages of particular importance were 1 Corinthians 8:6; Romans 1:3-4;
Colossians 1:15; Ephesians 4:6. Issues of God's foreknowledge and
human freedom were often discussed in connection with Romans 1:1;
9:11-13; Philippians 2:13,[26] which does not imply that the Fathers all came
to the same conclusions. Paul is the main source cited in discussions of
grace, faith, justification, and the ascetic life.

By the time of Tertullian (fl. 200–220 CE), the letters of Paul enjoy
near-canonical status. Although there is no fixed NT, there *is* widespread
recognition of the four gospels, Acts, and thirteen letters of "Paul." It
took more time for there to be widespread recognition of the other letters
(including Hebrews) and Revelation.

The teachings of Paul were simplified and changed with time. The
idea of imaginative participation in the death of Christ, of dying and
rising with Christ, and of being transformed into Christ's likeness almost
disappear from discussion. There grew up instead an emphasis on grace,
holiness, participation in the sacraments, and obedience to the church's
teaching. Thus it is the Paul of the Pastorals who dominates.

23. *Haer.* 3.22.1; Wiles, *Divine Apostle,* 81.
24. *Against Marcion* 5.14. Gerald Bray, ed., *Romans.* ACCS NT 6 (Downers Grove: Inter-
Varsity, 1998), 202.
25. Tertullian, *On the Resurrection of the Flesh* 10; Irenaeus, *Haer.* 5.10.2. Bray, *Romans,* 209.
26. Wiles, *Divine Apostle,* 98–110.

Varying concepts of atonement or redemption occur throughout the ancient literature. In any given theologian, certain ideas subside and another emerges as primary, such as the concept of recapitulation for Irenaeus. The notion of Christ's death as a sacrifice was common, but this could mean several different things. The emphasis could be on the death as a fulfillment of the "types" or symbols of the OT (as with many Alexandrian theologians), or it could be on Christ vicariously "paying" or taking on the penalty for sin (as with Augustine and Gregory the Great). Origen used the concept of the death as a ransom-payment, but mixed it with other ideas: the death as a way of tricking Satan into overstepping his bounds; the resurrection as a cosmic victory over death; the whole life of Christ, not just his death, having a saving effect, inaugurating a process of believer transformation.[27] Atonement turns out to be considerably more complicated, and the diversity of views much greater, than is usually recognized.

Paul in the Twenty-first Century

We have seen that Paul's teachings were appropriated in a number of different ways in the time immediately after his life. They can be read in a number of different ways today as well:

- as a guide for practicing faith in a multi-ethnic community;
- as truth and inspiration for genuine faith-living and not simply following rules;
- as teachings that are helpful for a spiritually vibrant church in which people have strongly held beliefs but are willing to alter behaviors out of consideration for others, thus allowing for a diversity of practices, and even beliefs, in the church;
- as a source of dogmas that are to be taken literally, including doctrines about salvation from the wrath of God through the sacrificial death of Christ, which paid a ransom price (derived from Rom 5:9; 8:3; 1 Cor 6:20; 7:23; etc.).
- as a unified body of thirteen or fourteen letters (whose differences are denied), which will be considered a source of rules to be strictly followed, but that will in fact be selectively enforced, since some of the rules are incompatible: for instance, women prophets taking turns and not all speaking at once or women keeping silent in the churches.

27. Hastings Rashdall, *The Idea of the Atonement in Christian Theology* (London: Macmillan, 1919), 258–61, 273, 287; Stephen Finlan, *Problems with Atonement: The Origins of, and Controversy about, the Atonement Doctrine* (Collegeville, MN: Liturgical Press, 2005), 67–68.

Obviously, Paul can be used in ways that will allow for diversity of understanding or in ways that suppress problems and prevent discussion. Paul can be used to encourage personal and first-hand religious experience or to impose strict conformity. For different people Paul's troublesome texts can stimulate lively discussion or dishonest suppression of secret doubts. In short, Paul's writings can be read honestly or dishonestly. The fundamentalist option is really an attempt to do the impossible: to deny that there are any differences between biblical writings and to claim that every text can be treated as absolute truth. Fundamentalist readings of Scripture have led to some of the worst violence in the past and present. Today it is fundamentalist readers of the Qu'ran who are causing the most violence; in centuries past it was fundamentalist Christians. (In the twentieth century it was ex-Christians.) Fundamentalism is one of the great problems in human history. We are now at a place where we can begin to understand this phenomenon, and to critique it. Responsible spiritual living now requires responsible intellectual reflection.

This leads to some final observations about Paul and about our own approach to the whole Bible, not just Paul. We can no longer mindlessly accept all the Bible as literal truth, especially when it advocates massacring nations (Num 31:17-18; Deut 7:2; Josh 11:20), or barbaric customs like testing a woman's fidelity by making her drink sweepings from the temple floor to see if they make her swell up and die (Num 5:12-31). We have to accept that biblical texts come to us through the hands of humans who were at a certain stage of cultural development and spiritual insight. Different texts come from people at different stages of development. "The spirits of prophets are subject to the prophets" (1 Cor 14:32). But God is patiently working to help us grow, "to help you to determine what is best" (Phil 1:10) and to move on to the higher stages ("The one who began a good work among you will bring it to completion by the day of Jesus Christ," Phil 1:6).

The Faith Experience

Reading Paul raises issues in our own faith-life. Faith for Paul was a lived relationship of trusting in God and Christ, illuminated by the Spirit. It is surely time for us to rediscover the faith *experience,* despite the vulnerability and uncertainty that go with it. One is always somewhat vulnerable when one trusts, especially when the assumptions one brings into the relationship prove to be childish or superstitious and need to be corrected through life-experience. We may find our sand castles of illusory security crumbling. We may find that some of our ideas need to change, and this will be unsettling. But we can gain a new kind of security, one that is anchored in eternal shores and not in the shifting sands of this life.

A mature Christianity does not require any more spiritual skills today than it did in the past, but it does seem to require more mental and social skills, including the ability to engage the Bible in debate and reflection, and skills for dealing with people with a wide range of different problems. But the same need to practice faith is still there. Faith need not be deeper or more intense than in the past, but it must be very alert. We must beware the dangers of fatigue, lethargy, and sadness in today's confusing world. We need a real faith walk so that we are not dominated by the discouraging, hostile, or seductive things in the environment. We need faith to help stabilize and direct us through this complicated life.

We need childlike faith even while emerging into full and responsible adulthood. We need Jesus the healer while yet overcoming patterns of magical thinking. We need science, religion, culture, and love. We need education, faith, and hope for living. We need to know there is a future for us and for all who love God.

> For now we see in a mirror, dimly, but then we will see face to face. Now I know only in part; then I will know fully, even as I have been fully known. And now faith, hope, and love abide, these three; and the greatest of these is love. (1 Cor 13:12-13)

Bibliography

Primary Sources

Clement of Rome. *Early Christian Fathers*. Translated by Cyril C. Richardson. New York: Touchstone, 1996.

Epictetus. *The Stoic and Epicurean Philosophers*. Edited and translated by Whitney J. Oates. New York: The Modern Library, 1940.

Heraclitus the Cynic. *The Cynic Epistles: A Study Edition*. Edited by Abraham J. Malherbe. SBLSBS 12. Missoula, MT: Scholars Press, 1979.

Ignatius of Antioch. *Early Christian Fathers*. Translated by Cyril C. Richardson. New York: Touchstone, 1996.

Martin Luther. *Martin Luther: Selections from His Writings*. Edited by John Dillenberger. Garden City, NY: Doubleday, 1961.

Philo of Alexandria. *The Works of Philo*. Translated by C. D. Yonge. Peabody, MA: Hendrickson, 1993.

Plato. *The Great Dialogues of Plato*. Translated by W. H. D. Rouse. New York: Mentor, 1956.

Seneca. *Epistulae Morales*, vol. II. Translated by Richard M. Gummere. LCL. Cambridge: Harvard University Press, 1962.

Testaments of the Twelve Patriarchs. *The Old Testament Pseudepigrapha*, 1:775–828. Translated by Howard Clark Kee. Edited by James H. Charlesworth. New York: Doubleday, 1983.

Secondary Sources

Arnold, Clinton E. *The Colossian Syncretism: The Interface between Christianity and Folk Belief at Colossae*. WUNT 2/77. Tübingen: Mohr Siebeck, 1995.

Bailey, Daniel P. "Jesus as the Mercy Seat: The Semantics and Theology of Paul's Use of *Hilasterion* in Romans 3:25." *Tyndale Bulletin* 51 (2000): 155–58.

Bauckham, Richard. "Pseudo-Apostolic Letters." *JBL* 107 (1988): 469–94.

Bauer, Walter. *A Greek-English Lexicon of the New Testament and Other Early Christian Literature.* Translated by W. F. Arndt. Second edition. Revised by F. W. Gingrich, and Frederick W. Danker. Chicago: University of Chicago Press, 1979.

Beker, Johan Christiaan. *Paul the Apostle: The Triumph of God in Life and Thought.* Philadelphia: Fortress Press, 1980.

Boyarin, Daniel. *A Radical Jew: Paul and the Politics of Identity.* Berkeley: University of California Press, 1994.

Bray, Gerald, ed. *Romans.* ACCS NT 6. Downers Grove: InterVarsity, 1998.

Brodie, Thomas L., Dennis MacDonald, and Stanley E. Porter, eds. *The Intertextuality of the Epistles: Explorations of Theory and Practice.* Sheffield: Sheffield Academic Press, 2006.

Brondos, David A. *Paul on the Cross: Reconstructing the Apostle's Story of Redemption.* Minneapolis: Fortress Press, 2006.

Büchsel, Friedrich. ἀγοράζω, ἐξαγοράζω. *TDNT* 1:124–28.

Bultmann, Rudolf. *Theology of the New Testament.* New York: Charles Scribner's Sons, 1951.

Bundrick, David R. "*Ta Stoicheia tou Kosmou* (Gal 4:3)." *JETS* 34 (1991): 353–64.

Burkert, Walter. *Structure and History in Greek Mythology and Ritual.* Berkeley: University of California Press, 1979.

Callahan, Allen Dwight. *Embassy of Onesimus: The Letter of Paul to Philemon.* Valley Forge, PA: Trinity Press International, 1997.

Campenhausen, Hans von. *The Formation of the Christian Bible.* Philadelphia: Fortress Press, 1972.

Christensen, Michael J., and Jeffery A. Wittung, eds. *Partakers of the Divine Nature: The History and Development of Deification in the Christian Traditions.* Madison, NJ: Fairleigh Dickinson University Press, 2007.

Collins, John J. *Apocalypticism in the Dead Sea Scrolls.* London: Routledge, 1997.

———. *Jewish Wisdom in the Hellenistic Age.* Louisville: Westminster John Knox, 1997.

———. *Scepter and the Star: The Messiahs of the Dead Sea Scrolls and Other Ancient Literature.* New York: Doubleday, 1995.

Collins, Raymond F. *First Corinthians.* SP 7. Collegeville, MN: Liturgical Press, 1999.

———. "'I Command That This Letter Be Read': Writing as a Manner of Speaking." In *The Thessalonians Debate: Methodological Discord or Methodological Synthesis?*, edited by Karl P. Donfried and Johannes Beutler, 319–39. Grand Rapids: Eerdmans, 2000.

Cotter, Wendy. "Women's Authority Roles in Paul's Churches: Countercultural or Conventional?" *Novum Testamentum* 36 (1994): 350–72.

Cumont, Franz. *The Mysteries of Mithra.* New York: Dover, 1956; translation © Open Court Publishing, 1903.

———. *The Oriental Religions in Roman Paganism.* New York: Dover, 1956, from the 1911 translation.

deBoer, Martinus C. "The Meaning of the Phrase τὰ στοιχεῖα τοῦ κόσμου in Galatians." *NTS* 53 (2007): 204–24.

Deissmann, Adolf. *Paul: A Study in Social and Religious History.* 2nd ed. New York: Harper & Brothers, 1957, from the 1927 translation.

Deming, Will. "Paul and Indifferent Things," In *Paul in the Greco-Roman World: A Handbook*, edited by J. Paul Sampley, 384–403. Harrisburg, PA: Trinity Press International, 2003.

Donfried, Karl P. *Paul, Thessalonica, and Early Christianity.* Grand Rapids: Eerdmans, 2002.

———. *The Theology of the Shorter Pauline Letters.* Cambridge: Cambridge University Press, 1993.

Dunn, James D. G. *The Epistles to the Colossians and to Philemon: A Commentary on the Greek Text.* NIGTC. Grand Rapids: Eerdmans, 1996.

———. "Once More: ΠΙΣΤΙΣ ΧΡΙΣΤΟΥ," In *SBL Seminar Papers, 1991.* SBLSP 30, edited by Eugene H. Lovering Jr, 730–44. Atlanta: Scholars Press, 1991.

———. "Pharisees, Sinners, and Jesus," In *The Social World of Formative Christianity and Judaism*, edited by Jacob Neusner, Ernest S. Frerichs, Peder Borgen, and Richard Horsley, 264–89. Philadelphia: Fortress Press, 1988.

———. *Romans 1–8.* WBC 38A. Dallas: Word Books, 1988.

———. "The Theology of Galatians: The Issue of Covenantal Nomism," In *Pauline Theology, Vol. I: Thessalonians, Philippians, Galatians, Philemon*, edited by Jouette M. Bassler, 125–46. Minneapolis: Fortress Press, 1991.

———. *The Theology of Paul the Apostle.* Grand Rapids: Eerdmans, 1998.

Ehrman, Bart D. *Lost Christianities: The Battles for Scripture and the Faiths We Never Knew.* Oxford: Oxford University Press, 2003.

———. *Misquoting Jesus: The Story Behind Who Changed the Bible and Why.* HarperSan Francisco, 2005.

Elliott, Neil. *Liberating Paul: The Justice of God and the Politics of the Apostle.* The Bible and Liberation. Maryknoll, NY: Orbis, 1994.

Elliott, Susan Margaret. *Cutting Too Close for Comfort: Paul's Letter to the Galatians in Its Anatolian Cultic Context.* JSNTSup 248. London: T&T Clark, 2003.

———. "The Rhetorical Strategy of Paul's Letter to the Galatians in Its Anatolian Cultic Context: Circumcision and the Castration of the *Galli* of the Mother of the Gods." Ph.D. dissertation, Loyola University Chicago (1997).

Engberg-Pedersen, Troels. *Paul and the Stoics.* Louisville: Westminster John Knox, 2000.

Enslin, Morton Scott. *The Ethics of Paul.* Nashville: Abingdon, 1957.

Fee, Gordon D. *Paul's Letter to the Philippians.* NICNT. Grand Rapids: Eerdmans, 1995.

Finch, Jeffrey. "Irenaeus on the Christological Basis of Human Divinization," in *Theōsis: Deification in Christian Tradition.* PTMS 52, edited by Stephen Finlan and Vladimir Kharlamov, 86–103. Eugene, OR: Pickwick Publishers (Wipf & Stock), 2006.

Finlan, Stephen. *The Background and Content of Paul's Cultic Atonement Metaphors.* AcBib 19. Atlanta: Society of Biblical Literature (Brill), 2004.

———, and Vladimir Kharlamov, eds. *Theōsis: Deification in Christian Tradition.* PTMS 52. Eugene, OR: Pickwick Publishers (Wipf & Stock), 2006.

Fiore, Benjamin. "Paul, Shame, and Honor," In *Paul in the Greco-Roman World: A Handbook,* edited by J. Paul Sampley, 228–57. Harrisburg, PA: Trinity Press International, 2003.

Gager, John G. *Reinventing Paul.* Oxford: Oxford University Press, 2000.

Garland, David E. *First Corinthians.* BECNT. Grand Rapids: Baker Academic, 2003.

Gaston, Lloyd. *Paul and the Torah.* Vancouver: University of British Columbia Press, 1987.

Gaventa, Beverly Roberts. *Our Mother Saint Paul.* Louisville: Westminster John Knox, 2007.

Glancy, Jennifer A. *Slavery in Early Christianity.* Oxford: Oxford University Press, 2002.

Gorman, Frank H., Jr. *The Ideology of Ritual: Space, Time and Status in the Priestly Theology.* JSOTSup 91. Sheffield: Sheffield Academic Press, 1990.

Gorman, Michael J. *Apostle of the Crucified Lord: A Theological Introduction to Paul and His Letters.* Grand Rapids: Eerdmans, 2004.

———. *Cruciformity: Paul's Narrative Spirituality of the Cross.* Grand Rapids: Eerdmans, 2001.

Gray, Patrick. "The Liar Paradox and the Letter to Titus." *CBQ* 69 (2007): 302–14.

Griffith-Jones, Robin. *The Gospel According to Paul: The Creative Genius Who Brought Jesus to the World.* New York: HarperCollins, 2004.

Grindheim, Sigurd. "Apostate Turned Prophet: Paul's Prophetic Self-Understanding and Prophetic Hermeneutic with Special Reference to Galatians 3.10-12." *NTS* 53 (2007): 545–65.

Haacker, Klaus. *The Theology of Paul's Letter to the Romans.* New York: Cambridge University Press, 2003.

Hanson, Anthony Tyrrell. *The Paradox of the Cross in the Thought of St. Paul.* JSNTSup 17. Sheffield: JSOT Press, 1987.

Harding, Mark. "Disputed and Undisputed Letters of Paul." In *The Pauline Canon,* edited by Stanley E. Porter, 129–68. Pauline Studies 1. Leiden: Brill, 2004.

Hays, Richard B. *Echoes of Scripture in the Letters of Paul.* New Haven: Yale University Press, 1989.

———. "ΠΙΣΤΙΣ and Pauline Christology: What Is at Stake?" In *SBL Seminar Papers 1991.* SBLSP 30, edited by Eugene H. Lovering Jr., 714–29. Atlanta: Scholars Press, 1991.

Heen, Erik M., and Philip D. Krey. *Hebrews.* ACCS NT 10. Downers Grove:, IL InterVarsity, 2005.

Hellermann, Joseph. *Reconstructing Honor in Roman Philippi:* Carmen Christi *as Cursus Pudorum.* SNTSMS 132. Cambridge: Cambridge University Press, 2005.

Hengel, Martin, and Anna Maria Schwemer. *Paul Between Damascus and Antioch: The Unknown Years*. Louisville: Westminster John Knox, 1997.

Hooker, Morna D. *From Adam to Christ: Essays on Paul*. Cambridge: Cambridge University Press, 1990.

Horbury, William. *Jewish Messianism and the Cult of Christ*. London: SCM, 1998.

Horrell, David G. *The Social Ethos of the Corinthian Correspondence: Interests and Ideology from 1 Corinthians to 1 Clement*. Edinburgh: T&T Clark, 1996.

Horsley, Richard A. "The Law of Nature in Philo and Cicero." *HTR* 71 (1978): 35–59.

————. "Rhetoric and Empire—and 1 Corinthians." In *Paul and Politics: Ekklesia, Israel, Imperium, Interpretation*, edited by *idem.*, 72–102. Harrisburg, PA: Trinity Press International, 2000.

Hughes, Frank W. "The Social Situations Implied by Rhetoric." In *The Thessalonians Debate: Methodological Discord or Methodological Synthesis?*, edited by Karl P. Donfried and Johannes Beutler, 241–54. Grand Rapids: Eerdmans, 2000.

Hurtado, Larry W. *How on Earth Did Jesus Become a God? Historical Questions about Earliest Devotion to Jesus*. Grand Rapids: Eerdmans, 2005.

Hyldahl, Niels. "Paul and Hellenistic Judaism in Corinth." In *The New Testament and Hellenistic Judaism*, edited by Peder Borgen and Søren Giversen, 204–16. Peabody, MA: Hendrickson, 1995.

Jefford, Clayton N. *The Apostolic Fathers and the New Testament*. Peabody, MA: Hendrickson, 2006.

Jewett, Robert. "Paul, Shame, and Honor." In *Paul in the Greco-Roman World: A Handbook*, edited by J. Paul Sampley, 551–74. Harrisburg, PA: Trinity Press International, 2003.

Johnson, E. Elizabeth. "Romans 9-11: The Faithfulness and Impartiality of God." In *Pauline Theology, Volume III: Romans*, edited by David M. Hay and E. Elizabeth Johnson, 211–39. Minneapolis: Fortress Press, 1995.

Johnson, Luke Timothy. *Reading Romans: A Literary and Theological Commentary*. New York: Crossroad, 1997.

————. "Romans 3:21-26 and the Faith of Jesus." *CBQ* 44 (1982): 77–90.

————. "Transformation of the Mind and Moral Discernment in Paul." In *Early Christianity and Classical Culture: Comparative Studies in Honor of Abraham J. Malherbe*. NovTSup 110, edited by John T. Fitzgerald, Thomas H. Olbricht, and L. Michael White, 215–36. Leiden: Brill, 2003.

————. *The Writings of the New Testament: An Interpretation*. Philadelphia: Fortress Press, 1986.

Käsemann, Ernst. *New Testament Questions of Today*. London: SCM, 1969.

Kee, Howard Clark. *Miracle in the Early Christian World*. New Haven: Yale University Press, 1983.

Kelly, J. N. D. *Early Christian Doctrines*. Rev. ed. New York: Harper & Row, 1978.

Klauck, Hans-Josef, with the collaboration of Daniel P. Bailey. *Ancient Letters and the New Testament*. Waco: Baylor University Press, 2006.

Kooten, George H. van. *Cosmic Christology in Paul and the Pauline School: Colossians and Ephesians in the Context of Graeco-Roman Cosmology, with a New Synopsis of the Greek Texts.* WUNT 2/171. Tübingen: Mohr Siebeck, 2003.

Kruse, Colin G. "The Offender and the Offence in 2 Corinthians 2:5 and 7:12." *EQ* 60 (1988): 129–39.

Levison, John R. "The Two Spirits in Qumran Theology." In *The Bible and the Dead Sea Scrolls: The Princeton Symposium on the Dead Sea Scrolls.* Vol. 2: *The Dead Sea Scrolls and the Qumran Community*, edited by James H. Charlesworth, 169–94. Waco: Baylor University Press, 2006.

Liddell, Henry George, and Robert Scott, revised by Henry Stuart Jones. *A Greek-English Lexicon.* 9th ed. Oxford: Clarendon Press, 1940.

Lightfoot, J. B. *Saint Paul's Epistles to the Colossians and to Philemon.* London: Macmillan, 1904.

Linman, Jonathan. "Martin Luther: 'Little Christs for the World'; Faith and Sacraments as Means to *Theosis.*" In *Partakers of the Divine Nature: The History and Development of Deification in the Christian Traditions*, edited by Michael Christensen and Jeffery A. Wittung, 189–99. Madison, NJ: Fairleigh Dickinson University Press, 2006.

Lohse, Eduard. "Pauline Theology in the Letter to the Colossians." *NTS* 15 (1968–69): 211–20.

Long, Fredrick J. "From Epicheiremes to Exhortation: A Pauline Method for Moral Persuasion in 1 Thessalonians." In *Rhetoric, Ethic, and Moral Perusasion in Biblical Discourse.* ESEC, edited by Thomas H. Olbricht and Anders Eriksson, 179–95. New York: T&T Clark, 2005.

Longenecker, Richard N. *Galatians.* WBC 41. Dallas: Word Books, 1990.

Lyonnet, Stanislas. "The Pauline Conception of Redemption." In *The Theology of Atonement: Readings in Soteriology*, edited by John R. Sheets, 168–97. Englewood Cliffs, NJ: Prentice-Hall, 1967.

MacDonald, Dennis Ronald. *The Legend and the Apostle: The Battle for Paul in Story and Canon.* Philadelphia: Westminster, 1983.

MacDonald, Margaret Y. *The Pauline Churches: A Socio-historical Study of Institutionalization in the Pauline and Deutero-Pauline Writings.* Cambridge: Cambridge University Press, 1988.

Malherbe, Abraham J. *Paul and the Popular Philosophers.* Minneapolis: Fortress Press, 1989.

———. *Paul and the Thessalonians: The Philosophical Tradition of Pastoral Care.* Philadelphia: Fortress Press, 1987.

Malina, Bruce J., and Jerome H. Neyrey. *Portraits of Paul: An Archaeology of Ancient Personality.* Louisville: Westminster John Knox, 1996.

Maly, Eugene H. "The Purpose of the Bible." In *The New American Bible.* Nashville: Thomas Nelson, 1987, vii–xiii.

Marshall, I. Howard. *The Acts of the Apostles: An Introduction and Commentary.* TNTC. Leicester, England: InterVarsity, 1980.

Martin, Dale B. *Slavery as Salvation: The Metaphor of Slavery in Pauline Christology.* New Haven: Yale University Press, 1990.

McCant, Jerry W. *2 Corinthians.* Sheffield: Sheffield Academic Press, 1999.

McLean, B. Hudson. *The Cursed Christ: Mediterranean Expulsion Rituals and Pauline Soteriology.* JSNTSup 126. Sheffield: Sheffield Academic Press, 1996.

McNamara, Martin. *Targum and Testament; Aramaic Paraphrases of the Hebrew Bible: A Light on the New Testament.* Shannon, Ire.: Irish University Press, 1972.

Meeks, Wayne A. *The First Urban Christians: The Social World of the Apostle Paul.* New Haven: Yale University Press, 1983.

Meissner, William W. *The Cultic Origins of Christianity: The Dynamics of Religious Development.* Collegeville, MN: Liturgical Press, 2000.

Milgrom, Jacob. *Leviticus 1–16.* AB 3. Garden City, NY: Doubleday, 1991.

Murphy-O'Connor, Jerome. *Paul: A Critical Life.* Oxford: Oxford University Press, 1997.

———. *Paul the Letter-Writer: His World, His Options, His Skills.* Collegeville, MN: Liturgical Press, 1995.

Neyrey, Jerome H. *Paul, in Other Words: A Cultural Reading of His Letters.* Louisville: Westminster John Knox, 1990.

Osiek, Carolyn, and Margaret Y. MacDonald, with Janet H. Tulloch. *A Woman's Place: House Churches in Earliest Christianity.* Minneapolis: Fortress Press, 2006.

Perkins, Pheme. "God, Cosmos and Church Universal: The Theology of Ephesians." In *SBL Seminar Papers 2000.* SBLSP 39. Atlanta: Scholars Press, 2000, 752–73.

Pervo, Richard I. *Profit with Delight: The Literary Genre of the Acts of the Apostles.* Philadelphia: Fortress Press, 1987.

Petersen, Norman R. *Rediscovering Paul: Philemon and the Sociology of Paul's Narrative World.* Philadelphia: Fortress Press, 1985.

Rashdall, Hastings. *The Idea of the Atonement in Christian Theology.* London: Macmillan, 1919.

Reasoner, Mark. *The Strong and the Weak: Romans 14.1–15.13 in Context.* SNTSMS 103. Cambridge: Cambridge University Press, 1999.

Roetzel, Calvin. *Paul: The Man and the Myth.* Edinburgh: T&T Clark, 1999.

Sanders, E. P. *Paul and Palestinian Judaism.* Philadelphia: Fortress Press, 1977.

Schenker, Adrian. *Versöhnung und Sühne: Wege gewaltfreier Konfliktlösung im Alten Testament mit einem Ausblick auf das Neue Testament.* Biblische Beiträge 15. Fribourg: Verlag Schweizerisches Katholisches Bibelwerk, 1981.

Schürer, Emil. *The History of the Jewish People in the Age of Jesus Christ (175 B.C. – A.D. 134).* Revised by Geza Vermes and Fergus Millar. Edinburgh: T&T Clark, 1973; originally 1901–9.

Schüssler Fiorenza, Elisabeth. *In Memory of Her: A Feminist Theological Reconstruction of Christian Origins.* 10th Anniversary Ed. New York: Crossroad, 1994.

———, ed. *Searching the Scriptures.* Volume Two: *A Feminist Commentary.* New York: Crossroad, 1994.

Seifrid, Mark A. *Justification by Faith: The Origin and Development of a Central Pauline Theme.* NovTSup 68. Leiden: Brill, 1992.

Stählin, Gustav. Περίψημα. *TDNT* 6:84–93.

Stowers, Stanley K. *A Rereading of Romans: Justice, Jews, and Gentiles.* New Haven: Yale University Press, 1994.

Sumney, Jerry L. "'I Fill Up What Is Lacking in the Afflictions of Christ': Paul's Vicarious Suffering in Colossians." *CBQ* 68 (2006): 664–80.

Teilhard de Chardin, Pierre. *The Phenomenon of Man.* New York: Harper & Row, 1959.

Theissen, Gerd. *The New Testament: History, Literature, Religion.* Translated by John Bowden. London: T&T Clark, 2003.

Thielman, Frank. "The Story of Israel and the Theology of Romans 5-8." In *SBL Seminar Papers 1993.* SBLSP 32, edited by Eugene H. Lovering Jr., 227–49. Atlanta: Scholars Press, 1993.

Tobin, Thomas H. *Paul's Rhetoric in Its Contexts: The Argument of Romans.* Peabody, MA: Hendrickson, 2004.

Welborn, L. L. *Paul, the Fool of Christ: A Study of 1 Corinthians 1–4 in the Comic Philosophic Tradition.* London: T&T Clark, 2005.

White, John L. *The Apostle of God: Paul and the Promise of Abraham.* Peabody, MA: Hendrickson, 1999.

Wiles, Maurice F. *The Divine Apostle: The Interpretation of St. Paul's Epistles in the Early Church.* Cambridge: Cambridge University Press, 1967.

Wiley, Tatha. *Paul and the Gentile Women: Reframing Galatians.* New York: Continuum, 2005.

Williams, Sam K. "Again *Pistis Christou.*" *CBQ* 49 (1987): 431–47.

———. *Galatians.* Nashville: Abingdon, 1997.

Winter, Bruce W. *Philo and Paul among the Sophists.* SNTSMS 96. Cambridge: Cambridge University Press, 1997.

Wire, Antoinette Clark. *The Corinthian Women Prophets: A Reconstruction through Paul's Rhetoric.* Minneapolis: Fortress Press, 1990.

Wright, David P. *The Disposal of Impurity: Elimination Rites in the Bible and in Hittite and Mesopotamian Literature.* SBLDS 101. Atlanta: Scholars Press, 1987.

Young, Frances. *The Theology of the Pastoral Epistles.* NT Theology. Cambridge: Cambridge University Press, 1994.

Index of
Modern Authors

Index of Ancient Texts

in Roman Catholic Canonical Order

"NRSV" given when numbering differs from Masoretic Text numbering.

9:6	14	23:33	16	2:7	65
9:8	14	23:37	17	2:7-8	100, 116
9:9	74	24:27	16	2:8	124
9:17-18	14	26:9-20	14	2:10	65, 100
9:17-26	12	26:20	15	2:12	100, 116,
9:18	74	27:1	145		156
9:20	14	27:3	145	2:14-16	149
9:21	13	28:30	17	2:14-15	101
9:22-24	73			2:16	101
9:27	78	*Romans*		2:17	101
9:30	78	1–2	97	2:19-21	101
11:26	12	1:1	xi, 97, 196	2:22	101
12:12	145	1:2	97	2:23	101
12:25	145	1:3-4	98, 196	2:25	97
13:9	14	1:5	98, 113,	2:26	101
13:46	15		135, 162	2:27	101
15	12, 15, 17,	1:6	98	2:28-29	62, 101
	79	1:7	98	2:29	184
15:5	18	1:8	98	3	102,
15:9	18	1:9-11	98		107–8
15:20-30	17	1:12	98	3:1	102
15:35	191	1:15	98	3:2	102
15:37-40	16	1:16	98	3:3-4	102
15:37-39	145	1:17	99	3:5	124
16:37	17, 144	1:18	99	3:5-6	102
17	15, 31	1:19-20	99	3:8	102
18	31	1:21	99	3:9	102
18:2	57	1:21-22	99	3:11-12	102
18:5-6	15	1:23	99	3:13	102
18:8	31	1:24	99	3:15	102
18:17	31–32	1:25	18, 99	3:20	102, 115
18:18	57	1:26	100	3:21	106, 112
18:24	57	1:27	100	3:21-22	102, 106
18:26	134	1:28	100, 130	3:21-26	112
19:22	135	1:29-30	100	3:22	111–12
20:7	145	1:32	100	3:22b-26	103, 106
20:13	145	2	100	3:23	102
21:4	145	2:1	100	3:24	39, 68,
22	178	2:3-4	100		106, 123,
22:4-16	14	2:5	100		152
22:7	14	2:5-8	64	3:24-25	67, 86
22:25	17	2:6	100	3:24-25a	102
22:25-28	144	2:6-7	84	3:24-26	161

Mos.

1.24	6
1.29	6
2.2	6

Opif.

36	100

Plant.

8-9	100

Som.

1.143	88
1.177	6

Spec. Leg.

2.45	9, 100

Rabbinic Literature

m. Yoma

6.4	85

Christian and Gnostic Literature

ACTS OF THECLA

5	171

BARNABAS

7.7-9	85

1 CLEMENT

1–2	188
2.1	189
5.2	189
7.4	189
17.6	188
19.1	188
20.3	189
20.11	189
21.6	189
23.3-4	188
25:1-6	189
30.3	189
34.8	189
37.3	189
37.5	188
42.1-5	189
43.3-6	190
44.4	190
47.1	189
47.3	189
47.3-7	188
49.5	189
50.5	189
60.4	189
61.1	189

DIDACHE

9:2	49

GOSPEL OF PHILIP

103-5	195
109	195
127	195

GOSPEL OF THOMAS

56	19
87	19
108	19
110	19

IGNATIUS OF ANTIOCH

Ephesians

1.1	191
6.1	190
8.1	191
10.1-3	192
12.2	191
20.2	191

Magnesians

3.1	190
6.1	190

Philadelphians

4.1	191
7.2	190

to Polycarp

4.3	191
6.1	190

Romans

4.2	191
6.3	191
7.2-3	191
8.1	192

Smyrnaeans

6.1	191
8.2	190

Trallians

2.1	190
3.1	190
7.2	190
8.1	191

IRENAEUS
Adv. Haer.

3.16.6	195
3.18.1	195
3.22.1	196
4.20.4	195
4.33.4	195
5.1.3	195
5.10.2	196

LUTHER
In. Galatians

2:19	106
5:17	106

TERTULLIAN
Adv. Marc

3.7.7	85
5.14	196

.